DISC

DATE DUE

THE FICKLE GLASS

AMS Studies in the Renaissance: No. 4

Other Titles in This Series:

THE FICKLE GLASS
A Study of Shakespeare's Sonnets

by
PAUL RAMSEY

AMS PRESS
New York

Library of Congress Cataloging in Publication Data

Ramsey, Paul, 1924–
    The fickle glass.

    Bibliography: p.
    Includes index.
        1. Shakespeare, William, 1564–1616. Sonnets.
    2. Sonnets, English—History and criticism.
    I. Title
    PR2848.R35   821'.3   77-15910
    ISBN 0-404-16032-8

MANUFACTURED IN THE UNITED STATES OF AMERICA

This book is dedicated

to

Marifrances and O. B. Hardison

"O learn to read what silent love hath writ!"

Metrical Sigla

i	iamb
i	weak iamb; stressed syllable light
I	strong iamb; unstressed syllable strong
t	trochee
t	weak trochee
T	strong trochee
p	pyrrhic
s	spondee
a	anapest
b	amphibrach, three-syllable foot stressed on second syllable
c	cretic, three-syllable foot stressed on first and third syllables
d	dactyl
v-p	verse-pause
∫	verse-pause (siglum placed within a verse)
x	metrically unstressed syllable
⁊	truncated foot, foot with only one stressed syllable
>	anacrusis; light, metrically uncounted syllable at beginning of line
<	feminine ending
61.1&3	the rhyme of lines 1 and 3 of Sonnet 61
yellowèd	*-ed* is syllabic
yellowèd	*-o-* lightly pronounced, metrically uncounted
what CAN	*what* unstressed, *can* stressed

NOTE: Any iamb can be marked i, any trochee t.
A few other markings are explained when they occur.

Texts Used, and a Note on Italics

For the metrical sections, Chapter Four and Appendix A, the text used for the sonnets of Shakespeare is, unless otherwise stated, *Shake-speares Sonnets* (London: 1609), Folger copy with the Aspley imprint, slightly regularized.

For the remainder of the book, the text used for the sonnets of Shakespeare is, unless otherwise stated, my not yet published text, with markings occasionally simplified.

For other work by Shakespeare, the text used is, unless otherwise stated, *The Riverside Shakespeare,* ed. G. Blakemore Evans and others (Boston: Houghton Mifflin Co., 1974). Brackets are given as in Evans's text.

The Bible used is *The Geneva Bible,* ed. Lloyd E. Berry (1560; facs. reprint, Madison, Wisconsin: The University of Wisconsin Press, 1969).

Other texts used are stated. Some indentation and spacing are silently altered. Italics throughout are mine, unless stated.

Acknowledgments

Sections of this book have been given as lectures at The Divinity School of Yale University and at meetings of the Shakespeare Association and of the Tennessee Philological Association. Appendix A was publish under the title "The Syllables of Shakespeare's Sonnets" in *New Essays on Shakespeare's Sonnets,* edited by Hilton Landry (AMS Press), and Chapter 8, in a somewhat abridged form, was published until the title "A Theology of a Love" in *The English Bulletin* (editor, Richard Jackson).

Mary Dacey Waller, Eileen Cross, Vicki Ash, and Diana Martin have typed with skill and patience. Many scholars, poets, critics, and friends (the classes pleasantly overlap) have supported this labor, and I am grateful. I would like to give special mention to the extensive help of Zetsumato Hayashi and Edward R. Weismiller. The artist Bets Ramsey — who is, I am happy to say, my wife — has reflected, suggested, proofread, and praised.

The University of Chattanooga, now the University of Tennessee at Chattanooga, has given me research grants; and the library staff of the University of Tennessee at Chattanooga, under the able direction of Joseph A. Jackson, has offered me thoughtful and courteous assistance. I would also like to thank the directors and staffs of a number of libraries where I have worked on this book: the Henry E. Huntington Library; the Pierpont Morgan Library; libraries of Yale and Harvard universities; the Library of Congress; the British Museum; the John Rylands Library, Manchester; the library of Trinity College, Cambridge University; and the Bodleian Library.

Lastly I wish to thank the Folger Shakespeare Library ("That is my home of love, if I have rang'd") for a Folger Senior Fellowship, and their directors, Louis B. Wright (now retired) and O. B. Hardison, Jr., and staff members and former staff members for much assistance over a period of years, especially Giles E. Dawson, Philip A. Knachel, James G. McManaway, the late Dorothy Mason, R. J. Schoeck, Anne Wadsworth, and Laetitia Yeandle.

Contents

PROBLEMS

The Problem of the Problems

The time wasted in dealing with problems connected with Shakespeare's sonnets has become a weary scandal, but the recent habit of cheerfully disclaiming attempts to solve these problems does not brush them aside. When I began this study, I intended to write about techniques, meaning, and value. But I found the way blocked.

The problems of the sonnets may not be entirely solvable; but they cannot be evaded. They loop and twist into each other, and to tug at one is to tighten others. Nor can one bypass the problems to come at aesthetic judgment. Aesthetic judgments about the sonnets necessarily presume and imply stated or unstated, lucky or dubious, judgments about the problems.

One cannot, for instance, say much about the rhythms of the poems without solving the problem of syllabification dealt with in Appendix A. It would lead a reader to prompt distraction to read, over and over, "an iamb, an anapest, or a semielision" (and that is the simplest case).

Hyder Edward Rollins, the more recent Variorum editor of the sonnets, points out that the authenticity has been normally assumed but seldom clearly defended.[1] It is hardly a trifling question. If the poems are not by Shakespeare, discussion of relationships between the sonnets and Shakespeare's poems or plays is foreclosed or radically changed; if the sonnets are not almost all, or all, by one poet, the discussion of relationship between the poems breaks down. To discuss relationships between poems is inevitably to deal with, covertly or openly, the order of the poems, which is to deal with chronology and dating.

Decisions or assumptions about order are vital to any sustained literary criticism of the sonnets. A number of books and essays, especially in recent years, have attempted to reach essential meanings and themes by discussing selected sonnets out of order.[2] This method casts doubt on interpretations of individual sonnets and can seriously harm more general interpretations, for instance interpretations which say or suggest that Shakespeare's sonnets end in reconciliation or triumph; Sonnets 126 and 152, which end the chief two sequences, are neither reconciling nor triumphant.

The long-lasting biographical frenzy over these poems has produced some lively and up-to-a-point healthy reaction. Still, whether and how far the poems are autobiographical are questions inevitably to be asked, or begged, and the answers matter. Who the people are, or are not, ties back in with questions of dating and order. One of the chief causes for biased handling of the problems is the wish to support some candidate; by the same token, any reasonable discussion of candidates will illuminate other problems. Problems link.

The sonnets are autobiographical in deep ways and in many specific ways; they are also and primarily poems. Some things are personal, some metaphorical, and some conventional; worse yet, a passage may be any two or all three at once; one needs to tell which, when.

Finding persons and influences can help us understand meanings in the sonnets. My support for Christopher Marlowe as the rival poet explains some meanings and reinforces some independent evidence about the dates; my support for Samuel Daniel as chief influence explains some meanings and also gives evidence for dating. The relation of Daniel and Marlowe to Shakespeare also shows something of Shakespeare's ways of emulations and his habits of feeling and thought.

The problems cannot be ignored; they can only be better or worse managed. Critics who wave aside the problems inevitably smuggle in answers, and there are various ways to go wrong. Students of the sonnets are misled by obtrusive modern assumptions, the thrill of discovery, or the pull of advocacy; by being too literal minded or not literal minded enough; by being more impressed with what fits a theory than what fails to fit; by the click of the false disjunction; by undue scepticism; or by confusions about "fact," internal and external evidence, or probability. This book will deal with some examples (and, it may be, offer some more) of each of these temptations. I would hope I can make the mild claim that the cards, trumps or not, are on the table.

To be more precise, one could escape the problems simply enough, by not writing about these poems. But that, for anyone once smitten, is too much to ask.

Chapter 1

Unity of Authorship, Authenticity, and Order

The chief and fundamental problem of the sonnets is their unity of authorship. Closely bound up by that question is their authenticity, the first question for the Shakespearean scholar.

Most serious critics and scholars (I shall not honor the Baconians and their cousins with a parenthesis every time they are an exception) accept these poems as Shakespeare's but, as Rollins points out,[1] seldom with much argument. The literary power of the poems no doubt has seemed sufficient testimony; yet the external evidence is less than obviously certain, and to identify authorship by internal evidence is a notoriously risky venture. Some argument is in order.

The poems are attributed to Shakespeare on the title page of the 1609 quarto. The edition may or may not have been authorized; but, either way, the title page's attribution is considerable evidence. Even unauthorized editions get the author right much more often than not. All of Thomas Thorpe's attributions to the other books he published are unquestioned, and almost certainly correct; therefore his authority is much greater than many scholars seem to grant. William Jaggard attributes two of these poems (Sonnets 138 and 144) to Shakespeare in the 1599 pirated *The Passionate Pilgrim*. Some of the poems in that book are certainly Shakespeare's (for instance, the sonnets from *Love's Labor's Lost*), and a number of others may be, though some of them are probably by other hands. Jaggard put these two poems first, which suggested that he really thought they were Shakespeare's (good tomatoes not infrequently appear at the top of the basket); and Shakespeare's sonnets were circulating in manuscript, according to Francis Meres's comment in 1598.[2] To combine the attribution of a possibly unauthorized book with that of a book certainly pirated,

5

hardly amounts to demonstration. From the standpoint of complete certainty, one can say that the attribution is dubious; but one should not let the shadows of doubt reach too far. From the standpoint of probability, the Meres-Jaggard-1609 evidence is good and converging.

If Sonnets 138 and 144 are authentic, then many others are. Sonnets 138 and 144 refer to an essential part of the sonnets' events and link very closely to other sonnets referring to the triangle, Sonnets 133-136 and 40-42. Sonnet 138 is very much like, in tone, theme, complex self-mockery and wit, a number of the other dark lady sonnets; and I know no other genuine parallels in the language.

Having gone that far, we are in the web, which web is the chief argument for the unity of authorship. The sonnets are deeply and intricately twisted into each other, in language, theme, tricks of style, syntactical links, imagery, rhythm (which is one reason so many rearrangements have tempted rearrangers). The very numerosity of the links makes it impossible to count them systematically. I find a total of ninety-four poems in the first 126 occurring in groups of three or more, ten other poems occurring in pairs, the criteria being close thematic and syntactical linkages, so close as to suggest very near proximity of time or thought. Many of the twenty-two poems not counted in groups have some strong links with adjacent poems. Virtually all critics admit the contiguity of the first group, Sonnets 1-17 or so. The triangle sonnets (40-42, 133-136, 144) are firmly linked in meaning to each other, as are the rival poet sonnets (78-80, 82-86). Hence the web suggests intense linking within the 1609 order, and closely allied themes and images recur and recur and recur. In short, once in the web, it is hard to shift loose. Only a handful of poems fail to tie in with others, which tie in with others, until almost all of the poems have direct and indirect connections.

One could exclude from the web only Sonnet 77, sent with a triple gift; Sonnets 153-154, the Bath sonnets, whose authenticity is doubted by some scholars; Sonnet 145 in tetrameter lines; and, more surprisingly, Sonnets 129 and 146, which are spiritual sonnets, a common Elizabethan kind. Sir Thomas Wyatt's "Farewell, love, and all thy laws forever," Sir Philip Sidney's two great sonnets "Thou blind man's mark, thou fool's self-chosen snare" and "Leave me, o Love, that reachest but to dust" are, with Donne's Holy Sonnets and Sonnets 129 and 146 of Shakespeare, among the best-known exemplars.[3] Sonnets 129 and 146 are among the favorites and accepted by almost all scholars; and Sonnets 77 and 145 are admirable poems.

I offer the following, mostly new, reasons for crediting the authenticity of Sonnet 145. First, it has decided links with Sonnets 144 and 146 (144.9&11 fiend & friend, 145.9&11 end & fiend, 146.6&8 spend & end; 145.10&12 day & away, 146.2&4 array & gay). Second, it links in heaven-hell themes to Sonnets 144 and 146. Third, it connects impressively with Sonnet 29: in rhyme, 29.2&4 state & fate, 29.10&12 state & gate, 145.2&4 hate & state; in the parallel phrasing of "my outcast state" (29.2) and "my woeful state" (145.4); in the heavenward-ness which is the crucial reversal of each; in the two strongest instances of enjambment in the sonnets, "Haply I think on thee, and then my state,/ Like to the lark at break of day arising/ From sullen earth, sings hymns at heaven's gate (29.10-12) and "'I hate', she alt'rèd with an end/ That follow'd it as gentle day/ Doth follow night who like a fiend/ From heav'n to hell is flown away" (145.9-12). Fourth, one can offer the other reasons for supporting the integrity of Sonnets 1-152.

The Bath sonnets are not certainly Shakespeare's, but probably are because (1) the two poems were evidently written by one author, (2) Sonnet 153 has the rhyme and word links, further discussed in Chapter Four, with Sonnet 152: "eye" and "lie" (152.13&14), "lies" and "eye" (153.13&14), (3) lines 153.3-4, "And his love-kindling fire did quickly steep/ In a cold valley fountain of that ground," are impressive in cadence, diction, and imagery. Not all good lines in Elizabethan poetry are Shakespeare's; but mastery of that order is significant.

The sonnets of the 1609 quarto are, then, with few if any exceptions, by one poet.

The 1599 and 1609 attributions are to Shakespeare. The numerous echoes to or from authentic plays, some of which echoes are discussed in Chapter Three, point to Shakespeare. The implied biography fits Shakespeare, at least before 1596 or so.

The speaker is named Will: "My name is Will" (136.14). So were many Englishmen, but more were not so named. The speaker is dissatisfied with his profession and of lower social standing than his friend. The profession is never clearly named; but the stage is consistent with all that is said, and some references suggest it, especially Sonnets 110-111. The speaker is an ambitious poet; he has a great, a fearfully great, insight into human complexity and weakness, which he shares only with the author of the plays.

The evidence is sufficient that these sonnets are, with few and probably no exceptions, Shakespeare's, and I shall assume so in the rest of this book.

The Order

I shall defend the view that the order of the 1609 edition is, at least
for Sonnets 1-126, Shakespeare's order, and essentially chronological
for Sonnets 1-126, with Sonnets 127-152 overlapping Sonnets 40-42 in
time, extending an indefinite length of time before or after those
poems. Sonnets 153-154 are probably where Shakespeare meant them
to be, but cannot be reasonably dated on the available evidence.

The Dark Lady Group

The internal evidence of the dark lady sonnets, Sonnets 127-152, is
insufficient to decide the question of their order. These poems shall
therefore be discussed first: the order of Sonnets 1-126 is the crucial
issue.

If the manuscript is a good one, whether or not Shakespeare directly
authorized the publication, then the dark lady sonnets are probably in
the correct order. If *A Lover's Complaint* is Shakespeare's, if all the
sonnets are Shakespeare's, and if Sonnets 1-126 are in the correct
order, then the manuscript is, with respect to order, almost certainly a
good manuscript. M. P. Jackson has in my judgment demonstrated
that *A Lover's Complaint* is Shakespeare's;[4] I have already given
reasons for believing that the sonnets are Shakespeare's; the order of
Sonnets 1-126 shall be defended in the following section.

Hence there is quite good reason to think that the dark lady sonnets
are in the proper order in the 1609 edition, unless internal evidence
outweighs the argument just given. In this section I shall maintain that,
first and most important, the internal evidence is inconclusive and
therefore does not outweigh those arguments; and, second, that on
internal evidence the 1609 order assumed as chronological is at least as
plausible as any rearrangement.

The dark lady sonnets have comparatively little order, whether in
chronological sequence or rearranged. They are, with two exceptions,
poems about a black-haired woman and represent several attitudes
toward her: (1) gay, gentle teasing (128, 130); (2) delicate tenderness
(143, 145); (3) witty obscenity, with shades of self-contempt and some

hostility to her (135, 136, 151); (4) anger, bitterness, hatred, thralldom (131, 133, 134, 137, 138, 139, 140, 141, 142, 144, 147, 148, 149, 150, 152); (5) something between, or mixed of, teasing and the strong emotions (127, 132).

Several of these deal directly with the triangle: Sonnets 133, 134, 135, 136, 144. Others speak of her infidelity or promiscuity and hence may concern the triangle: Sonnets 137, 138, 139, 140, 141, 152.

A few of these poems are clearly linked, Sonnets 133-136 most definitely. Sonnet 134 is linked to Sonnet 133 grammatically (by the "so" in line 134.1) and in subject. Sonnets 135 and 136 are linked to each other by the Will puns and to line 134.2, "I myself am mortgag'd to thy Will." Sonnet 134 ends "Him have I lost; thou hast both him and me;/ He pays the whole, and yet am I not free," and Sonnet 135 begins by echoing that phrasing, "Who ever hath her wish, thou hast thy Will,/ And Will to boot and Will in overplus." Sonnet 140 echoes a rhyme of Sonnet 139 ("slain" and "pain," 140.2&4 and 139.13&14) and, more important, carries over a metaphor of death and mortal illness.

Sonnet 127 seems closely tied to Sonnets 131-132 in the handling of the "mourning" and "black" references, and two poems, Sonnets 129 and 146, interrupt their contexts, Sonnet 129 being particularly intrusive, a fierce attack on lust between two gay and gentle poems.

The separation of Sonnets 127 and 131-132 is well enough explained on a chronological scheme, since a poet is likely to pick up a theme in a poem written three or four poems ago (or, for that matter, three or four years ago). The intrusion of Sonnets 129 and 146 is also explainable on the chronological scheme, since moods change rapidly; and it takes no wizardry at psychoanalysis to believe that Shakespeare's moods were highly changeable. Further, Sonnets 129 and 146 belong to a different genre of sonnet from all the others, being meditative sonnets on traditional religious themes, not love sonnets. If the poems are chronological in order, Shakespeare may not have noticed the clash of these two poems with their contexts or may have noticed and stuck with his scheme. These poems are not part as such, wherever they are put, of either sequence, though of course they could have been inspired by the guilt and hatred fostered by the tangled affair with the unknown woman (unknown, too well known, not likely to be known). C. F. Tucker Brooke and Brents Stirling in their rearrangements put Sonnet 146 as a conclusion, a palinode,[5] but what reason except wishing is there to suppose that Shakespeare ended with a high Christian rejection of the sonnets' themes? What evidence we have is otherwise.

Brooke's rearrangement is one of the most careful and thoughtful. What it shows for the dark lady sequence is how little order at best there is in those poems. If we had only Sonnets 127-152 we would not be entitled to a theory supporting the order or to a theory of clear dislocation. These poems do not represent enough narration or development to build upon. Shakespeare wrote some poems to a woman over a period of time; the order could well be chronological or not. No rearrangement gives them more sequence than they have or that one might expect. The entanglement happened; darker moods predominate; the poems end harshly.

He might, in 1609, have wished to end the poems with a large Christian statement; he might very well and grimly have so ended when he wrote *Macbeth* or *Othello*; but, if he ordered Sonnets 127-152 in the 1590s and before showing the collection to his "private friends," it does not fit what we know of his career to assume that he did end so; and if he did not deliberately order Sonnets 127-152 we have no textual right to impose that order on the poems.

To reorder toward Sonnet 146 involves some complex and wholly unproved assumptions, something like the following: (1) Shakespeare did change these poems from their chronological order sometime in the 1590s or 1600-1609, but Thorpe got hold of an earlier manuscript or a descendant of it, with poems either in the earlier order or loose; or (2) Shakespeare wrote Sonnet 146 after the other poems; the chronology fits the thematic order the reorderer intuits, had Shakespeare decided to publish the poems (which, on this assumption he did not do, since the 1609 edition, again on this assumption, has the poems out of order). No respectable evidence exists for any of those assumptions; if better or other assumptions are involved, reorderers should make them explicit. The burden of proof is theirs, and reorderers seldom say what the reordering genuinely means and assumes.

One could pull out and separate Sonnets 129 and 146, not as a grand last word, but simply as a different kind of poem, as Sonnets 153 and 154 are separated. Do that, and the point of greatest moment between my view and the views of Brooke and Stirling is resolved. I feel deeply, not thereby claiming proof, that "More perjured I, to swear against the truth so foul a lie" is a profounder, more appropriate way, and a way more consonant with Sonnet 126, to end the dark lady sonnets than is a high Christian reversal and transcendence of the sonnets' hopes and themes.

Sonnets 1-126

The general impression of chronology in the poems to the young man is very considerable. The first seventeen or so are plausibly early. They are not love poems in the full sense. The poet is impressed by the beauty of his young friend and wishes him to marry and have offspring; it is later that the real glories and complexities emerge. The poems from Sonnet 100 on (Sonnet 100 refers to a gap of silence) have a number of indications that the relation was by then a long-standing one.[6] In Sonnet 100 the poet complains to his Muse that "thou forget'st so long" (100.1); in Sonnet 102 he says, "Our love was new and then but in the spring" (102.5) and "Not that the summer is less pleasant now" (102.9). Sonnet 104 speaks of three years and the changes that are occurring. Literal or not, and why not literal?, the three years mean a span of time. In Sonnet 108 the poet says, "I must each day say o'er the very same/ ... Ev'n as when first I hallow'd thy fair name" (108.6,8). In other sonnets he says, "Alas, 'tis true I have gone here and there" (110.1) and "Now all [unfaithfulness] is done" (110.9); "Those lines that I before have writ doth lie,/ Ev'n those that said I could not love you dearer" (115.1-2); "I have frequent been with unknown minds" (117.5); "... ruin'd love when it is built anew/Grows fairer than at first" (119.11-12); and "O, thou my lovely boy . . . / Who hast by waning grown" (126.1,3). These poems were certainly written late in the relation; they are last in the order. Where there are events, the sonnets about them are contiguous: the triangle sonnets addressed to the young man (40-42) are together, the rival poet sonnets (78-86) are together. Several poems about absence are together, more than once; several poems about the young man's corruption are together, more than once; several poems about not writing poems are together.

Many poems are clearly consecutive, linked in subject and by grammatical references. Sonnet 126 seems a very natural envoy. That is, much of the order is right, and much of the order is chronological.

Further, what order is to be expected? The poems were written over a period of time, "day-to-day reflections"[7] which show the concerns of a deeply engaged and vacillating mind.

The poems have sequences, not a fully articulated story. They represent events when events happen. For the rest they show the stops and starts, hopes and fears, changes and continuities of a relationship which ended. The sequence from Sonnet 100 to Sonnet 126 is tragically continuous in its very inconsistencies, the apologies for silence, the last flaring of the ideal, the fadings, the guilt, the turning away.

Certainly the sequence is not a random disorder. Much is straight, and if much, why not all? The rearrangers need to explain, persuasively, why so much is in clear order. If so much is in order, does not that in itself powerfully support the notion that the poems were transmitted in a bound book or with the order clearly marked in the manuscript?

What is meant, anyway, by the correct order? If Shakespeare did not, deliberately, put them together in order, there is no authorized order and never has been. I think he did, and in essentially chronological order. The evidence of chronology is too strong to permit one to believe that he assembled them on some other principle, say, topical; and for some one other than Shakespeare, except possibly the young man, to have reassembled the 126 poems into the sequence which shows as many marks of chronology as it does, is fantastically unlikely, a miracle of genius or luck. Even the young man is distinctly less likely as arranger than is Shakespeare, since the young man did not receive the dark lady poems as addressee, he may well not have received a number of the poems addressed to him, and received any he did receive spasmodically, one or in groups, over a period of time. (If the young man did assemble the poems in chronological order, without Shakespeare's help and without knowledge of Shakespeare's intent, and the manuscript so assembled found its way to Thomas Thorpe, then that order is largely "right," that is, chronological, at least for Sonnets 1-126, but unauthorized.)

The simplest guess is that Shakespeare kept copies in a copybook as he went. The next simplest is that Shakespeare some time after he had written the poems put them into chronological order with no doubt some, now ineradicable, errors of memory. That manuscript or a copy of it, in a copybook or with clearly marked order, got to Thorpe through Shakespeare or some intermediary, and Thorpe followed the order. Something very near to that is the likelihood.

To put a dilemma bluntly, either Thorpe followed a manuscript in Shakespeare's order or not. If the former, the 1609 edition has essentially the right order. If the latter, the 1609 edition could not have as many marks of essentially chronological order as it does.

If a man writes poems over three years or so, there will be gaps, discontinuities, shifts of attitude in those sonnets compared to a play or to a poem such as *Lucrece*. Events happen between; the mind shifts its view; moods change. Sonnet 75 is about the vacillation in the poet's mind which the poems often reflect.

It has been urged, for instance by W. H. Auden,[8] that poems praising the purity of the young man follow poems lamenting his corruption, a truth supposed inconsistent with a chronological view of the sequence. The inconsistency is real enough. In Sonnets 33-35, 40-42, 57-58, and 69 the poet speaks of the young man's moral failings; then in Sonnet 70 he writes, "Thou present'st a pure, unstainèd prime;/ Thou hast pass'd by the ambush of young days,/ Eith'r not assail'd, or victor being charg'd" (70.9-11). I paraphrase as "You have kept your innocence over a period of time, either not having been tempted or else having successfully resisted all temptation." The explanation is not, however, dislocation. Sonnets 69 and 70 are unmistakably paired, dealing with slanders of the young man's reputation, and Sonnet 69 ends, "But why thy odor matcheth not thy show,/ The soil is this, that thou dost common grow," which I paraphrase as "The reason that your reputation does not fit the innocence of your beauty is that you grow in common soil: you are common, not innocent."

Since the inconsistency occurs in two linked sonnets, it must be in the mind rather than in the disarrangement of poems. The poet explains the procedure in line 88.4 when he says that he shall "prove thee virtuous, though thou art forsworn." The conventions of praise and the natural gracing of love cover up ugliness as best they may. The praise of the young man's virtue, though desperately intense at times, is rarer than the praise of his beauty and part of a convention of praise which Shakespeare absorbed and strongly would believe: for instance, Sonnets 18, 26, 54, 79, 105, 109. The dispraising speaks with another and hurt voice. There was little virtue to praise.

Rearrangers of the sonnets often break natural links in the 1609 order and do not appear to restore lost grammatical links. Grammatical links are frequent and, if the dislocations had occurred, then restoration should restore a number of syntactical links. But this does not happen. Further, rearrangers often group poems on one topic together. It is far more likely and natural that a poet writing over a period of time would return to themes than he would write all of his poems on a given topic at one time.

Some of the best rearrangers, including Brooke and Stirling, accept much of the 1609 order. Stirling finds, in the 1609 order of Sonnets 1-126, thirty-four groups (ninety-six poems) of "intensively linked" sonnets, sonnets so linked by syntax, word repetitions, echoes, or other close tissue as to be "virtually certain" in their order.[9] He further finds groups linked by "close association" to be Sonnets 1-17, 18-19, 33-42, 43-52, 62-68, 76 with 78-80 and 82-86, 87-96, 97-108, 122-126 (eighty-one poems).[10] Brooke leaves unchanged the order of Sonnets 1-35, 43-58, 66-70, 97-108, 117-126, changing poems which come between these groups.[11]

To admit so much is virtually to give away the argument. Assuming, as I do, that the poems were written over a period of time, some singly, some two or more at a sitting, others in close proximity in time, some after gaps of time, one would expect just the sort of thing Stirling admits to in the 1609 order: general chronology, small groups with firm connections, larger groups with more general connections, and some gaps and inconsistencies of attitude within and between groups.

Both Brooke and Stirling, then, give very strong if unintentional evidence for the 1609 order and fail to explain the partial dislocation, though both try. Brooke speaks of a "gust of wind"[12] in the printer's shop (which blows none of us any good). The presumption of that view is that the sheets were separate and unnumbered but carefully in the right order and that the gust of wind left the majority of the poems in correct groups, which groups were regathered from the floor in the proper order. It is not a likely hypothesis, nor does Brooke offer a better one.

Stirling tries at some length to describe how the (presumably unmarked but ordered) sheets might have been shuffled, and admits circularity in his proceedings: "But I cannot pretend that I failed to see a pattern forming once I began placing singles. . . . Consequently, the results should be checked for a wishful begging of the question."[13] One appreciates Stirling's honesty, and care, but with that admission, plus a two-poems-to-a-sheet hypothesis,[14] plus a belief that twenty-seven poems occurred one to a sheet,[15] plus the admission that he sometimes suspects dislocation but followed the 1609 edition "in doubtful case[s],"[16] plus a basic tendency to follow the 1609 edition, plus the "near-misses,"[17] plus most of all the lack of verifiability in his crucial judging of what is coherent, one has a family of hypotheses sufficiently flexible to get around almost any problem and to have little value as proof. The hypothesis of a manuscript with marked order makes far greater sense.

One suspects that the clear coherence of the first group leads reorderers astray. Stirling's notion is of poems consisting of several sonnets, for which the group of sonnets, Sonnets 1-17, is the model.[18] The test of that notion is the restored coherence, including syntactical, and other close tissue in the restored poems as compared with the first group. It is a test which, in my judgment, Stirling's regrouped poems do not pass. What happened is rather that Shakespeare began by writing a coherent series of poems urging a young man to marry, then continued writing poems to the young man for another three years or so, but without again planning or binding a series of over fifteen so closely.

The 1609 order fits what one could expect from a chronological view and does not fit what one would not expect: the deliberate sequential building of a poem. A poet writing poems will often start a poem which has little in common with a poem he wrote the previous week; he will often be led by an association to write a poem off to the side. A poet deliberately writing a longer poem will not do that (formal digressions work differently); hence offshoots in the sonnets are valuable in showing what one reasonably should expect. One could of course take many examples of buildings and offshootings; I shall take two which I believe make the point clearly.

Sonnets 67, 69, and 70 deal with the theme of the young man's bad company and reputation and, as I showed earlier in this chapter, take inconsistent attitudes toward his character. The first quatrain of Sonnet 67 complains of the young man keeping impious company, then turns naturally to two departures from the subject. The second quatrain begins, "Why should false painting imitate his cheek,/ And steal dead seeing of his living hue?" That is, it raises the questions of cosmetics. The rest of the poem moves away from that topic and from the topic of bad company to the idea of the young man as exemplar of beauty. Then Sonnet 68 unites the themes of cosmetics and exemplary beauty, beginning and ending with the theme of exemplary beauty in relation to the past, the substance of the poem being Shakespeare's most powerful attack on cosmetics, false beauty. The poem ends with a map and a seeing:

And him as for a map doth nature store,
To show false art what beauty was of yore.

Sonnet 69 begins with a reference naturally following from the map of beauty and the "show": "Those parts of thee that the world's eye doth view." Sonnets 69 and 70 then return to the idea of corrupt company which Sonnet 67 began with. Thus the progress is topic, departure, association, then return to topic. Sonnet 68 is not about bad company or slander at all, yet it fits in seamlessly and unmistakably, even being grammatically linked to Sonnet 67 by the first word in line 68.1, "Thus."

Sonnets 97-99 give another example of the procedure, without return. Sonnets 97 and 98 are poems about absence, an absence expressed in beautiful flower imagery in Sonnet 98. Sonnet 99 continues the flower motif and drops the absence motif, turning to the theme of the young man as exemplar of beauty.

Such is not the procedure of a man writing a coherent poem or of a man writing disconnected poems, but it is very much the procedure of a man writing poems to a loved one, sometimes in rapid succession. The procedure fits the chronological theory.

What results from such a chronological sequence? Is there a sonnet story? Yes. There is an aesthetic and psychological exploration of the heights, changes, depths, tangles, and failures of love, a love presented in Sonnets 1-126 as chronological. For reasons I shall give in the next chapter, I hold that the aesthetic account reveals a biographical relationship which covered a span of time. Shakespeare befriended a young man, fell in love with him, was variously delighted and repelled by him throughout some time, encountered competition for the young man's affection: Shakespeare's mistress, a rival poet or poets, other women, and, I suspect, other and cruder men. Shakespeare found the passion entangled with his own professional fears and hopes (and with all that he knew), fading, flaring, vacillating, glorying, hurting, and finally passing. Such is the story told by the 1609 order. It is, so long as men can breathe and eyes can see, beautiful; it is tragic, transcendent, at times ugly, at times weak and bitter; profound, ennobling, troubled, transient. It is the story of human love, never told better.

Chapter 2

The Biographical
Questions

Of all the problems connected with Shakespeare's sonnets, the questions of biography are the most often scoffed at and the least relevant to aesthetic criticism. Yet they are highly relevant to dating and tangentially relevant to much else. If, as I shall argue, Marlowe is the rival poet, the rival poet sonnets were written before Marlowe's death in 1593. Could we pin down, as I have not, the identities of the young man and the dark lady, we could probably establish dates more firmly and could just possibly learn much more.

Speculating biographical enthusiasms for varied candidates for persons represented by Shakespeare's sonnets, have crammed bookcases and led little where; and a promoting cause, the romantic view of poetry as primarily self-expressive, is un-Elizabethan. Thus, led by the sceptical wit of Hyder Edward Rollins, many modern commentators greet any biographical interpreting of the sonnets with quick scorn and predictable polemics.

Yet Rollins, for all his attacks on biographicizing, does not deny biographical reality to the persons involved. He speaks in frustrated agnosticism about the young man's (and the other persons') existence; and at times seems to lean, in spite of himself, toward believing in their existence.[1] In fact, writers who speak hard words against biographical interpreting of the sonnets seldom out and out deny, and often assume, the historicity of the persons concerned.[2] That is not surprising; the sense of actuality in the sonnets is very strong, the personalities of the young man and the dark lady memorable and distinct.

The most evident argument for a biographical interpretation is that the feelings and persons do seem real, personal, and specific. An answer is equally evident: Shakespeare was a great dramatist, and the feelings and persons in his plays also seem real, personal, and specific, even though we know that many of the persons are invented.

Another argument against a biographical view is that the poems

17

partake of the flourishing sonnet tradition. Shakespeare was trying his hand at the genre as he tried or was to try others: the longer narrative, *Venus and Adonis* and *Lucrece*; the lament, *A Lover's Complaint*; the metaphysical poem, *The Phoenix and Turtle*. That is importantly true, but does not decide the issue whether the persons in the sonnets represent (somewhat, or sometimes, or largely) actual persons or not.

Conventions come out of actualities, and help to create actualities. Lovers write to lovers, and poets thereby learn a genre to practice as richly or dully, involutely or simply as they wish. Convention and actuality have many relationships. Some poets are lovers, some lovers poets. All poetry is biographical (even autobiographical, since poets use their own experience and feelings). All poetry is literary, since poets learn from reading poems. In one strict, true, and formal sense, no poem is autobiographical: each poem is an invention, an imagined speech or speeches, the speaker(s) being part of the invention; each poem is an artifact for public or private aesthetic display and cherishing. Yet some poems are directly autobiographical in intent ("this is I; heed how I feel"); those poems are affected by the demands and limitations of form and genre, and the rhetoric available at a given time. Hyperbole, distancing, invention, rationalization, complexities of context, invention — and real experience and real feeling.

Rollins writes that the young man "may have existed, . . . [or] may be a fictitious, a conventional, a dramatic figure."[3] He is surely, in some sense, each of the last three: fictitious, since in poems, which are fictions (things made); conventional, since in sonnets written in a tradition; dramatic, since written about by a great dramatist. He was also, almost certainly, an actual person.

Had Shakespeare invented a story to build poems on, it would have been more dramatic and coherent, more realized, than the manifestly present yet incomplete story in these poems.[4] Further, special details occur, such as the copybook in Sonnet 122 and the unsolved details in the rival poet sonnets (to be discussed later in this chapter), to undo any nonbiographical view, since only biographical information would make those details clear.

A story is told, a story that takes time and has an ending (Sonnet 126) but no denouement, a broken story that fits and fails to fit the conventions of the sonnet tradition. What is normal in the tradition? Sonnets that praise and idealize patrons? Yes. Sonnets that scold a patron, or that apologize to him for giving away a copybook received as a gift? No. Sonnets that idealize beauty, or mock the idealization of beauty? Yes. Sonnets that worry about rival poets and make obscure

jokes about "compeers by night"? No. Sonnets about patrons, or
ladies? Yes. Sonnets that complain about the patron making love to
the lady? No. (At least in England.)

A collection or sequence of sonnets is not a drama or formal
narrative. Even so, if the poems are nonbiographical, why did Shakespeare bother to invent so much action and then stop frustratingly short
of telling more? Were the triangle invented, Shakespeare would hardly
tell that tale in one brief group of poems a third of the way through the
sequence to the young man (Sonnets 40-42), and in another run
(Sonnets 133-136) plus a separated sonnet (Sonnet 144) in the dark
lady sonnets. No rearrangement solves the narrative problem.

Too much and too little, is the argument. The sonnets have too
much jagged specificity to ignore, too little development and complet-
ing of the events to be an invention. The most rational hypothesis to
explain that feature of the sonnets, is actual persons and events. What
else are we to think? That Shakespeare deliberately arranged things so
as to trap people into accepting the arguments offered above, or
similar arguments? That Shakespeare wrote some 500 sonnets creating
a full story and that only these 154 poems remain, Sonnets 1-126
somehow having preserved chronological order? Are there better
hypotheses?

Also, in a poem involving the dark lady, her husband, the young
man, her other lovers, and the poet, the poet says, "My name is Will"
(136.14).

Four persons enter the poems: the speaker-poet, his young friend,
the dark lady (I shall normally use the traditional if spooky title
without further apology), and another poet. There are also some other
rival poets and probably the dark lady's husband. Fortunately, the
most important biographical question has a true answer, supplied by
Thomas Thorpe in 1609: the speaker-poet is William Shakespeare.

There are few real clues to the dark lady. Lascivious brunettes are
always in supply and no law requires that their names be preserved for
posterity. We learn that this one played a musical instrument, walked
on the ground, was probably married, and had dark hair and eyes, but
nothing specific enough to be much help.

Rowse's Candidate for the Dark Lady

A. L. Rowse's candidate, Emilia Bassano Lanier, has provoked
much clamor and publicity, polemics and puffing.[5] Rowse has by a

good measure failed to establish his case. His opponents have scored some points, but certainly have not proved that she was not Shakespeare's dark lady, though in angry moments some seem so to claim.

Suppose one were to grant some points in Rowse's favor and agree that Mrs. Lanier and Shakespeare's dark lady meet with certainty the following conditions: female, alive and living in London in the 1590s, accomplished on the virginals (or similar musical instrument), younger than Shakespeare, married and adulterous, dark of hair. Even so, one could not say that there is better than one chance in some dozens that they are the same person. Surely dozens of women and maybe hundreds fit all those conditions. The odds actually have to be put higher. It is uncertain that Emilia Lanier had dark hair, though, being of Italian descent, it is likely that she did. It is uncertain that she played the virginals, though, since she was of a musical family and married a musician, she may well have. It is uncertain that the dark lady was married, though line 152.3 ("in act thy bed-vow broke") makes it probable that she was. It is not at all clear that the dark lady was younger than Shakespeare. Sonnet 138 says that the poet is old and the dark lady unjust, but ladies can be both unjust and old. That leaves, as certain (granting the date, and the historicity of the dark lady, both of which I do) only that she was female, alive and living in London in the 1590s. Since the estimate of one chance in some dozens was based on hypothetical certainty for all those points discussed, the odds surely have to be set at one out of some hundreds. Emilia Bassano's liaison with Henry Carey, Lord Hunsdon, the patron at one time of Shakespeare's company, affects the odds very slightly, being the sort of evidence that catches the eye to little result.

Still, one chance out of some hundreds is some chance; it does not mean that odds of several hundred to one have been established against her candidacy; it means that, since no conclusive evidence so far has been offered against her candidacy,[6] there is at least one chance out of some hundreds and that further evidence might narrow the odds or might exclude her.

The names Emilia and Bassano have some appeal. Emilia in Shakespeare's *Othello* has a name not in Shakespeare's primary source; she is a salty Italian woman who wittily defends adultery, yet ends well. That Bassanio in *The Merchant of Venice* in some ways reflects the young man of the sonnets is a view I accepted (see the next chapter) before Rowse announced his candidate. I offer no guess how much those coincidings affect the odds, certainly not enough to create a probability; but they have interest.

Emilia Bassano Lanier remains a possible candidate; her candidacy has not been refuted and is far from being established; it seems frustratingly unlikely that definite evidence will settle the question either way. Rowse's knowledge of the Elizabethan age and his confidence cannot change possibility into probability, much less certainty. Truth is a stubborn lady.

The Young Man

That one young man is referred to in Sonnets 1-126 is virtually certain. I thought once that some or many of them might be to a woman or women, but could not sustain such a view. Whenever a pronoun is given it is masculine, and too many links and ties occur to doubt that they were all written to one young man. Sonnet 76 says, "O know, sweet love, I always write of you" (76.9), which, if exaggerated, is good evidence.

The full name of the young man is unknown and may well remain unknown. Certain things about him, once his actuality is granted, are definite. He was younger than Shakespeare; he was of higher social rank than Shakespeare; he had an affair with Shakespeare's mistress; Shakespeare thought him promiscuous (a number of lines hint it and line 61.14 says it, "with others all too near"); he was the recipient of poems, probably love poems, by at least two other poets and probably several (the "every alien pen" of line 78.3 is hyperbolic but suggests at least more than two); he was unmarried when Shakespeare wrote Sonnets 1-17, and his mother was alive at the time of lines 3.9-10, "Thou art thy mother's glass and she in thee/ Calls back the lovely April of her prime"; he had a streak of cruelty and a high opinion of himself.

Less definite, but still highly likely, are some other things. His first name was William (the punning Sonnets 134-136 strongly if not quite conclusively seem to pun on his name, and the "Mr. W. H." of the dedication corroborates); he was handsome (men in love make some bad mistakes about looks, but I doubt that Shakespeare did; men who are noticed to look like their mothers [line 3.9, just mentioned] are often handsome); his father was dead when Shakespeare wrote Sonnet 13 (line 13.14, "You had a father; let your son say so," is definite about that unless the idiom has changed); he may well have had at least one book dedicated to him, though not necessarily a book still extant or even a published book. He was fair of complexion and probably blond.[7] He was born in 1570-1575 or very close to those limits (several years younger than Shakespeare, old enough in 1590 to 1592 to be urged to marry). He was probably alive in 1609 when Thorpe dedicated the book to him. Memorial dedications are less common than dedications to living persons.

There is little reason to doubt these; each is distinctly implied once or certified by numerous references, and neither convention nor literary decoration nor invention is, for reasons I have given, a sufficient explanation. Convention and truth are of course compatible. It is conventional to say in love poems that the loved one is beautiful; a man writing love poems normally believes that his loved one is beautiful.

The probability is high that his last name began with the letter H, since the dedication says so. The text of the dedication is as follows: TO.THE.ONLIE.BEGETTER.OF. / THESE.INSVING.SONNETS. / M$^{r.}$ W.H. ALL.HAPPINESSE. / AND.THAT. ETERNITIE. / PROMISED. / BY. / OVR.EVER-LIVING.POET. / WISHETH. / THE.WELL-WISHING. / ADVENTVRER.IN. / SETTING./ FORTH. // T. T.

Even though I have read lengthy and tangled discussions, I still find the dedication beautiful and clear: "The well-wishing adventurer, Thomas Thorpe, in setting forth on the venture of publishing the book, wishes the only source and inspirer of the sonnets, Master W. H., to have all happiness and the eternity promised to him in the sonnets by the ever-living poet William Shakespeare."

What is obscure? "Begetter" as "procurer of the copy," a reading required for special pleading, gets virtually no support from the *Oxford English Dictionary* or from normal reading. A Muse or inspirer causes poems to be brought forth in a poet as a begetter causes a child to be conceived in a womb.

Thorpe, then, is saying that the young man of the sonnets is Master W. H. Thorpe may have lied, may have been mistaken, may have deliberately reversed or otherwise have disguised the initials,[8] or the printer may have made another mistake, in one of the letters, but those possibilities stop well short of probability. The punning sonnets offer corroboration of the W, since Will begins with W. Even without the punning sonnets, the odds are high that, if his initial was W, his first name was William, because over 95% of British men in the sixteenth and seventeenth centuries with the initial W were named William, according to random samples I took from the *Short-Title Catalogue* and the *Dictionary of National Biography.* According to the *Oxford Dictionary of Christian Names,* between 1550 and 1599, 22½% of all English males were named William.

Something, then, though not very much. I have an irrepressible hunch (I claim it only as such) that he was a Catholic, which ties in with one plausible reading of Sonnet 124, implying opposition to Elizabeth's persecution of Catholics. To hint that the establishment is a real heretic and to say that "th' inviting time . . . calls" (124.8) for rebellion is strong talk, and more plausible if Shakespeare is addressing a Catholic.[9] Sonnets 1-17 do suggest that Shakespeare was in some way close to the young man's family (perhaps by kinship? or employment?).

Finding his name would solve a long bruited puzzle, might make the dating more firm, add a footnote or two, and could even open several doors. The search would require some travel to no sure inn. It would take, in the words of Franklin B. Williams in a somewhat different context (he wisely and smilingly refused the Master W. H. journey), study of "lists of knights, registers of universities and inns of court, and heraldric visitations, with a wry realization that not one of them can be trusted to be complete"[10] and the further wry realization that, even if the search succeeded, possibly little more than a name might be found. It is perhaps worth adding here that, for all the speculation and contention, no one has ever really looked very hard, in lists, registers, visitations, or — what may be a hint of some merit — recusant rolls. There would only be a hundred or so W. H.'s highly enough placed with the proper dates.

So much is what I believe can be said. But the cases made for Henry Wriothesley, Third Earl of Southampton, for William Herbert, Third Earl of Pembroke, and for William Hatcliffe, have been offered with learning by important scholars and warrant some considering.

If the view taken here of the dedication is right, neither earl is the young man. Mr. W. H., as has often been said, would not be used of an earl; and the way in which the earls' supporters handle the dedication is at least suspect. The likelihood of an actor-player being on intimate terms, innocent or otherwise, with either of these men is not very great. Some of the sonnets could hardly have been sent or perhaps even written to a highly placed aristocrat. Poems, yes, but not these poems. As best as I can judge from the portraits I have seen, either man might be considered handsome enough but neither blond enough. One may add a piece of negative evidence of some value: much is known about both these men, but no reference in their papers or letters or in comments about them has ever revealed Shakespeare as friend or close acquaintance.

Sonnet 25 speaks authoritatively against the candidacy of any very highly placed aristocrat since it places Shakespeare and his friend safely away from the "public honor" (25.2) and "proud titles" (25.2) of "great princes' favorites" (25.5) who can die at a frown. To say that Shakespeare is separate from that world but the friend in the midst of it, makes utter nonsense of the couplet: "Then happy I that love and am belov'd/ Where I may not remove, nor be remov'd." Shakespeare can hardly be saying, "You may be beheaded tomorrow, but I and my love are safe."

The dedication argument seems to me very nearly conclusive, the Sonnet 25 argument nearly as strong, the other arguments cumulative but not demolishing. My case for Marlowe as rival poet excludes Pembroke: the dates do not fit.

What evidence is there for either of the earls? Most of the elaborate arguments offered for either man consist of refuting arguments for the other or finding events and qualities in the life of the proposed candidate which fit the poems.

Arguing against either man has a special trap, the persuasive click of the closing disjunction. Evidence against Southampton is felt to be strong evidence for Pembroke, and vice versa; but it is not.[11] It is easy to forget under polemical pressure that two inconsistent, debated doctrines may both be false. John Dover Wilson writes, "If Southampton, then, be ruled out we are left with William Herbert."[12] Not to mention all other named or unnamed candidates.

What fits, impresses; yet should not impress very much. Advocates of Southampton tie in the sonnets written in absence with documented or speculated trips Shakespeare or Southampton took; but most people are absent from most people most of the time. Such parallels are virtually worthless as evidence; but, when heaped up, begin to overwhelm even good minds. C. F. Tucker Brooke writes, "The Earl of Southampton fits the date so exactly that it seems supererogatory to consider other suggestions."[13] Even suggestions as to the hundreds of other young men who fit the dates? Or the distinct ways in which Southampton does not fit? Hundreds of details each fit thousands of men. What evidence is crucial and truly narrowing?

Two pieces of evidence exist for Southampton, one for Pembroke.

The evidence for Pembroke is the remark in Heminge's and Condell's dedicatory letter to the First Folio that William, Earl of Pembroke and his brother Philip, Earl of Montgomery "haue prosequuted both them [Shakespeare's plays], and their Author liuing, with so much fauour."[14] But, while enough to give a start to an eager looker, that passage is very little evidence that Pembroke and Shakespeare were close personal friends. Many people liked and like Shakespeare's plays; and, in an age of patronage, some signs of favor from two lords to a playwright hardly prove intimacy of one of the lords with him. One cannot argue from the common to the extraordinary with much convincingness. Further, in accord with the style of such dedications, "so much fauour" means any favor at all, perhaps no more than an admiring remark or two after a performance.

Of the two pieces of evidence for Southampton, one is weak and the other stronger. The dedication of *Lucrece* is said to parallel closely Sonnet 26 and to show an intimacy of friendship.[15] But the dedication to *Lucrece* and Sonnet 26 do not parallel each other in any specific way at all: "lord," "love," and "duty" occur in each, but how commonplace can flattery be? If they did closely parallel each other, it would have some import, but would establish beyond doubt nothing about Southampton in relation to the young man, since Shakespeare often echoes himself in various contexts; and the dedication to *Lucrece* is formal and obsequious; it professes limitless love and duty, as dedications often did.

The other piece of evidence is better. Southampton was Shakespeare's only certain dedicatee and may well have been his patron, though, to be strict, it is not certain that he ever spoke a word or gave a shilling to Shakespeare. Elizabethan writers often dedicated books in hope and were often disappointed. Shakespeare's dedicating *Lucrece* to Southampton suggests that the dedication of *Venus and Adonis* had had some effect, but even that is not sure. The second dedication may mean "Thank you; further gifts would be appreciated"; but it may also mean "I am sorry my last request had no response; please be helpful this time."

Sir Sidney Lee claims that twenty sonnets refer to patronage: Sonnets 23, 26, 32, 37, 38, 69, 78-86, 100, 101, 103, 106-107.[16] If Shakespeare had only one patron or dedicatee, Southampton, and if the sonnets tell that the young man is Shakespeare's patron or dedicatee, Southampton gets the verdict and court may close. At least that is a kind of evidence which, if right, means something, so those sonnets are worth regarding.

In Sonnet 23, the poet after lamenting that he had forgotten "to say,/ The perfect ceremony of loues right [right and rite]" (23.5-6, 1609 ed.), then says, "O let my books be then the eloquence,/ And domb presagers of my speaking brest" (23.9-10, 1609 ed.).

The word "books" is usually emended to "looks," and the emendation may be right, especially in context of Sonnet 24, but the emendation begs the question with respect to the Southampton question and "books" makes fairly clear sense in context.

According to the *Oxford English Dictionary, book* originally meant a leaf or sheet, hence "books" could conceivably mean written sheets or poems (the sonnets already sent), but not most probably. The *Oxford English Dictionary* gives no Elizabethan examples of the meaning "poems" for *books* and, except for the meaning "legal documents," Shakespearean usage of *books* appears generally consonant with modern usage, literal or metaphorical.

A metaphorical meaning of "books" is possible but strained, a literal reading more natural, and the most obvious referents for a literal meaning are *Venus and Adonis* and *Lucrece*, though the reference could be to *A Lover's Complaint* (if a version existed that early) and lost longer poems. Thus Sonnet 23 can reasonably be taken as evidence for Southampton.

Lines 26.1-3, "Lord of my love, to whom in vassalage/ Thy merit hath my duty strongly knit,/ To thee I send this written ambassage," are in dignified language which would be appropriate to a patron or a loved one, and line 26.3 is ambiguous. "This written ambassage" probably means the poem itself, but could also mean some other writing sent with the sonnet. The poem probably does not implicate patronage, but might. Sonnets 32, 37, 100, 101, 103, 106, and 107 have no remotely likely references to patronage which I can discover. Sonnet 38 asks the young man to inspire Shakespeare's verse, which does not implicate patronage. Sonnet 69 says that poets praise the young man. Sonnets 78-86 are about the rival poet as a rival for the young man's affection and inspiration.

Is the rival poet also a rival for patronage? Possibly. Sonnets 78, 80, 82, and 86 have some passages which may suggest so. Lines 78.3-4 sound very much, out of context, as though the young man were patron to other poets, but the context makes that possibility dubious and at most secondary.

So oft have I invok'd thee for my Muse,
And found such fair assistance in my verse,
As ev'ry alien pen hath got my use,
And under thee their poetry disperse.
Thine eyes, that taught the dumb on high to sing
And heavy ignorance aloft to fly,
Have added feathers to the learnèd's wing
And given grace a double majesty.
Yet be most proud of that which I compile,
Whose influënce is thine, and born of thee;
In others' work thou dost but mend the style,
And arts with thy sweet graces gracèd be.
But thou art all my art, and dost advance
As high as learning my rude ignorance.

The context makes clear that the chief reference is to the young man as inspirer; the assistance is in the verse, not pocketbook. There may be no reference to patronage, even in lines 78.3-4 which mean primarily and maybe exclusively, "Every other poet follows me in seeking inspiration for his poetry and sends his poems forth under the influence of your beauty." But patronage may also be suggested: the truth that several poets sought the young man's influence hints that the young man was well enough placed and moneyed to be of some mundane use to the admiring poets.

Lines 80.9-10 and 86.1-2 could refer to patronage as well as to affection and inspiration or in Sonnet 86 something more physical, but they do not have to: respectively, "Your shall'west help will hold me up afloat/ Whilst he upon your soundless deep doth ride" and "Was it the proud full sail of his great verse/ Bound for the prize of all-too-precious you."

The passages discussed neither prove nor discourage the view that the young man was in some sense Shakespeare's patron. Patronage is a vague relation. It may be one gift once; it may be a close and long-lasting relation such as that of the Pembrokes to Samuel Daniel. One could claim, on the basis of the passage quoted from Heminge and Condell, that William and Philip Herbert were Shakespeare's patrons, since they showed him some marks of favor. Shakespeare may have received some patronage from several men, and the young man may have shown patronage to several poets who never published anything.

Hence dedication, a public and specific act, and for extant books a clearly verifiable act, is better evidence. Lines 82.1-4 speak of dedication in a distinct if entangled way.

I grant thou wert not marri'd to my Muse,
And therefore mayst without attaint o'erlook
The dedicatèd words which writers use
Of their fair subject, blessing ev'ry book.

The lines may mean, "Since you are not exclusively committed to my poetry, you may without fault read books written by other poets dedicated to you," or "Since you are not exclusively committed to my poetry, you may without fault read poems dedicated to you as books of poems are dedicated to dedicatees." Neither meaning implies that Shakespeare had dedicated a book to the young man, though such a dedication might add to the private joke. Even if the lines did imply that Shakespeare dedicated one or more books to the young man, it would not establish the case for Southampton since Shakespeare may have dedicated lost or unpublished works to other dedicatees, but it would be an impressive piece of evidence for Southampton. But a hint is not an implication, and the lack of any book dedicated to the young man by Shakespeare could also serve a private joke. Literally, saying "the dedicated words which writers use" rather than "the dedicated words which other writers also use" would seem to imply that Shakespeare has not dedicated a book to the young man, an interpretation which would rule out Southampton, unless Sonnet 82 is earlier than *Venus and Adonis*.

I would say on the evidence that the odds are better than even that the young man was in some sense a patron of Shakespeare and other poets; and there is the lively, ambiguous hint about dedication. Hence the books–patronage–dedication argument for Southampton has some merit, but not enough to establish a probability. I find no serious corroborating evidence, and I think the anti-Southampton arguments strongly outweigh it. The reader, as always, must judge for himself.

Leslie Hotson devotes his vast scholarship and polemical skills to supporting a case for William Hatcliffe. The argument is founded on what Hotson calls an "incredible clue,"[17] namely, that since Shakespeare refers to the young man in sovereign metaphors the young man must have been a Prince at a festival at an Inn of Court. The clue is literally incredible: Shakespeare might have made a passing allusion or two to a friend's being a Prince of Purpoole; he could not have made that a major theme in some of the world's most serious love poetry. The rest of Hotson's journey takes us no nearer, since no evidence of any credibility emerges. The clue and the hope lead; all else is battered to conform. Any analogy can "prove" a point; any evidence against a point can be dismissed as conventional.

Hotson refers many general passages and features of the sonnets to highly specific events and relations, then dismisses what seems quite specific as merely conventional. References to truth and beauty in the sonnets refer to the white and blue of William Hatcliffe's colors,[18] while the specific references to age, which suggest to most scholars a date later than the 1580s, are by Hotson (1) dismissed as merely conventional,[19] and (2) used to show that Shakespeare was older than his friend.[20] Using the precisely same evidence as conventional, hence worthless, against one's case, but solid as evidence for one's case is a method not highly persuasive. Hotson also uses Sonnet 138 to show Shakespeare young and the dark lady old.[21] By such methods one can "prove" anything, that is, sadly, nothing. It is sad because Hotson is a scholar to whom our debt is heavy.

Thus, pending the appearance of better candidates or arguments, we are left with Master William H., a familiar and invisible figure, whose last name eludes us. My inferences about him will be accepted by those who accept them.

Homosexuality

To raise the question of the youth is inevitably to raise the question of homosexuality. Whether the relation was overt or not cannot be finally decided on the available evidence, but some things may be said.

Shakespeare says that there is a sexual element in his feeling for the young man, referring in Sonnet 20 to the young man as "the master-mistress of my passion" (20.2) who "for a woman" (20.9) was "first creatèd" (20.9). The relation is, then, in a sense overt: Shakespeare speaks of it.

In the same sonnet he says in distinctly plain language that the relation was not physically overt: "But since she [nature] prick'd thee out for women's pleasure,/ Mine by thy love and thy love's use their treasure" (20.13-14).

That is funny and clear. To say that the relationship was physically overt is to call Shakespeare a liar, or at least a cynical jokester. Nor will it do to say the relation changed after Sonnet 20: Shakespeare calls the relation "pure" in line 110.14. It would be pleasant to accept the testimony of Sonnet 20 and consider the matter closed.[22] Unfortunately, the subject is one about which human beings do not always tell the truth. We need to look at what evidence we may find.

Citing Renaissance friendship is mostly beside the way. It is beside the point polemically since as rapidly as the old-fashioned can say, "Ah, there is no trace of homosexuality here; these are Renaissance friendship poems," the newer-fashioned may reply, with probable additions of jargon, "Ah, but what physical desires empower such friendship?"

It is beside the way in quality. Friendship then as now was a great thing, and could be praised as such; but it is a different thing. The friendship of Hamlet and Horatio is beautiful, tender, and noble. Shakespeare, who on the evidence was a good friend to his friends, understood friendship and expresses it magnificently. But Hamlet and Horatio are not in love. Shakespeare is in love with the young man, and I do not see how anyone who has been in love and who has read these poems can dispute the point. Damon and Pythias in Richard Edwards' play *Damon and Pythias* (1571) and Pyrocles and Musidorus in Sidney's *Arcadia* are deep friends; that relationship, shallow in Edwards, subtle in Sidney, is not the relationship of the sonnets. Pyrocles and Musidorus clasp each other in the arms and weep as they do so, but in manly innocence. They are idealistically and passionately in love with women.

C. S. Lewis makes the necessary comment that the language of Shakespeare in the sonnets "is too lover-like for that of ordinary male friendship; and though the claims of friendship are sometimes put very high in, say, the *Arcadia*, I have found no real parallel to such language between friends in sixteenth-century literature."[23]

Nor does it serve to cite, as is frequently done,[24] variant meanings of the words *lover* and *friend*. To an Elizabethan, *friend* can mean "lover" as it can nowadays in some sophisticated usage, and *lover* can mean "friend" in a normal modern sense, but *lover* can also mean "lover" and *friend* "friend." In *Measure for Measure,* Lucio says to Isabella, "Your brother [Claudio] and his lover [Juliet] have embraced" (I.iv.40), and Juliet is pregnant. We are told a few lines earlier "He hath got his friend with child" (I.iv.29). The use of the words *friend* and *lover* proves nothing either way.

The case for overt homosexuality depends on general likelihoods and specific hints of language. It is likely that a man passionately in love for over three years will consummate or seek to consummate his passion. The young man was not one to pass up any pleasure he wanted; and Shakespeare admits in the sonnets his weakness and susceptibility to temptation. One can argue that the complaints of mutual infidelity show an overt relation, since that is usually what infidelity means: to make physical love with someone other than the person entitled to one's physical love. In lines 93.1-2 Shakespeare says, "So shall I live, supposing thou art true,/ Like a deceivèd husband," but does not tell us in what precise respects he is like that husband beyond supposing wrongly that the friend is true. If the friend is untrue, to what? to a chaste love? or to a physically realized love? Here, as many a place, either answer works, as it does in the *had*s of lines 52.14 and 87.13. The word *had* suggests to a modern ear physical possession, but that is not the primary meaning in line 52.14, "Be'ng had, to triumph; being lack'd to hope," or in lines 87.13-14, "Thus have I had thee as a dream doth flatter,/ In sleep a king, but, waking, no such matter." Line 52.14 refers to presence as opposed to absence; in Sonnet 87 the poet fears the friend's abandoning him. Either passage is perfectly consistent with physical possession and perfectly consistent with spiritual but not physical possession. A dream may be a dream of physical possession, or not.

Some other phrases suggest overtness, and many will read that way. In lines 57.1-2, "Being your slave, what should I do but tend/ Upon the hours and times of your desire?" "desire" reads very naturally as a pun. In line 87.9 the phrase "Thy self thou gav'st," if said of a woman, would certainly suggest consummation. Few other phrases, if any, are so striking, but many phrases are consonant with overtness. But no phrase has to read that way, and circularity bedevils any attempt to canvass the evidence. Many phrases can be read either way; the way one reads them depends on the view taken. If any phrase unambiguously states or implies overtness, I have not found it.

The evidence against overtness is the stronger evidence:

(1) The specific denial of Sonnet 20. If Shakespeare is lying, to whom? To the young man? He would have known. To friends to whom he planned to circulate the poems? Possibly, but the poems began as very private: when Shakespeare first wrote them, he probably had no larger audience in mind. One can speculate that Sonnet 20 was written when Shakespeare began to circulate the poems, written precisely as a blind, a protection of the relationship. That is possible but less than probable.

(2) The repeated identification of beauty and virtue. Infidelity in these poems is to turn from virtue to stain. To have written Sonnet 144, "Two loves I have, of comfort and despair," with its religious notes opposing the holy love for his friend to the profane love of the dark lady, in order to mask an overt homosexual relationship, is a little hard to imagine.

One could argue against this that one may be idealistic about a physical affair or point to Shakespeare's capacity for rationalization. Again, perhaps so, but again not probably so. While Elizabethans could be sophisticated about overt homosexuality, as in the coy passages in Marlowe's *Hero and Leander* discussed later in this chapter, it is a long way from that to making overt homosexuality a standard of purity. Here the Renaissance friendship tradition is relevant, since deep, physically innocent friendship between men was taken as a standard and a source of virtue. Shakespeare does reveal his capacity for rationalization in the sonnets, but he also reveals what he is rationalizing about.

(3) Negative evidence here is impressive. One has no doubt about the overtness of Shakespeare's relations with the dark lady; even without the specific sexual puns of Sonnets 135, 144, and 151, one would still be positive. The dark lady poems also reveal strong and specific sexual guilt. In general the sonnets are very revealing poems: had there been an overt relationship, it would be evident in the poems. But it is not evident.

(4) The love has a familial quality. Attempts to prove that the young man was Shakespeare's son are faulty enough in terms of evidence and methodology, but touch one strain of feeling. Sonnets 1-17 are not very apt to have been written by an active homosexual to his lover, and they incorporate a quality which appears and reappears throughout the poems.

The probability is against overtness, but certainty is not to be had. If the relation was overt, the complications of purity, love, guilt, inner division become very strange indeed. Sonnet 20 catches wittily and lightly what the sonnets, and *Venus and Adonis, Lucrece,* and *A Lover's Complaint,* largely are about, and are: the collision between great sexual passion and a great and passionately held ideal of chastity.

The Rival Poet

We probably know the rival poet's name; we need to find out which name. The sonnets make clear that he was a poet whom Shakespeare admired and feared and who had a substantial reputation before Shakespeare did; thus, he is a poet whose name has very likely survived.

To be unsure, he may have been a good poet now forgotten, who never published a book or whose books have vanished; he may have been a poet whom Shakespeare nervously overrated. But those are the less likely alternatives. A poet so highly reputed probably wrote several published books; and Shakespeare's literary judgment is not lightly to be put aside.

Of the possible known candidates, Christopher Marlowe has the best *prima facie* case, to which I shall add some new and I think conclusive particulars.

The rival poet sonnets tell a good deal about the rival poet, after reasonable allowances for poetic hyperbole, satire, and veiling. Some references are highly specific, but lost to us. The "compeers by night" (86.7) and the "affable familiar ghost/ Which nightly gulls him with intelligence" (86.9-10) are unmistakably private jokes which have stayed private. The ghost can hardly be Mephistopheles ("affable" indeed!) as some defenders of Marlowe claim,[25] or Homer (an affable coney catcher, a con man?) as defenders of Chapman are prone to insist.[26] The references may be to collaborators or to spying, either of which would fit Marlowe, but we cannot be sure.

Certain truths about the rival poet, however, emerge plainly:

(1) He was a poet of substantial reputation before Shakespeare had a substantial reputation. Marlowe with others qualifies here.

(2) He was a poet Shakespeare admired and feared. The rival poet sonnets are at once laudatory, even a little awe-struck, and satiric; a little mocking, but also more than a little frightened. Shakespeare as a young man no doubt admired and envied at least several poets. Young poets do. Two we can be certain Shakespeare admired, simply because they influenced him much, are Samuel Daniel and Christopher Marlowe.

(3) He was probably better educated than Shakespeare, according to the most natural reading of lines 78.5-7: "Thine eyes, that taught the dumb [Shakespeare] on high to sing/ And heavy ignorance [again Shakespeare] aloft to fly/ Have added feathers to the learned's wing" [the rival poet's or poets']. Marlowe was a Cambridge man and a scholar.

(4) He was original, offering "a fresher stamp [than Shakespeare could offer] of the time-bett'ring days" (82.8). Marlowe is one of the most original poets ever.

(5) He was a poet who wrote love poems to a man. The poems of the rival poet to the young man might just possibly be poems seeking patronage and offering conventional praises, as in the proliferation of dedicatory sonnets in the period, but Shakespeare certainly makes the

poems of the rival poet sound like competitive love poems. They are
inspired by the young man's "eyes" (78.5), respond to his "lovely
argument" (79.5), and praise not only his "virtue" (79.9), but the
"beauty" (79.10) in his "cheek" (79.11). They are "bound for the prize
of [the] all-too-precious" young man (86.2), and they must sing
lovingly because Shakespeare, hearing them, says "'Tis so, 'tis true"
(85.9).

Several other candidates, Spenser, Barnes, Daniel among them,
wrote love poems to women, which makes it less likely that they wrote
love poems to a man. Shakespeare in the sonnets writes love poems
both to a man and to a woman, but that is unusual. Richard Barnfield
in *Cynthia* (1595) wrote love sonnets to a man, but qualifies on
virtually no other ground; his poetry could hardly be called a "proud
full sail."

Marlowe does, in *Hero and Leander,* praise the physical beauty of a
man, Leander, in a way much more suggestive than anything in
Shakespeare's sonnets:

> His body was as straight as Circe's wand;
> Jove might have sipp'd out nectar from his hand.
> Even as delicious meat is to the taste,
> So was his neck in touching, and surpass'd
> The white of Pelops' shoulder. I could tell ye
> How smooth his breast was, and how white his belly,
> And whose immortal fingers did imprint
> That heavenly path with many a curious dint,
> That runs along his back, but my rude pen
> Can hardly blazon forth the loves of men,
> Much less of powerful gods . . . [27]

                                                    (1.61-71)

There is a knowing smile for a private audience in those and in other
lines of the poem, especially the Neptune passage (2.153-226). "The
loves of men" is a coy sort of pun.

(6) A man who writes love poems to a man is likely to be a
homosexual, overt or sublimated. (Probably more than likely, but that
raises psychological issues irrelevant to the present concern.) The
evidence, external and internal, is that Marlowe was overtly homosexual. The external evidence is that of Richard Baines who quoted
Marlowe as saying "That all they that loue not tobacco & boyes were
fooles."[28] Baines's testimony is inherently credible and has been partly
substantiated by scholarship on other points.[29]

The internal evidence is stronger. It is hard not to believe that the author of the passage quoted from *Hero and Leander* was homosexual, the "I could tell ye" sounding very much like a boast to a special audience. The Ganymede episodes in *Dido*, the playing up well beyond the sources of the homosexual nature of Edward's attachment to Gaveston in *Edward II*, and the Neptune–Leander episode in *Hero and Leander* fondle the theme and leave no serious doubt.[30]

(7) One needs to account for the brevity of the rivalry, a point not previously noted. Sonnets 78-86 are accepted as the standard rival poet sonnets. I believe that there may be some further references in Sonnets 87-99, but that is all. The rivalry flares up and vanishes. Other explanations are of course possible, but Marlowe's death is a precise and dramatic explanation.

(8) An old and still an impressive piece of evidence is the simple truth that "the proud full sail of his great verse" (86.1), with its pun on *proudful*, fits Marlowe better than it does any other poet in contention.

These considerations are short of conclusive, but they are converging. Just on them, it is fair to say that Marlowe has a substantially better claim than any other candidate. Before looking at some special evidence, I shall examine the claims of George Chapman, Marlowe's chief rival as rival poet, recently supported by Martin Seymour-Smith in his valuable edition of the sonnets.

What Seymour-Smith with others considers the "striking evidence"[31] that Chapman claimed to have been inspired by the spirit of Homer is unpersuasive, since it sorts badly with the passage in Sonnet 86 it is supposed to explain:

> Was it his sprite, by spirits taught to write
> Above a mortal pitch, that struck me dead?
> No, neither he, nor his compeers by night
> Giving him aid, my verse astonishèd.
> He, nor that affable familiar ghost
> Which nightly gulls him with intelligence,
> As victors, of my silence cannot boast.
>
> (86.5-11)

References to inspiration and to familiar spirits are commonplace in the period; and Homer cannot fit the plural "spirits" or the "affable" or "gulls."

Looked at in terms of the conditions I have stated, Chapman does better than some candidates but worse than Marlowe. Chapman has nothing striking to recommend him and some evidence against him.

(1) He was not, so far as we know, a poet of substantial reputation in the early 1590s, his first published work, *Skià Nuktòs, The Shadow of*

Night, appearing in 1594. Its preface strongly suggests that he is a nervous beginner struggling for recognition.

(2) Chapman is, despite his massively irritating pomposity and his clotted pedantry, a good poet. Marlowe is a better poet. We know Shakespeare admired Marlowe; we have no idea whether he admired Chapman's work or not.

(3) Marlowe and Chapman both qualify as learned men; Marlowe probably had a better formal education than Chapman, apparently self-educated.

(4) As original, they qualify equally well. Both are highly original.

(5) Chapman did not write love poems to a man, so far as we know, and it is hard to imagine him writing very personal love poems to anyone. It is "philosophical conceits" that his pen "seriously court-eth."[32]

(6) I know of no evidence that Chapman was homosexual.

(7) Nothing in Chapman's known biography accounts for the brevity of the rivalry.

One could sum the case at this point by saying that Chapman and Marlowe, largely on (8) the evidence of line 86.1, "the proud full sail of his great verse," stand out among known candidates. Spenser fits that description better than Chapman and only a little worse than Mar-lowe, but the *Amoretti* speak pleasantly against his candidacy. Mar-lowe fits no requirement less well than Chapman, and several require-ments much better. The objection that Marlowe died too early is no objection for anyone convinced, as I am (and was before I explored the rival poet question), that the sonnets were probably written in the early 1590s, a conclusion I shall defend in the following chapter.

So much for probabilities; now an attempt at proof.

An important piece of evidence is an echoic allusion in lines 80.7-8 and context, to *Hero and Leander.* If Shakespeare is offering a deliberate echoic allusion to Marlowe, he is *saying* by means of the parody that Marlowe is the rival poet. Here is the passage[33] from *Hero and Leander*:

> A stately builded ship, well rig'd and tall,
> The Ocean maketh more majesticall:
> Why vowest thou then to liue in *Sestos* here,
> Who on Loues seas more glorious wouldst appeare?

A. L. Rowse notes an allusion[34] by Shakespeare to the first two lines quoted, in lines 80.11-12, "I am a worthless bote,/ He of tall building, and of goodly pride" (1609 ed.). Those two lines, taken by themselves, are some evidence, since *tall* and *build-* get repeated, but the reference is not in itself sure; many a noble craft sails on Elizabethan poetic seas and *tall* and *build-* are hardly surprising terms to use about a ship.

The rest of the allusion, which Rowse does not note, is more striking, and supports Rowse's evidence and position. Earlier in the sonnet Shakespeare says, "My sawsie [saucy] barke (inferior farre to his)/ On your broad maine doth wilfully appeare" (80.7-8, 1609 ed.), line 80.8 echoing one of Marlowe's lines closely.

Marlowe:

Who *on* Loues sea *m*ore glorious wouldst *appeare*?

Shakespeare:

On your broad *m*aine doth *w*ilfully *appeare*

Cadence, words, rhyme, grammatical placing are similar, as are features of sound pattern, for instance the initial *m* before *w* before *appeare*. The "broad maine" of Shakespeare means precisely the "Loues seas" of Marlowe. This reference reinforces the likelihood of lines 80.11-12 being an allusion, and the reinforcement is mutual.

Being an echo of Marlowe proves nothing; Shakespeare is rich in such echoes. If, however, it is a deliberate echo, a mocking reference, it proves that Marlowe is the rival poet. Deliberateness is certainly hinted in the "wilfully," which means "deliberately," and supported by the competitive impudence of "sawsie barke." Other reasons strengthen that likelihood.

Marlowe is the greatest influence on Shakespeare. Shakespeare frequently echoes Marlowe; he also parodies him,[35] garbles him for comic effect,[36] and on one certain and another probable occasion alludes to Marlowe as he echoes him.

The most famous and unmistakable echoic allusion occurs in *As You Like It,* when Phebe, having just tumbled into love with Rosalind-Ganymede, says, "Dead shepherd, now I find thy saw of might,/ 'Who ever lov'd that lov'd not at first sight?'" (III. v. 81-82). This is at least a double and probably a triple allusion to Marlowe, to the line quoted from *Hero and Leander* (1.176), to the lyric "The Passionate Shepherd to His Love," and to the shepherd Tamburlaine. The first two references in the allusion need not be friendly;[37] the Tamburlaine reference is unfriendly. To identify Marlowe and Tamburlaine is to identify Marlowe with overweening pride and to join the chorus of hostile voices.[38] For that matter, parodying and garbling for comic effect raise at least a suspicion of unfriendly feelings.

The second echoic allusion to Marlowe in *As You Like It* is disputed but fascinatingly like. Touchstone says, "When a man's verses cannot be understood, nor a man's good wit seconded with the forward child, understanding, it strikes a man more dead than a great reckoning in a little room" (III. iii. 12-15). This echoes the important phrase in *The Jew of Malta,* "infinite riches in a little room," in which Barabbas blasphemously echoes the medieval notion of Christ, the Infinite, within Mary's womb,[39] and fits with deadly accuracy the official report of Marlowe's death: he was stabbed, struck dead, by Ingram Frizer in a room in a quarrel ostensibly over the reckoning, the bill.[40]

Some scholars reject that allusion because it is harsh and offends against their hopes about Shakespeare's attitudes toward Marlowe.[41] The evidence we have is against Shakespeare feeling kindly toward Marlowe. The allusion is more than harsh: it is a judgment, reflecting God's judgment on atheism and blasphemy, the pun in "reckoning" catching overtones of the awesome judgment of Barabbas implicit in "infinite riches in a little room."

One may shy away from the thought of the genial Shakespeare's taking such a view, but stern retribution is one of his voices. Witness the couplet of Sonnet 141, "Only my plague thus far I count my gain,/ That she that makes me sin awards me pain," and the couplet of Sonnet 147, "For I have sworn thee fair and thought thee bright,/ Who art as black as hell, as dark as night," both, as I shall argue in Chapter Three, written well before 1599 or 1600, the probable date of composition of *As You Like It.* In *Othello* and *Macbeth* retribution has a stern enough voice.

Some relation of influence exists between *Hero and Leander* and the sonnets of Shakespeare, as proved by the following couplets:

Marlowe:

Whose name is it, if she be false or not,
So she be faire, but some vile toongs will blot?
(1598, sig. Clv; 1.285-286)

Shakespeare:

But whats so blessed faire that feares no blot,
Thou maist be falce, and yet I know it not.
(92.13-14, 1609 ed.)

If any two passages in English show influence by internal evidence, these do. To read them aloud is to waive doubt. One of these couplets rang in the ear of the author of the other couplet.

The existence of the other echoic allusions and the distinct relation of *Hero and Leander* to the sonnets[42] corroborate the likelihood of the echoic allusion in Sonnet 80 to Marlowe, itself highly likely on internal evidence.

I further think that lines 86.1-2, "Was it the proud *full saile* of his great verse,/ Bound for the prize of (all to precious) you" (1609 ed.), parodies the passage in *Hero and Leander* where Leander attempts the resisting Hero by scaling the ivory mount of her breast.

> And euery lim did as a soldier stout,
> Defend the fort, and keep the foe-man out:
> For though the rising yu'rie [ivory] mount he scal'd
> Which is with azure circling lines empal'd,
> Much like a globe, (a globe may I tearme this,
> By which loue *sailes* to regions *full* of blis)
> (1598, sig. E2v; 2.271-276)

The *full* and *sail* and the military word *prize* are apposite, and competitively witty; and that Marlowe is lurking behind Sonnet 86 gets a corroboration from line 86.7, "No, neither he, nor his compiers by night" (1609 ed.). I do not know who those compeers were or for what the "Schoole of night" in *Love's Labor's Lost* stands,[43] but that notorious textual crux has a connection with the compeers which I think, in conjunction with the other evidence presented, establishes the case for Marlowe as rival poet. For, in the school-of-night passage, Shakespeare is parodying a passage in Marlowe's *The Massacre at Paris*.

Shakespeare in *Love's Labor's Lost* certainly echoes and almost as certainly parodies Marlowe as a joke is made about a school of night, very close in Shakespeare's text to a separate parody of Marlowe;[44] in the rival poet sonnets Shakespeare makes a joke about compeers by night in a context in which he certainly echoes and in which there is good evidence that he is parodying Marlowe. The same joke occurs twice, Marlowe in its midst. The mutual corroboration is strong, for the rightness of the reading "Schoole of night" and for the existence of deliberate parody of Marlowe in the rival poet sonnets. Shakespeare, by parodying Marlowe as he satirizes the rival poet, is telling us something: the name of the rival poet. *The Massacre at Paris* passage[45] follows:

If euer *Hymen* lowr'd at marriage rites,
And had his alters deckt with duskie lights:
If euer sunne stainde heauen with bloudy clowdes,
And made it look with terrour on the worlde:
If euer day were turnde to vgly night,
And night made semblance of the hue of hell,
This day, this houre, this fatall night,
Shall fully shew the fury of them all.

The passage certainly struck Shakespeare's ear, since unmistakable echoes appear in the sonnets. The cadence, three words each in the same places, and other exactly placed sounds appear in the fifth line quoted (I. ii. 5) and line 15.12 of Shakespeare's sonnets:

If euer *day* were turnde *to vgly   night*
To change your *day* of youth   *to sullied night*
(1609 ed.)

Another parallel is almost as striking:

If euer *sunne stainde heauen* with bloudy clowdes
(Marlowe, line 3 above)

Suns of the worlde may *staine,* when *heauens sun stain*teh [staineth]
(33.14, 1609 ed.)

Those echoes seem to me certain. Two others are likely. "Rites" appears in the first line of the passage from Marlowe and in Shakespeare's line 17.11, "And your true rights [a pun on *rights* and *rites*] be termd a Poets rage" (1609 ed.). The rites are contrastive in Marlowe's and Shakespeare's passages, with "lowr'd" and "rage" respectively. The word *hue* appears in the sixth line quoted of Marlowe's passage, twice in line 20.7 of Shakespeare's sonnets (a line where a private joke has often been suspected, though never successfully explained), and in the school-of-night passage in *Love's Labor's Lost.* Shakespeare was listening.

There are three reasons for believing that the influence is from Marlowe to Shakespeare's sonnets: (1) we know that Marlowe influenced Shakespeare much and do not know that Shakespeare ever influenced Marlowe; (2) the passage in Marlowe relates to several of Shakespeare's sonnets, and it seems somewhat more plausible that Shakespeare had the passage from Marlowe echoing while Shakespeare was writing the sonnets rather than that Marlowe combined several memories of Shakespeare in a brief context; (3) the passage in Marlowe is parodied in *Love's Labor's Lost,* in the school-of-night passage, which follows:

> *King.*   O paradox, Blacke is the badge of Hell,
>   The hue of dungions, and the Schoole of *night:*
>   And beauties crest becomes the heauens well.
> *Ber*[owne].   Diuels soonest tempt resembling spirites [*sprites*] of *light.*
> (1598, sig. F2; IV. iii. 254-256)

Shakespeare is mocking gloomy poetry and motives. What shows he had the passage in Marlowe specifically in mind is the echoing of sound, which is distinct.

The rhyme:

> Marlowe: rites & lights & night & night
> Shakespeare: night & sprites & light
>   [note singular and plural in each]

Other echoes:

> Marlowe: the hue   of hell
>
> Shakespeare: The badge of Hell, / The hue

> Marlowe: And night   the   hue of hell
>
> Shakespeare: The hue   the Schoole of night

Shakespeare is echoing Marlowe. The immediate context of *Love's Labor's Lost* is one of parody, including a parody of some of Shakespeare's own sonnets (to be discussed in the next chapter) and a distinct, separate parody of Marlowe. The passage is joking. Therefore, the echo of Marlowe is deliberate parody.

The same joke, compeers-by-night and school-of-night, occurs both in the sonnets and *Love's Labor's Lost* in a context of parody and in a context in which Shakespeare is closely echoing Marlowe. In the rival poet sonnets, the parody occurs when Shakespeare is satirizing the (chief) rival poet.

The inference is plain and with the support of the other evidence conclusive:

Marlowe is the rival poet.

Chapter 3

The Date of Composition

In this chapter I shall argue that Shakespeare wrote his sonnets in the early 1590s, probably from 1591 to 1594, give or take a little. How far, if any, he revised them between 1595 and 1609 cannot be told. My guess would certainly be that he made some and perhaps extensive stylistic revisions. The evidence for the time of first composition is multiple and converging, and strongly suggests that the sonnets as we know them had their substantial shape and order, and most of their language, by 1595.

Specific evidence points to that dating; so do certain clusters and pushes of accumulating evidence. Francis Meres in *Palladis Tamia* (1598) speaks of Shakespeare's sugared sonnets among his private friends, a highly probable reference to at least a good number of these poems; and two of the sonnets, Sonnets 138 and 144, were published in *The Passionate Pilgrim* in 1599. These references set a *terminus ad quem* for some sonnets and quite possibly for all. How long the poems had been circulating, and how long written before circulating, we are not told. It is plausible, considering the privacy and intensity, that Shakespeare would have waited a while before showing the poems to his literary friends.

In his sonnets Shakespeare makes clear that he is distinctly older than his friend and that he considers himself a "pupil pen" (16.10), who compared to the rival poet or the "better" poets (32.13) of the age, is an apprentice unfamed and uncertain of his skill. In the 1600s it would be simply false to call himself a novice lacking fame and almost as much so in the late 1590s, when he was a celebrated poet and playwright. On the other hand, the references to age sort so badly with a date in the 1580s that the main proponent of such a date, Leslie Hotson, dismisses those references as mere convention when they hurt his case, solid evidence when they help it, a remarkable method of argument I have earlier discussed.

The double push of the pupil-pen and age references locate the sonnets almost certainly within the 1590s. The pupil-pen references seem hard to square with a date in the late 1590s. One can see some such references as conventional-modest, but the accumulation of references, including those which show fear and envy of the rival poet, strongly suggest a poet who in truth has not yet arrived to fame. The age references may suggest a date in the late 1590s a little more easily than in the earlier 1590s, but only a little. The difference between thirty and thirty-five is not, after all, very much. A man pushing thirty can seem dreadfully old to himself, especially in comparison with someone several years younger.

Sonnets 62 and 73 taken literally will not square with the 1590s or with 1609. Sonnet 73 ("That time of year thou may'st in me behold") shows the speaker at the grave's edge, his youth ashes. In Sonnet 62 hyperbole is working early and late: the poet believes that "no face so gracious is as [his]" (62.5) until his mirror shows him "beatèd and chopp'd with tann'd antiquity" (62.10), which would make him at least 85. The bust in the Stratford church, with however much accuracy, shows Shakespeare smooth faced in his late years. More than hyperbole or mere convention is at work, since Shakespeare is moralizing against his self-love, especially in line 62.12 where he recognizes that his "self-loving" is "iniquity." A passage in *The Prayse of Nothing*, whether or not Shakespeare had read it, makes an appropriate gloss as exemplifying an influencing tradition, by lamenting the "waywarde qualities of olde age," of men who "bestow the remnant of their life in making Sonets, in smothing their wrinckled skin, . . . & carrolling w[ith] ratling voyce their amorous *Villanella*: although without hazarding the losse of some tooth, they open not their hanging chappes, more fearfull then the graue." [1]

In *Willobie His Avisa* (1594), probably written by a friend of Shakespeare's, [2] Shakespeare is called the "old player." [3] The passage is joking and means an old player at the game of seduction as well as an old actor, but it implies that Shakespeare had been on the stage for a good while and does in 1594 call Shakespeare old. The book refers to a real or imagined love affair, recently past, of Shakespeare's; and may twit him about his love poems.

The much discussed Sonnet 107 seems to refer to some occasion of national celebration, but which one is lost in the generality and ambiguity of the language. In immediate context Sonnet 106 relates the present to the Middle Ages ("antique," 106.7) and Sonnet 108 relates the present to antiquity and to eternity. Hence the "now" (107.9) of the sonnet can mean "now in this age" rather than "now in this year," as has not to my knowledge been observed before. The discussion of the "mortal moon" (107.5) as a reference to the Armada, whether *pro* or *contra*, usually seems to assume that, if the Armada is meant, the poem must have been written in 1588 or 1589. But that is not so.[4] One can celebrate a victory years afterward. James Dickey's "The Driver," a beautiful celebration of the end of World War II, was written (according to Mr. Dickey in a letter to me) in 1961, some fifteen years after the event.

The phrase in line 123.2, "pyramids built up with newer might," is odd enough and may plausibly refer, as Hotson claims,[5] to the obelisks brought to Rome by Pope Sixtus V in 1586, 1587, 1588, 1599, but that only gives a *terminus a quo* of 1587 (1587 rather than 1586 since "pyramids" is plural), which is useless, since virtually no one dates the sonnets earlier than that.

Line 98.4, "That heavy Saturn laugh'd and leapt with him [April]," has been taken as a clue with some value for dating, but I do not see how the language can reasonably be construed to mean that Saturn was in opposition in the night sky[6] or that Saturn rose just after sunset,[7] or to mean that sun and Saturn were in Taurus.[8] Saturn may mean only the spirit of winter in contrast to the "sprite of youth" (98.3), referring to the pleasant mixture of chill and warm freshness on some April days. Saturn as the chilling planet was commonplace enough not to require astronomical or astrological definiteness. If the reference is to the visible planet, it is not clear, at least to me, what is being seen.

In short, the dating sonnets are no help at all to me. Anyone who can profit from them is welcome.

The best single internal allusion for dating, discussed less than the "mortal moon" reference, is in Sonnet 100:

> Where art thou, Muse, that thou forget'st so long
> To speak of that which gives thee all thy might?
> Spend'st thou thy fury on some worthless song,
> Dark'ning thy power to lend base subjects light?
> (100.1-4)

The "worthless song" seems to refer clearly to something that Shakespeare has been writing and "song" applies better to a poem than to a play or plays. The only longer poems ascribed to Shakespeare are *Venus and Adonis, Lucrece,* and *A Lover's Complaint,* involving the base subjects of seduction and rape. If *Venus and Adonis* or *Lucrece* is the referent, Sonnet 100 was probably written before 1595.

Dating by persons is the most often practiced method of dating the sonnets, suspect because, when identifications come first, dates tend to get shoved into line. I have argued that Pembroke's case is insubstantial, Southampton's better though unconvincing. Pembroke makes for later dates, Southampton for earlier. Supporters of Southampton are likely to extend the period of composition to accommodate 1593 and 1594 (the *Venus and Adonis* and *Lucrece* dedications) with 1603 (Southampton's release from prison as the putative occasion of Sonnet 107). Apart from the weak reed of Sonnet 107, Southampton would fit dates in the early 1590s well.

The dark lady does not affect the dating significantly. Since, as I believe I have proved, Christopher Marlowe is the rival poet, the rival poet sonnets were written before his death on May 30, 1593, and the sonnets toward the end of the young man's sequence probably after that time, his death being the most plausible reason for the cessation of the rivalry.

The sonnets of course do not have *a* date, since 154 is not 1. The span could conceivably be anywhere from less than a year to over twenty-five years, but some good evidence limits. Sonnet 104 tells us that the poet has known the friend for three years, or at the least, two and a half (since the poem does not say that the poet has seen three springs follow three winters). Sonnet writers are neither on oath nor famed for scrupulous accuracy; still, it takes a peculiar brand of literal-mindedness to deny the basic literalness of the three years. Why should a poet writing poems to a loved one say that they met or fell in love three years before, when he means three weeks or twelve years before? Sonnet 104 fits too tightly in context not to be to the young man. The first sonnets may have been written sometime after the meeting, hence two to three years is a plausible period of time for the writing of Sonnets 1-104, and Sonnets 100-126 would not likely cover more than a year, probably less. The gap of time in Sonnet 100 is only one of the indications that the relationship was breaking up. Thus the sequence of time is Sonnets 1-126 and the span of time two to four years, give or take very little.

The evidence for dating the dark lady sonnets, Sonnets 126-152 (I do not attempt to date Sonnets 153 and 154), is less firm than that for dating the sonnets to the young man, but several reasons suggest they were written during or overlapping the span of time of the young man sonnets, and perhaps covering less time. Two of the dark lady sonnets, Sonnets 127 and 132, were written before the parody of them in *Love's Labor's Lost* discussed later in this chapter. If *Willobie His Avisa* refers to this affair (the odds are perhaps .3 — that is, substantial but not enough to establish a probability — that it does), then the affair was over by 1594. The dark lady sonnets which refer to the triangle, overlap, and were consequently near in time to, Sonnets 40-42. The comparative fewness of the poems, and the explosiveness and rage of the affair, may suggest brevity, though that is not certain. Lovers can go on shouting at each other for years.

One cannot square a very long period of time for the sequence to the young man with Sonnet 126, the last in the young man sequence, in which Shakespeare calls the young man "lovely boy" (126.1) and says, as in Sonnet 104, that the young man has not changed in appearance or has only barely and frighteningly begun a hint of change.

Marlowe as rival poet means that the poems were written between 1590 and 1595, with 1591 or 1592 to 1594 a likely span, which other evidence supports.

Parallel passages and recurrent notions connect the sonnets more often with earlier plays and *Venus and Adonis* (published 1593) and *Lucrece* (published 1594, probably written 1593-1594) than with later work. The relations with the two poems is particularly dense, especially with *Lucrece*. Parallel passages are tricky to identify and some disagreement about specific parallels is inevitable, but the bulk of the parallels found, for instance by Hermann Isaac [Conrad] and Horace Davis,[9] is strikingly higher between the sonnets and *Venus and Adonis, Lucrece, Love's Labor's Lost, Romeo and Juliet,* and *A Midsummer Night's Dream,* all composed probably in 1591-1596, than with any later work. One can reply to this, "Of course, there are more connections; these are the plays and poems dealing the most with sexual love and romantic love." But in later plays dealing largely with romantic love, the connections are fewer; and I would argue that Shakespeare wrote most about romantic love in the earlier period for good reasons: he was in love and troubled about love, and the sonnet tradition in England was at its height.

In this same period, especially in *Romeo and Juliet* and *Love's*

Labor's Lost, Shakespeare shows in his plays the greatest interest in love poetry and in sonnets. None of the sonnets in the plays[10] is very beautiful, though the love duet of Romeo and Juliet is charming; they have comparatively workaday purposes or are displays of wit; they are neither visibly early nor late in style. They are flexible, skilled, work out well within the form.

In *Love's Labor's Lost* sonnets appear, the sonnet tradition is mocked, and Shakespeare parodies his own sonnets on at least one occasion and very likely on another. Since one cannot parody an unwritten poem, the parody gives a previously unnoticed *terminus ad quem* for the parodied sonnets.

The King speaks a mock-gorgeous super-sonnet (sixteen lines, rhyming *ababcdcdefefddgg,* the very rhyme scheme parodying by exaggerating the Shakespearean sonnet form). The poem mocks the tears, hyperboles, and commonplaces of the sonnet tradition, with a moment or two which are funny at Shakespeare's own expense.

> So sweete a *kisse* the *golden Sunne* giues not,
> To those fresh *morning* dropps vpon the Rose,
> As thy *eye* beames, when their fresh rayse haue smot.
> The night of dew that on my cheekes downe flowes,
> Nor shines the siluer Moone one halfe so bright,
> Through the transparent bosome of the deepe,
> As doth thy face through teares of mine giue light:
> Thou shinst in euerie teare that I do weepe,
> No drop but as a Coach doth carrie thee:
> So ridest thou triumphing in my wo.
> Do but beholde the teares that swell in me,
> And they thy glorie through my griefe will show:
> But do not loue thy selfe, then thou will keepe
> My teares for glasses, and still make me weepe.
> O Q[u]eene of queenes, how farre doost thou excell,
> No thought can thinke, nor tongue of mortall tell.
>   (Sigs. E2v-E3, 1598 ed.; IV. iii. 25-40)

Shakespeare himself is not the only target but may well be one of the targets.[11] Lines 1-2 steer impishly near Sonnet 33:

> Fvll many a glorious *morning* haue I seene,
> Flatter the mountaine tops with soueraine *eie,*
> *Kissing* with *golden* face the meddowes greene;
> Guilding pale streames with heauenly alcumy.
>   (33.1-4, 1609 ed.)

The four words I have italicized are repeated, two of them (*kiss-* . . . *golden*) in parallel sequences, and *sun,* implicit in lines 33.1-4, appears in line 33.9 as well as in the mock sonnet. The conceit is moderately commonplace but the collocation of items is not. A listening ear hears more, including the near triple rhyme of "mountaine tops" and "morning dropps" and the rhyme of "streames" and "beames."

Lines 8-14 of the mock sonnet manage to attack three themes Shakespeare reiterates in the sonnets: the self-love of the youth, especially Sonnet 3, which also has windows and mirrors; the eyes-mirror-heart-window folderol, especially Sonnets 24, 46, 47; and the extensive tears and woe of Sonnets 30 and 31. The last line of the mock sonnet laughs at one of Shakespeare's faults, the padding out of a line with tautology, line 118.13 being the most outlandish example, "But thence I learn and find the lesson true," which says twice that the following line will state what it states.

The other example of parody in *Love's Labor's Lost* is to me decisive. It has often been noted as a parallel and is so close that it has been used to emend a corruption in line 127.9, "eyes" to "brows."

King.   By heauen, thy Loue is blacke as Ebonie.
Berow[ne].   Is Ebonie like her? O word deuine!
A wife of such wood were felicitie.
O who can giue an oth? Where is a booke?
That I may sweare Beautie doth beautie lacke,
If that she learne not of her eye to looke:
No face is fayre that is not full so blacke.
King.   O paradox, Blacke is the badge of Hell,
The hue of dungions, and the Schoole of night:
And beauties crest becomes the heauens well.
Ber.   Diuels soonest tempt resembling spirites [sprites] of light,
O if in blacke my Ladyes browes be deckt,
It mournes, that painting [and] vsurping haire
Should rauish dooters [doters] with a false aspect:
And therefore is she borne to make blacke fayre.
Her fauour turnes the fashion of the dayes,
For natiue blood is counted paynting now:
And therefore redd that would auoyde disprayse,
Paintes it selfe blacke, to imitate her brow.
Duma[ine].   To looke like her are Chimnie-sweepers blake,
Long[aville].   And since her time are Colliers counted bright.
King.   And *AEthiops* of their sweete complexion crake.
Duma.   Darke needes no Candles now, for darke is light.
(Sigs. Flv-F2, 1598 ed., italics in text; IV. iii. 243-265)

The parallels to Sonnet 127 and the couplet of Sonnet 132 are several.

Sonnet 127

In the ould age blacke was not counted faire,
Or if it weare it bore not beauties name:
But now is blacke beauties successiue heire,
And Beautie slanderd with a bastard shame,
For since each hand hath put on Natures power,
Fairing the foule with Arts faulse borrow'd face,
Sweet beauty hath no name no holy boure,
But is prophan'd, if not liues in disgrace.
Therefore my Mistersse [Mistress'] eyes [brows] are Rauen blacke,
Her eyes so suted, and they mourners seeme,
At such who not borne faire no beauty lack,
Slandring Creation with a false esteeme,
Yet so they mourne becomming of their woe,
That euery toung saies beauty should looke so.

(1609 ed.)

Lines 132.13-14

Then will I sweare beauty her selfe is blacke,
And all they foule that thy complexion lacke.
(1609 ed.)

The couplet just quoted is certainly parodied by the following lines from the passage quoted from *Love's Labor's Lost:*

That I may sweare Beautie doth beautie lacke,
. . . .
No face is fayre that is not full so blacke.
(1598 ed.; IV. iii. 247, IV. iii. 249)

The resemblances between the whole passage in *Love's Labor's Lost* and Sonnet 127 are very thick. The rhyme of *lack* and *black*, the mourning-brows conceit, the complex relating of the black-is-fair theme to the anticosmetics theme, the face-fair-full-black of line IV. iii. 249 of *Love's Labor's Lost* to the fair-foul-false-face of line 127.6 are only some of the echoes, which is to say parody.

Love's Labor's Lost was published in 1598, that is, before March 25, 1599, and had been, according to the title page, "presented before her Highnes this last Christmas" and "newly corrected and augmented by W. Shakespere." One is more likely to correct and augment a play for a royal performance than just afterward. Hence, if one assumes the title page's veracity, the revised version was probably completed by the previous Christmas, probably Christmas 1597.

The parodying passages were more likely than not in the earlier version, since the revisions are almost certainly much less than half of the play. The earlier version was probably a good bit earlier. The reference in Robert Tofte's *Alba* (1598) certainly makes it sound some time ago: "LOVES LABOR LOST, I once did see a Play."[12] The "once." could mean "at one time," hence the previous week, but it is more plausible that it means what it does in our present idiom, a good while back, a likelihood strengthened by context. The next stanza begins, "This *Play* no *Play*, but Plague was vnto me,/ For there I lost the Loue I liked most" (italics in text). Title pages are not always trustworthy; Tofte's witness is independent.

Thus the parody gives for the sonnets parodied a firm *terminus ad quem* of 1598, a highly probable one of 1597, and a strongly probable one of some years before. Thus the parody in *Love's Labor's Lost* is good evidence for a date for the sonnets in the first half of the decade.

Stylistic evidence is frequently adduced in discussing problems of dating Shakespeare's plays, and has some value since Shakespeare wrote a number of plays, several examples in several kinds, and therefore relevant comparisons exist. For the sonnets we lack the comparisons, the sonnets in the plays being few and different in kind from the sonnets published in 1609.

The style of Shakespeare's sonnets is mature, rich, complex, fresh, and lyric. Stress the maturity, and one is apt to reach for a somewhat later date; stress the fresh lyricism, or the love of heavy rhetoric, and one is apt to turn to an earlier date.

Critics deserving respect[13] feel that the sonnets must have been written after *Lucrece,* but I demur for three reasons: *Lucrece* is in a different genre; rhetorical display exists as much in the sonnets as in *Lucrece; Lucrece* and the sonnets are rich in echoes of each other.

Looked at in a different way, the argument by style for a later date for the sonnets is too good: it takes us past the late 1590s to the time of the great tragedies. C. S. Lewis, arguing for "agnosticism" rather than a "later" date,[14] says that he "can easily conceive one who had achieved Shakespeare's mature dramatic technique still writing some of the sonnets we have."[15] Precisely; it is indeed conceivable. But it is highly unlikely, for cumulative reasons given in this chapter. It is impossible in theme: the sonnets represent a religion of love, a magnificent but finally unsuccessful effort to make romantic love a sufficient religion;

the great tragedies represent something else. The evidence of style gets in its own way, a point to which I shall return.

The young man and the dark lady appear in protean ways in the plays. That is knowledge, not speculation; a poet cannot undergo such profound emotional experience without it variously affecting his work. But finding the traces is something else again, since the imagination and the intellect of a poet alter what they touch. The young man and the dark lady may appear in images, colors of emotions, vanished and floating ways. Perhaps in no single instance is enough of a shape retained for one to say, "Here it is." But, if the young man does appear in recognizable form in the plays, it is surely in Bassanio,[16] extravagant, careless, charming, dearly loved by an older man of whom it is said, "I think he only loves the world for him" (II. viii. 48). *The Merchant of Venice* was written by 1598, and Antonio's emotion reflects some sadness of distance. Once again, the yielded date is the 1590s and probably early rather than late.

Lucrece and the sonnets have many echoes of theme, cadence, and phrasing; *Lucrece* was heavily influenced by Samuel Daniel's *The Complaint of Rosamond*. Since Edmond Malone's comments in the eighteenth century,[17] it has been widely agreed that Daniel's *Delia* and Shakespeare's sonnets show influence one way or the other (reciprocal influence is also possible), and Claes Schaar's careful and learned study[18] has strengthened that tradition. To be among those four works by Daniel and Shakespeare is to be in a world where sounds shimmer on sounds, echoes thicken, voices and themes merge. I shall attempt to demonstrate the reality of the web by listing some of the many echoes between *Delia* (1592) and Shakespeare's sonnets, beginning with Daniel's Sonnets 46, 27, and 31, which have multiple relations with various of Shakespeare's sonnets.

Sonnet 46 of *Delia* follows:

Let others sing of Knights and Palladines,
In aged accents, and vntimely words:
Paint shadowes in imaginary lines,
Which well the reach of their high wits records;
But I must sing of thee and those fair eyes,
Autentique shall my verse in time to come,
When yet th'vnborne shall say, loe where she lyes,
Whose beautie made him speake that els was dombe.
These are the Arkes the Tropheis I erect,
That fortifie thy name against old age,
And these thy sacred vertues must protect,

Against the Darke and times consuming rage.
Though th'error of my youth they shall discouer,
Suffice they shew I liu'd and was thy louer.

(1592)

The close relation to Shakespeare's Sonnet 106 ("When in the Chronicle of wasted time") is apparent in subject and theme; in each poem, poetry celebrating medieval beauty is related to the loved one addressed. Sonnets 106-108 of Shakespeare extend and vary the arguments of Daniel's sonnet. Daniel separated himself and his loved one from the writers who celebrated heroic antiquity. Shakespeare, in several ways, makes antiquity subservient to his love.

Line 46.12 of *Delia, "Against* the Darke and times consuming *rage,"* strikes the ear as a mightily Shakespearean line. The truth is, if my argument is right, the other way around: some mighty lines in Shakespeare, including the following ones, are very Daniellian:

1609   64.4   And brasse eternall slaue to mortall *rage*
1609   13.11-12   *Against* the stormy gusts of winters day
                          And barren *rage* of deaths eternall cold.

Lines 17.5,7 of Shakespeare's sonnets come very close in rhyme, idea, phrasing to lines 46.5,7 of *Delia:*

Delia: But I must sing of thee and those faire eyes
               When yet th'vnborne shall say, loe where she lyes
1609:   If I could write the beauty of your eyes
               The age to come would say this Poet lies

As often in echoes, meaning and grammar shift. Shakespeare responded to what he heard.

Shakespeare's line 17.1 repeats even more closely *Delia's* line 46.6.

Delia: Autentique shall *my verse in time to come*
1609:   Who will beleeue *my verse in time to come*

The "Antique song" of Shakespeare's line 17.12 picks up the idea of *Delia* 46.1-3 and possibly the sound of "Autentique" (46.6).

The "graue" (31.9), in idea, and "tropheis" (31.10) of Shakespeare likely come from *Delia* 46.7, "loe where she lyes," and 46.9, "Tropheis," respectively. Note in both the unusual spelling "tropheis," a form not given in the *Oxford English Dictionary.*

The rhyme of *Delia* 46.13&14, "discouer" & "louer," appears in

Shakespeare's rhyme 32.2&4, "couer" & "Louer," a repetition probably significant in the context of comparisons of poets (Shakespeare's
lines 32.4-8 and *Delia* 46.1-4).

Shakespeare's Sonnet 87 is, in the cadence of its feminine lines, a
very Delian-sounding poem. Sonnet 27 in *Delia* links both to Shakespeare's Sonnet 87 and Sonnet 30.

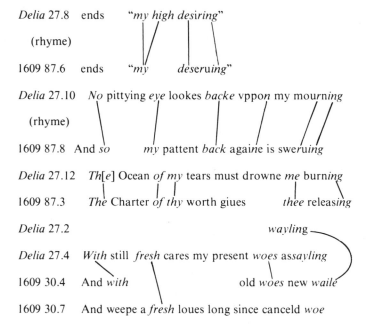

Delia 27.8   ends   *"my high desiring"*

   (rhyme)

1609 87.6   ends   *"my   deseruing"*

Delia 27.10   *No* pittying *eye* lookes *backe* vppo*n* my mou*rning*

   (rhyme)

1609 87.8   And *so*   *my* pattent *back* agai*ne* is swe*ruing*

Delia 27.12   *Th[e]* Ocean *of my* tears must drowne *me* burn*ing*

1609 87.3   *The* Charter *of thy* worth giues   *thee* releas*ing*

Delia 27.2   *wayling*

Delia 27.4   *With* still *fresh* cares my present *woes* ass*ayling*

1609 30.4   And *with*   old *woes* new *wailé*

1609 30.7   And weepe a *fresh* loues long since canceld *woe*

Delia 27.13, "And this my death shall christen her *anew*" links
to 1609 30.12 "*new* pay" and to the elaborate funereal-religious-love
paradoxes of Sonnet 31.

Sonnet 31 in *Delia* links to Sonnets 129, 25 and 95 of Shakespeare.

Delia 31.13   ends   *waste* in v*aine*

1609 129.1   ends   *waste* of sh*ame*

Delia 31.5   *spreads* her *glorie*

1609 25.5   *spread*

1609 25.8   *glory*

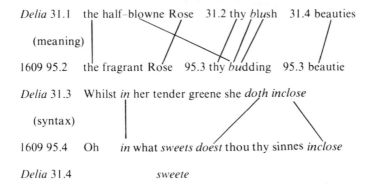

Delia 31.1   the half–blowne Rose   31.2 thy *blush*   31.4 beauties

(meaning)

1609 95.2   the fragrant Rose   95.3 thy *budding*   95.3 beautie

Delia 31.3   Whilst *in* her tender greene she *doth inclose*

(syntax)

1609 95.4   Oh   *in* what *sweets doest* thou thy sinnes *inclose*

Delia 31.4   *sweete*

Delia 31 and Shakespeare's Sonnet 33 have several links.

Delia 31		1609 33	
31.8	clowdes	33.12	cloude
31.3	greene	33.3	greene
31.8	shining	33.9	shine
31.11	howers	33.11	houre
31.10&12	now & brow	33.10&12	brow & now

Other echoes abound between the two books. Not only the repeated word but the imitative harshness of sound suggest relationship in the following example.

Delia 47.9   Els *harsh* my style, vntunable my Muse
1609 11.10   *Harsh,* featurelesse and rude, barrenly perrish

Line 3.1 in Shakespeare's sonnets, "*Looke* in *thy glasse* and tell the face thou *vewest,*" is a very Delian line in sound and connects with at least the following lines in *Delia.*

1.9   *Looke* on the deere expences of my youth
33.3   Receiuest hast this message from *thy glasse*
33.5 [cadence]   Fresh shalt thou see in mee the woundes thou mad*est*
23.1   *Looke in* my griefes, and blame me not to morne [mourn]

Here and elsewhere Shakespeare heard and absorbed the grace of Delian freshness.

Sonnet 1 in *Delia* and Shakespeare's Sonnet 4 each develop a metaphor of the cost accounting of love and have an echo.

Delia 1.7   Heere haue I *summ*'d my *s*ighe*s*
1609 4.8   So great a *summe* of *s*umme*s*

Sonnet 1 in *Delia* links also with Shakespeare's Sonnets 30 and 49.

Delia		1609	
1.6	accounts of	30.11	account of
1.7	I summ'd my sighes	30.2	I sommon
		30.3	I sigh
1.9	deere expences	30.13	deare
		30.8	expence

Delia 1.6   *cast* th'accounts of *all*
Delia 1.7   *summ*'d
1609 49.3   *cast* his *vtmost summe*

To cast one's utmost sum is to cast all.
Sonnet 25 of *Delia* links to Shakespeare's Sonnet 30.

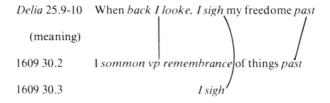

Delia 25.9-10   When *back I looke, I sigh* my freedome *past*

(meaning)

1609 30.2   I *sommon vp remembrance* of things *past*

1609 30.3   *I sigh*

Echoes are to be heard; it is finally the cadences that convince or fail to convince. The echoes in Shakespeare of *Delia* are not only of word, phrasing, meaning, metaphor, but—again and again—of sound.

The Daniel and Shakespeare relationship is one of the strongest arguments for dating the sonnets in the early 1590s. I shall put the case bluntly, then discuss some uncertainties and complications.

The Complaint of Rosamond influenced *Lucrece*; *Delia* influenced Shakespeare's sonnets; *Lucrece* and the sonnets have echoes. *Delia* and *The Complaint of Rosamond* were written by 1592. *Lucrece* was written in 1593 or 1594. The sonnets then were written when the influence of Daniel was heavy, namely in the early 1590s.

The web of relations between Daniel and Shakespeare set as a web neither a *terminus a quo* nor a *terminus ad quem*. Nor do, as such, the web of relations between *Venus and Adonis, Lucrece, The Two Gentlemen of Verona, Romeo and Juliet, Love's Labor's Lost,* and the sonnets. But both webs richly and mutually suggest proximity in time, that time being the early 1590s.

If *Delia* influenced Shakespeare's sonnets, setting a date of composition for the poems in *Delia* (1592) will set a *terminus a quo* for the sonnets.

Some of Daniel's sonnets were published in the 1591 pirated edition of Sidney's *Astrophel and Stella*. In 1592, Daniel issued an authorized edition of his own sonnets, and added sonnets to later editions through 1601. That is, he had written some sonnets by 1591, many by 1592, and continued writing sonnets, though more sparingly, for the next decade. Daniel states in the preface to *Delia* (1592) that the poems were the *"priuate passions"*[19] of his youth, which suggests a date of composition for the bulk of them during the mid-1580s or even earlier. This may be the correct date, in which case, if Shakespeare is the debtor, Shakespeare could have been influenced any time thereafter. If Daniel is the debtor, the mid-1580s date for his sonnets becomes unbelievably early. But the statement, a gentlemanly derogation of his literary efforts, may well not be true. Daniel did go on writing sonnets, and some of the most intense and bitter were written between 1592 and 1594,[20] which suggests a continuity of composition and feeling. In the 1601 edition he or someone engaged in a puzzling emendation of the 1592 line 26.6, "That was with blood and three yeeres witnes signed," the "three" becoming "fiue" in the 1601 edition.[21] If the "three" was literal in 1591 or 1592, then the "fiue" would be literal in 1593 or 1594, when the love ended. I am not sure that this is the correct explanation, but it explains an oddity plausibly, and gives the date of composition for the poems published in 1592 to be about 1588-1591 or 1588-1592.

In Edmund Spenser's *Colin Clouts Come Home Again*, probably written in 1591, in a passage in which he refers to Daniel by name, Spenser-Colin says that Daniel appeared "well in that well tuned song/ Which late he sung unto a scornful lasse" (lines 418-419),[22] a clear reference to *Delia*, the "late" sorting well with the suggested dates 1588-1591 and working against Daniel's claim to have written the poems earlier. Spenser then goes on to recommend to Daniel that he attempt poetry containing "tragick plaints and passionate mischance" (line 427), which Daniel does beautifully in *The Complaint of Rosamond*, published in 1592. Spenser may have had a gift of prophecy or a large power of influence, but it is more likely that he and his friend Daniel, both members of the Pembroke circle in 1591, had been discussing a poem Daniel was projecting or had begun.

Schaar holds that the influence is mostly from Shakespeare to Daniel.[23] If that be so, 1592 becomes a *terminus ad quem* for many of Shakespeare's sonnets. Assuming that Daniel is the debtor, my tentative dating of Daniel's sonnets puts the date of Shakespeare's sonnets back to the 1580s, and Daniel's statement in the preface of *Delia* would put Shakespeare's sonnets all the way back to the early 1580s. Those consequences are in themselves a good reason to doubt Shakespeare's priority, since other evidence, especially the references to age, make a date in the 1580s extremely implausible.

Scharr's basic arguments are that Daniel, an inferior and imitative poet, was incapable of the best phrases Daniel and Shakespeare share; and that Daniel handles awkwardly what he gets from Shakespeare. Daniel and Shakespeare both, like many other good poets, imitated and emulated much; hence, either might on that ground be the borrower. Daniel is an exciting and graceful poet, capable not only of melodious commonplace but also of distinctive phrasing.[24] Nor does he stumble in some passages where Schaar finds that he does. In lines 46.5-8 of *Delia* Daniel writes:

> But I must sing of thee and those faire eyes,
> Autentique shall *my verse in time to come,*
> When yet th'vnborne shall *say, loe where she lyes,*
> Whose beautie made him speake that els was dombe.
>
> (1592 ed.)

Schaar points out the resemblance to Shakespeare's Sonnet 17, including line 17.1, "Who will beleeue *my verse in time to come* (1609 ed.), and line 17.7, "The age to come would *say this Poet lies*" (1609 ed.), and finds Daniel the more likely borrower because of the awkwardness of the imitation, including the unusual verb "autentique."[25] Here one must disagree: the passage in Daniel is beautiful, as is the whole sonnet, and "autentique" is a lively verb-coinage. Even if it were awkward, it is not a word Schaar finds that Daniel imitated from Shakespeare, and therefore does not show Daniel the borrower. The phrases echoed are graceful in Daniel, and line 46.6 could have been filled out easily and euphoniously a number of ways. The distinctiveness of "autentique" shows rather that Daniel is capable of distinctive phrasing.

Much of Schaar's book demonstrates learnedly and with critical acumen that Daniel's style is in general simpler than Shakespeare's. That is true but not relevant to the question of influence. Schaar also gives some examples of Daniel's revisions of his sonnets being influenced by Shakespeare's sonnets.[26] However, since Schaar also admits some influence from Daniel to Shakespeare, that does not answer the question whether the chief and earlier influence was to or from *Delia*.

Schaar establishes past doubt that influence exists, but his arguments do not establish Shakespeare's priority. Four reasons may be offered for Daniel's priority. The second and third reasons are new.

First, each of several of the *Delia* sonnets has links with several of Shakespeare's sonnets, as we have seen, Sonnet 46 of *Delia* being the most striking example. It is more plausible that Shakespeare was impressed, as he should have been, by some of Daniel's finest sonnets, and reflected them in several places, than that Daniel managed to make some of his best and most coherent sonnets by bringing together a number of echoes of Shakespeare.

Second, Shakespeare in Sonnet 32 in a context where, as we have seen, he is echoing Daniel,[27] describes himself as inferior to the better poets of the age, which suggests that he was conscious of the imitation.

Third, the assumption that Daniel influenced Shakespeare explains a mistake in Shakespeare, the "rhyme" in lines 25.9&11 of "worth" and "quite." Sonnet 44 of *Delia* has several connections with Shakespeare's Sonnet 25.

Daniel's Sonnet 44

Drawne with th'attractiue vertue of her *eyes* [1]
My toucht hart tunres [turnes] it to that *happie* [2] *cost* [3]:
My *ioy*full [4] *North* [5] where all my *fortune* [6] *lyes* [7],
The leuell of my hopes desired *most* [8, 3].
There where my Delia *fayrer* [9] then the *sunne* [10],
Deckt with her youth whereon the world smyleth:
Ioyes [4] in that *honour* [11] which her beautie wonne,
Th'eternall *volume* [12] which her *fame* [13] compyleth.
Florish *faire* [9] Albion, *glory* [14] of the *North* [5]
Neptunes darling helde betweene his armes:
Deuided from the world as better *worth* [15],
Kept for himselfe, defended from all harmes.
Still let disarmed peace decke her and thee;
And Muse-foe Mars, abroade farre fostred bee.
(1592 ed., omitting the italics in text)

Shakespeare's Sonnet 25

Let those who are in fauor with their stars,
Of publike *honour* [11] and proud titles *bost* [3: rhyme],

Whilst I whome *fortune* [6] of such tryumph bars
Vnlookt for *ioy* [4] in that I *honour* [11] *most* [8, 3];
Great Princes fauorites their *faire* [9] leaues spread,
But as the Marygold at the *suns* [10] *eye* [1],
And in them-selues their pride *lies* [7] buried,
For at a frowne they in their *glory* [14] die.
The painefull warrier *famosed* [13] for *worth* [5, 15],
After a thousand victories once foild,
Is from the *booke* [12] of *honour* [11] rased quite,
And all the rest forgot for which he toild:
Then *happy* [2] I that loue and am beloued
Where I may not remoue, nor be remoued.

(1609 ed.)

Fifteen connections is several, and I omit some. I list the fifteen for convenience.

Daniel's Sonnet 44	Shakespeare's Sonnet 25
1. eyes	1. eye
2. happie	2. happy
3. cost, rhymes with *most*	3. bost, rhymes with *most*
4. ioyfull, Ioyes	4. ioy
5. North	5. Daniel's "North" rhymes with *worth* [15]
6. fortune	6. fortune
7. lyes	7. lies
8. most	8. most
9. fayrer, faire	9. faire
10. sunne	10. suns
11. honour	11. honour
12. volume	12. booke
13. fame	13. famosed
14. glory	14. glory
15. worth	15. worth

The echoes are there, as are further cadences, although the poems are not on the same subject in any direct way. Influence is unquestionable. If it goes from Daniel to Shakespeare, it explains very naturally why Shakespeare wrote down "worth" rather than the "fight" he presumably intended. Daniel's poem was sounding and rhyming in his ears. Influence the other way or the assumption that the error is scribal or compositorial produces an exceedingly unlikely coincidence.

The fourth argument, already noted, is simply that the predominant influence from Shakespeare to Daniel puts the sonnets of Shakespeare earlier than other evidence will allow.

None of this discussion sets a firm *terminus a quo*, since the dates offered for the composition of *Delia,* while plausible enough, have no claim to certainty. A firm *terminus a quo* is, however, offered by the passage in Marlowe's *The Massacre at Paris* which, as I showed in the previous chapter, certainly influenced Shakespeare's Sonnets 15 and 33, and probably influenced Sonnets 17 and 20. *The Massacre at Paris* was written after the death of Henry III on August 2, 1589.[28] The *terminus a quo*, then, for Sonnets 15 and 33 and probably Sonnets 17 and 20 is August, 1589. Sometime in 1590 or later is more likely since it takes some time for a play to get written, performed or read, and echoed. Since Sonnets 1-17, the most tightly woven group, must have been written in close proximity of time, it is safe to say that the sonnets were not begun before late 1589 and probably not before, at the earliest, sometime in 1590. Marlowe as rival poet yields a date prior to May 30, 1593, for Sonnets 78-86, and for several reasons (the cessation of the rival poet sonnets, the gap of time mentioned in Sonnet 100, the three years mentioned in Sonnet 104 taken in conjunction with the probablility of a starting date no earlier than late 1590) the sonnets must have ended sometime after Marlowe's death.

The sonnets must have been begun before 1593, since it is implausible that the first eighty-six sonnets including the rival poet sonnets (written when Marlowe was alive) were written in the first five months of 1593, especially since Sonnet 104 mentions a three-year span. If Sonnet 104 was written after Marlowe's death, Sonnets 1-104 were written in 1590-1593, 1591-1594, or 1592-1595, and Sonnets 105-126 probably took no more than a year.

Even if Marlowe's death is not taken into account, the pupil-pen references, the relations between Daniel and Shakespeare, the *Love's Labor's Lost* parody, the *terminus a quo* of 1590, the three-year reference and the other evidence, yield possible dates of something like 1590-1596 as outside limits. It is doubtful, even when one grants that the three-year span refers literally to knowing, not to writing, that these poems took much less than three years to write. Too much is developed and changed within them. The years 1591-1594 seem to me, all told, the best dates; the convergence of evidence on the early 1590s is firm.

The age? Who, approaching thirty, grievously in love with a younger person, does not feel old? The style? The evidence of the style gets in its own way, early and late, overrhetorical and lyrical, penetrating and strange. Revision may be a part, perhaps an important part, of the explanation. I have a further explanation to offer, that high genius has causes which bring it to flower. This chapter has touched three causes, which met and became one: the poetry of Marlowe, the poetry of Daniel, a young man. It is precisely in the sonnets that Shakespeare's style matured,[29] that diverse styles — in conflict in Sonnet 1 — found their true union and voice.

TECHNIQUES

Chapter 4

The Metrical Rules
of the Sonnets

Did Shakespeare write by rule or by ear? Decidedly by both. He worked normally within precise, stateable rules, whether or not he stated them, and he superbly listened.

A rule of practice is not necessarily overtly intended; yet it is not an accident or random either. Poems are intended to be expressive; rhythms are deliberately expressive. How far a poet formulates his sense of rhythm varies; even free-verse poets have some formulation of their rhythmical practice; and, on the other hand, the poet most conscious of metrical technique, a Coleridge, a Robert Bridges, is still writing by ear: the rhythms are felt, heard, within the framing of principles.

Shakespeare certainly knew some of his metrical rules. He intended the sonnet form, three cross-rhyming quatrains followed by a couplet. He knew he allowed unstressed extra syllables at the ends of lines; if Appendix A is right, he was aware that he allowed no extra syllables within lines. The variant doublets discussed in Appendix A must be intentional because they are so showy.

Shakespeare also refers to meter within the sonnets and offers metrical imitations and jokes. In lines 17.5-6, he writes, "If I could write the beauty of your eyes,/ And in fresh numbers number all your graces." The pun on "numbers" ("meter" and "counting") and the heavy yet nimble sound of its repetition are deliberate, witty, not casual. In line 12 of the same poem, he speaks of his verse as the "stretched miter [meter] of an Ántique song" (siglum added). The force and quantity of "stretch-" and the rapid rush of three comparatively light syllables leading to the self-deprecating pun of "Antique" ("antic" and "antique") are metrically playful. Shakespeare is seldom more artfully displaying his art than when he decries it as artless and old-fashioned. In Sonnet 76 he laments his barren style in fruitful meters, line 76.2 being the unusually bright, quick, varied, thus happily self-contradictory dance of "so far from variation or quicke change."[1] Shakespeare, then, is in the sonnets unmistakably conscious of meter.

Toward another extreme, he almost certainly did not say to himself, "I shall allow in the sonnets slightly more verse-pauses after syllable 1 than after syllable 3," but that is a rule of his practice. He knew that he was varying his rhythms more than Daniel and other sonnet writers, but we cannot tell how far he put to himself in clear language what the allowed variations were. If he did put the rules in clear (or unclear) language, it may not have been our language or even the language of Elizabethan writers on poetry. We do not know what Shakespeare thought about meter[2] because he did not leave us any treatises on meter. We can tell what he did metrically because he did it. And did it, in important senses, on purpose.

Some Metrical Fundamentals

Since tacit metrical assumptions can be variously confusing or question begging, I shall, before looking at the specific evidence, offer some general ideas about meter.

Verse is language in meter. Meter means measure. Various features of language can be made into metrical framings. Accentual-syllabic verse, the most important and widespread verse in England and America from the late sixteenth to the twentieth century, also much used in the Middle Ages and still widely used, consists of certain patternings of stress, or accent, with syllables.

Stress is whatever gives prominence to a syllable, involving loudness, pitch, length, juncture, timbre, and attack, with loudness and pitch predominant and usually mutually reinforcing. Metrical stress, ictus, is relative or comparative. All syllables have some stress or would be silences, and many actual degrees of stress exist. In meter, a syllable is stressed if it has more prominence than the other syllable or syllables in the foot. A metrical foot does not represent a heard rhythmical unit, since phrasing and pausing in a line are independent of the feet. Feet divide a line metrically to show fundamental patterns of metrically stressed and unstressed syllables, with some allowed variations.

Ockham's Razor, an important principle in metrics and elsewhere, can be stated, "Do not multiply entities without necessity."[3] The Razor has two edges: it includes two truths, both important: (1) one should use the simplest explanation which covers all the evidence; (2) one should not simplify; the explanation should cover all the evidence. Some things are complicated. One should be careful not to reduce everything to one of two alternative explanations, when both may have occasionally applied, even when one is predominant. A lion cage is occupied some of the time by people, or sparrows, but should not thereby be called a people cage or a sparrow cage.

Thus one should realize for instance (see Appendix) that, even though disyllabism seems to account for all the textual evidence, something like semielision may also have occasionally occurred: it did at least for a moment, discussed in the Appendix, in the mind of George Puttenham. A danger of the Razor is that it tends to exclude the unusual just because it is unusual: it requires some imagination not to tidy up the untidy too nicely. But the Razor is, after cautions, a very valuable principle. It is essential in describing feet, since without it any wild description which fits would be allowable: for instance, scanning a regular iambic pentameter as anacrusis trochee cretic amphibrach truncated foot (>tcbz — see Metrical Sigla). Five iambs make better sense; the description is simpler yet tells more: it shows the pattern.

It also shows a reason for this book's use of the foot concept rather than the stress-maxima or other methods of metrical description. The foot concept, properly understood, is (in some ways, at some times) highly elegant. To reduce x / x / x / x / x / to iiiii rather than >tcbz is a pretty achievement. The stress-maxima description of that basic pattern is more cumbersome, and the stress-maxima method describes several matters, at least for my purposes, less clearly and well than the foot concept that poets have deliberately used for some centuries.

The stress-maxima system as developed by Morris Halle and Samuel Keyser is a thoughtful treatment of the central problem of metricality in relation to describing what has been traditionally called the iambic pentameter; it has been offered in a spirit of genuine scholarship and carefully revised in relation to criticism of the position by scholars.[4] It thus deserves our respect, has opened and illuminated some issues and possibility, and has been of distinct value to me in this study, especially in one respect. Their view of unmetricality led me to reassess my earlier view that Shakespeare simply allowed trochees in the first four feet and allowed strong trochees in the fifth foot. Were that his practice, a number of his lines would be unmetrical by the Halle-Keyser principles somewhat modified by the principle of relative stress. That puzzled me; the puzzlement led me to the rules (discussed later in this chapter) by which Shakespeare justified trochees in the sonnets. Thus I am grateful for the Halle-Keyser explorations.

I also understand well enough the enthusiasm felt by some critics for a new system which apparently reduces to clarity and to a single principle of metricality the admittedly bulky and partly unexplained machinery of the traditional system. Not only has there been little useful said in the traditional system to explain how, why, and when substitutions are allowed (I hope my discussion of justified trochees is a step in the right direction), but there are such positive embarrassments as the traditional description of feminine endings as "extra-metrical," a phrase that clearly implies, "Some of the things in our system are not in our system."

But the Halle-Keyser system has its own awkwardnesses and exceptions (sometimes slightly hid by language). Thus they also allow the logical scandal of "extra-metrical syllables," and their relating of positions to syllables (a position is a syllable except when it is no syllable or two syllables) is as least as inelegant and unexplained as anything in the traditional system. But pots can call kettles black all day long without getting the meal prepared. Both systems (like other systems dealing with complex matters) have their oddities, exceptions, and logical problems. All in all, I find the foot system more useful for my purposes than the Halle-Keyser system in my attempts to describe Shakespeare's metrical practice and principles, especially in relationship to the handling of trochees, the comparisons with Daniel, and the discussion of metricality.

Further, the Halle-Keyser attempt to reduce metricality to a single rule is unhistorical, since what is allowed varies from poet to poet, period to period, and even within the practice of the same poet. Shakespeare in the plays allows internal feminine endings (a light extra syllable within the line before a strong pause); in the sonnets he does not. Shakespeare in the sonnets allows trochees with internal pause when the syllable preceding the trochee is strong (Rule 3, to be discussed in the next section of this chapter); Daniel in *Delia* does not (that is, no trochees occur justified merely by that reason). Wallace Stevens allows, as do many other poets, light anapests; Shakespeare in the sonnets does not (see Appendix A). Thus internal feminine endings are metrical in Shakespeare's plays, unmetrical in Shakespeare's sonnets. Trochees with internal pauses when the trochee is preceded by a strong syllable are metrical in Shakespeare's sonnets, unmetrical in

Daniel's *Delia*. Wallace Stevens's light anapests are metrical in "Sunday Morning," would be unmetrical in Shakespeare's sonnets.

In the Halle-Keyser system, two syllables can occupy one position under certain conditions (those conditions fit the examples in Stevens's poem). Thus the light anapests in Stevens's poem are metrical by the Halle-Keyser system, but unmetrical by the rules inferable from Shakespeare's sonnets. In the Halle-Keyser system, a stress-maximum in a weak position is unmetrical; when the syllable in a weak position is preceded by a strong syllable, it is not a stress-maximum, hence not unmetrical. Thus trochees with internal pause when the trochee is preceded by a strong syllable are metrical in the Halle-Keyser system, metrical for a narrower reason in Shakespeare's sonnets, but unmetrical in Daniel's *Delia*. To define unmetricality by a single rule just does not, unfortunately, fit what happens in poetry.

Hence, after reflection, I have stayed with the foot system as herein defined.

Trochees

Since Shakespeare does not allow anapests in the sonnets (see Appendix), and since real pyrrhics and spondees are rare, to discuss substitution in Shakespeare's sonnets is primarily to discuss trochees.

Trochees occur frequently in Elizabethan verse though the prosodists have little to say about them. Daniel, who showed more public interest than Shakespeare in metrical theory, uses in *Delia* many trochees in the first foot and some internal trochees after a verse-pause.[5] Yet in *A Defence of Ryme* he seems to hold that trochees are not allowed in iambic verse.[6] In general the metrists of the period do not recognize the existence of trochaic substitution,[7] and Campion actually chides English poets for using trochees in iambic lines.[8] The gap between theory and practice is sizable. Shakespeare may, then, have been conscious of his trochaic variations, or may have extended the practice of Daniel and others without theoretically formulating what he did. In any event, the trochees are there. Counting, as usual, presents problems.

The first difficulty, a problem for more than trochees, is that we do not know much about Elizabethan habits of stressing sentences and phrases. Lexical stress as such gives little problem in the sonnets. Thus in line 35.6, "Authorizing thy trespas with compare," modern editions are almost certainly right in stressing "authorizing" on the second syllable, an allowable Elizabethan pronunciation.

It is harder to be sure about phrasal stressing,[9] and a slight shift in comparative stress within phrasings would often change an iamb to a trochee or vice versa. Lacking other evidence, one assumes that phrasal stressing is essentially the same for Shakespeare as for us, and one has the dim consolation that mistakes made on that assumption are probably undiscoverable. The assumption has some negative and not entirely circular confirmation simply because it works out in Shakespeare's verse without visible violence or oddities.

The second problem in counting trochees is that the pull of the iambic pattern is strong and affects speech pattern. How far it pulls in a given instance is hard to tell, and Elizabethan practice may have pulled it further than ours toward the iambic measure. Elizabethan practice did not pull it all the way to a wrenched iambic reading of every line; had that happened, no gain would have occurred between poets such as Googe, Turberville, and Gascoigne, and poets which include Sidney, Spenser, and Shakespeare. The later poetry achieves a beauty and variety which exclusively iambic reading would ruin.

Thirdly, some lines can be read legitimately and expressively with different scansions. English pronunciation has strong phrasal patterns but patterns which include alternatives; and our sense of rhythm, of shades of meaning, and of emphasis affect which syllable in a group gets the primary stress and which syllables what degree of lesser stress, within the limits of what is idiomatically allowable. When adjacent syllables are each fairly heavy, a slight change of procedure or of actual stress will change scansion markedly, as in lines 30.1 and 30.4 respectively.

In line 30.1 the heavier syllables in relation to the whole line are "WHEN to the SESSions of SWEET SIlent THOUGHT," which yields the scansion tipsi. Applying the principle of relative stress rigorously, one gets without any change of actual stress the scansion tipti or tiiti since "-ions of" is either a pyrrhic or an iamb and "sweet si-" normally stressed is a trochee. Both "sweet" and "si-" are strong but "sweet" stronger.

In line 30.4 the following syllables are heavy: "AND with OLD WOES NEW WAILE my DEARE TIMES WASTE." I scan the line tttii, since "old" and "new" are in normal pronunciation slightly stronger in this context than "woes" and "waile." The second and third trochees are justified by Rule 5, to be discussed. The metrical pressure is such though that the line could also be read tiiii with a slight, legitimate shift of stress. The first foot could even be read as an iamb, a little less naturally, since *and* is a word which can take much or little stress.

Such problems make exact statistics for metrical substitution inherently impossible, but do not thereby make counting meaningless. In Shakespeare's sonnets, the alternative or problematical instances are few enough so that preponderances still obtain.

Suppose that my count of trochees in Table 1 for the first foot (321) and for the second foot (30) were each off by a factor of two in opposite and narrowing directions, a fantastically high percentage of error, there would still be a strong preponderance (160 to 60) in favor of the first foot. Since problematical instances of trochees are fewer than clear instances and would probably tend in counting to average out (some iambs being considered trochees, some trochees iambs), conclusions such as mine that Shakespeare used about 5% trochees in the sonnets are reasonably reliable if necessarily imperfect. He certainly used some trochees and fewer than 10% in the sonnets. To know that is to know something, and the margin of error is less than that.

Table 1 contradicts two standard opinions, that Shakespeare allowed trochees only in the first foot or after a caesura;[10] and that Shakespeare did not allow any trochees in the last foot of iambic lines.[11] I shall try to show that he allowed trochees justified by five rules and that trochees justified by Rule 4 or Rule 5 (to be discussed) occur in the last foot of lines.

Trochees and Verse-Pause

I prefer the term *verse-pause* to the term *caesura*, restricting the term *caesura* to verse-pauses which occur at a regular place in the line as part of a poem's pattern.

Verse-pauses are hard to define but usually easy to recognize. A verse-pause is not merely a "breathing-place,"[12] as Campion called it, since our sense of phrasal completeness may be met even when there is no actual stop. That sense of completeness involves pausing or syntactical sense or kinds of juncture, and I cannot furnish a simple definition. As with substitution, different correct verse-pauses are sometimes possible within a line. Nonetheless we can in most instances see clearly enough whether a verse-pause is required or not. Thus in line 25.2, "Of publike honour and proud titles bost [boast]," a verse-pause comes after "honour," and one may occur after "-tles," but none after "of" or "proud" or "tit-." In line 25.13, "Then happy I that loue and am beloued," a verse-pause may occur after "I" or "loue" or both, and it seems wrong to omit both.

Verse-pauses occur at the end of every or virtually every line. Even in the rare strong overflows (for instance, lines 29.11-12, "Like to the lark at break of day arising/ From sullen earth" [modernized]), I hear at least a hint of a pause. The enormous majority of lines in Shakespeare's sonnets have a definite pause at their end. Internal verse-pauses occur after every possible syllable, distributed as shown in Table 2.

Verse-pauses occur after the syllables in the following frequency (that is, the most verse-pauses occur after syllable 4, the fewest after syllable 9): 4 6 5 7 2 8 1 3 9.

With verse-pauses after syllables 4, 5, and 6 counted as medial, 1834 out of 2411 verse-pauses (76%) are medial.

These figures will later be discussed in comparison with Daniel's *Delia* and for comparison of groups within Shakespeare's sonnets.

Trochees most frequently come after verse-pauses; but a number of examples of trochaic substitutions do not immediately follow verse-pauses, and some of the evidence is unambiguous, including the following examples.

In line 2.14, "And see thy blood warme when thou feel'st it could [cold]," "warme," whether an adjective complement coordinate with "could" or an infinitive, cannot be separated from "blood" by a verse-pause and is clearly more stressed than "when." Thus the scansion is iitii with no verse-pause before the trochee, the trochee justified by Rule 3, to be shortly discussed.

In line 6.11, "Then what could death doe if thou should'st depart," no separation is possible between "death" and "doe," and "doe" is stronger than "if." To stress "if" would make the line unbearably awkward. Thus a trochee occurs in the third foot and not after a verse-pause, yielding the scansion iitii, the trochee justified by Rule 3, to be shortly discussed.

Two other lines scanning iitii with no verse-pause before the trochee are line 19.10, "Nor draw noe lines there with thine ántique pen" (siglum added) and line 55.12, "That weare this world out to the ending doome," the trochees justified by Rule 3, to be shortly discussed.

In line 40.12, "To bear loues wrong, than hates known iniury," "known" is distinctly stronger than "in-" and cannot be separated from "hates," yielding for the last three feet the scansion iti with no verse-pause before the trochee. This line is unmetrical by the rules I shall adduce.

In line 129.14, "To shun the heauen [one-syllable] that leads men to this hell," the "men" is stronger than "to" and not to be separated from "leads," yielding the scansion iiiti with no verse-pause before the trochee, the trochee justified by Rule 3, to be shortly discussed.

A fact of practice can, therefore, be stated: Shakespeare in the sonnets uses trochees in any of the first four feet, some after verse-pauses, some not, with trochees in the first place or after a verse-pause predominating. The question is, what sorts of trochee? The primary answer is, trochees justified by certain rules.

Rules for Justifying Trochees

(1) & (2)

The first two rules are the traditional ones:

(1) Trochees are allowed after a verse-pause (caesura).
(2) Trochees are allowed in the first foot.

Rule 2 is for the sonnets of Shakespeare a subclass of Rule 1, since verse-pauses occur after every, or nearly every, line. Examples of Rules 1 and 2 are very frequent.

Internal trochees after a verse-pause:

13.7 You[r] selfe again *after* your selfes decease
14.13 Or else of thee *this I* prognosticate

And over a hundred others.

Trochees in the first foot:

2.12 *Proouing* his beautie by succession thine
3.1 *Looke in* thy glasse and tell this face thou vewest

And over three hundred others.

(3)

The third rule is that Shakespeare allows trochees with internal verse-pause (that is, with a pause after the first syllable of the trochee)

when the trochee is preceded by a strong syllable. These are comparatively rare (about two dozen) and most of them are medial (in the third
foot).

Some examples are awkward or problematical (e.g., line 39.3, "What
can mine own *praiseʃto* mine own selfe bring"); some are rhythmically expressive, for instance, the following:

> 7.6 Resembling strong *youthʃin* his middle age
> 50.13 For that same grone doth put *thisʃin* my mind
> 64.7 And the firme soil *winʃof* the watry maine
> 129.14 To shun the heauen that leads *menʃto* this hell.

Two of these lines, including a line from one of the best-loved sonnets, use this variation to achieve the effect of powerful struggle.

> 29.3 And trouble deafe *heauenʃwith* my bootlesse cries
>   (The "heauen" is one syllable)
> 51.11 Shall naigh noe dull *fleshʃin* his fiery race

Three trochees have internal verse-pause but with a light syllable
preceding the trochee.

> 116.1 Let me *notʃto* the marriage of true minds
> 121.9 Noe, I *amʃthat* I am, and they that leuell
> 139.3 Wound me *notʃwith* thine eye but with thy toung

As I have stated the rule, these lines are unmetrical. Simplify Rule 3
to "Shakespeare allowed trochees with internal verse-pause," and
they become metrical, though very exceptional. The problem inherent in such a choice will be discussed in the sections "A Principle"
and "Metricality" in this chapter.

(4)

The fourth rule is that Shakespeare allows strong trochees in pyrrhic-
spondaic situations, that is, a strong trochee preceded by two light
syllables whether the previous foot counts technically as a light iamb,
light trochee, or pyrrhic.

When the combination is thought of as a double foot, that is, applying the rule of comparative stress to the two feet taken jointly, the

scansion would be pyrrhic followed by spondee. The notion of the double foot is inelegant by Ockham's Razor; hence I do not use it in actual scansion or in compiling the tables; but it is useful in showing a not infrequent relationship.

Note that such a combination is iambic in structure, light followed by heavy.

Some of these trochees are in lines very pleasant of rhythm, for instance, the following:

19.8 To the *wide world* and all her fading sweets
30.2 I sommon vp remembrance of *things past*

(5)

The fifth rule is that Shakespeare allows reconciled trochees, an often lovely class. I stipulatively define "reconciled trochee" to mean a strong trochee pulled toward, but not to the iambic: that is, a foot with the ictus on the first syllable but with some special linguistic force given also to the second syllable. Stress, as I have said, consists of whatever gives emphasis to a syllable, and involves at least loudness, pitch, quantity, attack, timbre, or juncture. In these feet, the first syllable gets an important component of stress, usually loudness and pitch; the second syllable some other component of stress. Clear examples occur in lines 1.6, 33.4, 98.5, and 116.9 respectively:

Feed'st thy *lights flame* with selfe substantiall fewell

Guilding *pale streames* with heauenly alcumy

Yet nor the laies of birds, nor the *sweet smell*

Lou's not *Times foole,* though rosie lips and cheeks
[*Times* was also italicized in the 1609 edition]

These feet read well with the first syllable given more loudness and pitch than the second, the second more quantity and a special juncture, musically fading to silence. Such feet are not justified by the other rules, are not to my ear iambs, yet fit the meter with a special grace.

The other examples are 2.8.3-4, 16.13.9-10, 30.4.3-4, 30.4.5-6, 30.12.3-4, 69.12.7-8, 80.12.3-4, 102.11.3-4, 104.7.9-10, 110.3.9-10,

130.2.9-10, and 137.7.3-4. Some of these, especially perhaps 80.12.3-4 and 137.7.3-4, are borderline. I hear them as somehow reconciled; if not reconciled, they should be listed with the unmetrical feet discussed later in this chapter.

A Principle

One cannot (at least I cannot) reduce the five rules for justification of trochees to an inclusive rule, a rule from which one could infer or with high probability predict each metrical or unmetrical occasion; they do however have something in common which can be at least roughly stated: it is not allowable to disrupt iambic flow. Trochees allowed by Rules 1 and 2 do not disrupt the flow because the flow has not begun; trochees allowed by Rule 4 do not disrupt iambic flow since the pattern light-light-heavy-heavy is a subclass or analogue of the pattern light-heavy; trochees allowed by Rule 5 do not disrupt the flow because such trochees are reconciled: something continues to pull toward the iambic. Trochees justified by Rule 3 are a borderline (and Shakespeare, as I have shown, uses them for effects of struggle or near disruption); hence such trochees are rare; hence Daniel in *Delia* does not allow them. The pattern light-heavy-heavy-pause is, however, distinctly less disruptive of iambic flow than the pattern heavy-light-heavy-pause. Therefore the decision to count trochees with internal pause as unmetrical except when preceded by a strong syllable, is justified by a fairly clear principle.

Trochees in the Fifth Foot

No trochees with distinctly weak second syllables occur in the fifth foot in the sonnets. But, judged by normal criteria, especially loudness and pitch, eighteen strong trochees occur in the fifth foot.[13] For instance, in line 98.5, "Yet nor the laies of birds, nor the sweet smell," "sweet" is by a normal reading both louder and higher in pitch than "smell," and consequently by normal standards, the fifth foot is a trochee.

Other examples of the "sweet smell" pattern occur in iambic placing, for instance, "ripe thoughts" in line 86.3, "That did my ripe thoughts in my braine inhearce," hence the Elizabethan stressing of such phrases was likely close to ours. Thus one can say that Shakespeare allows certain strong trochees in the fifth foot. All of these are justified either by Rule 4 or Rule 5.

Pyrrhics and Spondees

The pyrrhic, two unstressed syllables, and spondee, two stressed syllables, are, in anything like pure form, rare in English poetry because, by the principle of relative stress, any discernible difference of stress counts in determining ictus or metrical stress. Hence, strictly counted, most apparent spondees are heavy iambs or heavy trochees. Furthermore, when strong stresses come together, we tend to alternate stress. Thus a "spondaic" showcase such as Milton's "Rocks, Caves, Lakes, Fens, Bogs, Dens, and shades of death" turns out in most reading to be TTIii or TTTii or possibly TIIii rather than sssii.[14]

Still, since we cannot always discern differences in stress, some pyrrhics and spondees do occur. Neither pyrrhics nor near-pyrrhics are allowed in the fifth foot. In Shakespeare's sonnets, I find only the following examples of real pyrrhics and spondees.

Pyrrhics	**Scanned**
When to the Sess*ions of* sweet silent thought (30.1)	tipTi
For blunt*ing the* fine point of seldome pleasure (52.4)	ipTii
Some fresher stampe *of the* time bettering dayes (82.8)	iipTi
For how *do I* hold thee but by thy granting (87.5)	iptti
To make of monst*ers, and* things indigest (114.5)	iipti
Let me not to the marri*age of* true mindes (116.1)	ttipT
Least guil*ty of* my faults thy sweet selfe proue (151.4)	ipTTT

Spondees	**Scanned**
Sweets with sweets warre NOT, IOY delights in ioy (8.2)	tTsii
Sauage, extreame, RUDE, CRUell, not to trust (129.4)	tisii
HAD, HAVing, and in quest, to haue extreame (129.10)	siiii

These examples are certainly few enough, and any one of them could be read with a light variation of stress which would change the pyrrhic or spondee to an iamb or trochee, not necessarily respectively. Like-

wise, many light or strong iambs or trochees could become pyrrhics or
spondees with a slight shift of accent, or a slightly different hearing of a
pattern. For instance, in such not uncommon lines as line 2.6, "Where
all the trea*sure of* thy lusty days," I hear the third foot as a very light
iamb rather than a pyrrhic, perhaps because of a slight rise in pitch. If
such feet are counted as pyrrhic, the number of pyrrhics would be
increased significantly.

Four of the lines I list as including pyrrhics or spondees (87.5, 114.5,
116.1, and 8.2) are unmetrical for reasons to be discussed in the section
"Metricality" later in this chapter. Thus it should be clear that real
pyrrhics and spondees are both rare and apt to occur in unusual
contexts.

Near pyrrhics and spondees are frequent in the sonnets and often
occur together, near pyrrhic followed by near spondee (discussed in
relation to Rule 3 for justifying trochees). Fifty-six examples of the
pyrrhic-spondaic combination (two lights followed by two heavys)
occur in the sonnets. However, for purposes of counting, I follow the
stricter practice of considering all such feet separately, as pyrrhics,
spondees, iambs, or trochees, usually trochees. I do not know any
example in English poetry of a real pyrrhic followed by a real spondee,
but the combination is possible as in the following invented line,
scanned ipsii:

Shall three of a sort, blank of hue, prevail?

The ugliness of my line may suggest why poets are not attracted to the
possibility.

Successive Trochees

Successive trochees occur in the sonnets, with one or more of the
trochees usually strong. Most of such trochees are justified by the
rules, but not all. I count twenty-six examples of two successive
trochees,[15] six examples of three successive trochees, no example of
four successive trochees, and one disputable example of five successive
trochees.

Three Successive Trochees

Thén if fór my loúe, thou my loue receiuest (40.5)   ttTii

The first trochee is justified by Rule 2, the second trochee is unmetrical, the third trochee is justified by Rule 3, since the first "my" receives some rhetorical stress.

Añd the fiŕme soile ẃin of the watry maine (64.7) *t*Ttii

The first trochee is justified by Rule 2, the second by Rule 4, the third by Rule 3.

Giv́e my lóue fame faśter then time wasts life (100.13) tTTi*l*

The first trochee is justified by Rule 2, the second and third trochees are unmetrical.

Óf the wíde world, dréaming on things to come (107.2) *t*Ttii

The first trochee is justified by Rule 2, the second by Rule 4, the third by Rule 1.

Iñ the oúld age blácke was not counted faire (127.1) *t*Ttii

The first trochee is justified by Rule 2, the second by Rule 4, the third by Rule 1.

Least guilty of mý faults th́y sweet seĺfe proue (151.4) ip*T*TT

The first trochee is justified by Rule 4, the second and third trochees by Rule 5. "My" and "thy" have rhetorical stress.

In Shakespeare's plays, there are several examples of five successive trochees, including the following:

Romeo! humors! madman! passion! lover!

Never, never, never, never, never

This is strange, Your father's in some passion[16]

The line in *Romeo and Juliet* is deliberate high-spirited comedy; the great line in *King Lear* moves away from the norm to a far world of grief; the line in *The Tempest* is a strange moment preluding a famous speech ("Our revels now are ended").

The one trochaic line in the sonnets sits ill among such company:

What can mine owne praise to mine owne selfe bring (39.3)

Several scansions are possible, none happy. One can force the reading to "What CAN mine OWNE PRAISE to mine OWNE selfe BRING" (iitii), but the more natural reading of the parallel *mine-own* groups is "WHAT can MINE owne PRAISE to MINE owne SELFE bring" (ttttT). If the *mine-own* groups are read differently from each other, then "WHAT can MINE owne PRAISE to mine OWNE selfe BRING (tttii) is possible.

Metricality

Here is a passage of prose, taken entirely at random, divided into appropriate "lines" and scanned.

Out of that study came the con*cept of*	tiiit
a non-*profit legal* foundation and	ittii
on March 5, 1973 [five, nineteen se*venty-three*], *the Pa-*	isiap
cific *Legal* Foundation was *incor-*	ttiii
porated as a non-*profit, tax-ex-*	ipitt
empt public interest legal org*ani-*	tiiip

By the rules adduced for Shakespeare's sonnets, summed at the end of this chapter, ten feet out of sixty, 17%, are unmetrical, and three of them are twice unmetrical. I have italicized the unjustified trochees, anapest, pyrrhic at line ends, and words divided at line ends (the cause three times of double unmetricality). In Shakespeare's sonnets, fewer than .2 of 1% of the feet are unmetrical by the same rules. Only 53% of the feet in the prose-as-scanned are iambs; over 90% of the feet in Shakespeare's sonnets are iambs.

That prose sample (other samples give comparable results) and comparison make incontestably clear that metricality exists, that rules for it can be adduced and applied, and that some discourse is much more metrical than other discourse.

Drawing rules from metrical practice does, however, have its puzzles. In one strict sense, when rules are inferred from practice, nothing is unmetrical, since Shakespeare's metrical practice, or that of any other poet, *is* the practice, all regularities, oddities, and singularities included. Nor can we merely say that what is statistically rare is unmetrical. One then has the problem of deciding how rare an occurrence has to be to be counted unmetrical, and drawing a statistical magical boundary seems arbitrary. Also that principle would count as unmetrical some very metrical happenings. Thus line 106.6, "Of hand, of foote, of lip, of eye, of brow" is the most fulfilled iambic pentameter in the sonnets, the iambic pattern having been reinforced by relative stress, quantity, parallelism, and verse-pauses. Since it is the only line in Shakespeare's sonnets with a pause after every foot, it is metrically unique; yet one could hardly call it unmetrical. For that matter, each line of poetry is rhythmically unique, yet not thereby, as such, unmetrical or unrhythmical.

One cannot exclude nor entirely rely on aesthetic judgment in making decisions about metricality. Some things do sound unmetrical: the prose I have just analyzed sounds like prose, not poetry; I knew, years before I studied Elizabethan metrics, that something was metrically wrong with line 89.2 as printed in all modern editions: "And I will comment upon the offense." (The "upon" should be stressed on the first syllable.) Yet some lines I shall classify as unmetrical are very graceful, for instance, line 87.5, "For how do I hold thee but by the granting," and a line that is consciously, mimetically rough may not violate any metrical rule, for instance, line 11.10, "Harsh, featurelesse, and rude, barrenly perrish."

Nor are unmetricalities necessarily mistakes. Line 87.5 is a pleasant extension of Shakespeare's practice, the sprung rhyme of lines 45.6&8 was an exhibition of literary fashion; the unmetrical line 8.2, "Sweets with sweets warre not, ioy delights in ioy," is expressive of the conflict; the opening of Sonnet 116, "Let me not to the marriage of true mindes/ Admit impediments" (line 116.1 is unmetrical) is prosaic, reflective, preparatory for the great surge of poetry to follow.

If puzzles precluded judgment, our silence would be long. Not to classify certain procedures as unmetrical is to break down the clearly established distinction between prose and iambic verse; and to say, for instance, that Shakespeare simply allowed trochees would be to describe his practice less accurately than to state the rules for justification, especially since an underlying principle can be (has been) given, namely, that disrupting iambic flow is not allowed.

By the rules derived in this chapter, the following are the only instances of unmetricality in Shakespeare's sonnets. What is unmetrical is italicized.

Strong trochees, not justified

8.2   Sweets with *sweets warre* not, ioy delights in ioy.
10.4   But that thou none lou'st is *most eu*ident.
30.6   For precious friends hid in *death's date*les night.
39.3   What can *mine owne* praise to *mine owne* selfe bring
         (Two examples)
40.12   To beare loues wrong, then *hates knowne* iniury.
62.12   Selfe, so *selfe lou*ing were iniquity.
100.13   Give my *loue fame* faster then time wasts life
         ("faster" is also unmetrical; see next group)

Trochees, not strong, not justified (italics in text omitted)

40.5   Then if *for my* loue, thou my loue receiuest
42.7   Thou doost *loue her* because thou knowst *I loue* her
         (Two examples)
87.5   For how do I *hold thee,* but by thy granting
100.13   Giue my loue fame *faster* than time wasts life
107.8   And peace proclaimes *Oliues* of endlesse age
114.5   To make of monsters, and *things in*digest
116.1   Let me *not to* the marriage of true mindes
121.9   Noe, I *am that* I am, and they that leuell
127.8   But is prophan'd, if *not liues* in disgrace
136.2   Sweare to thy blind soule that *I was* thy Will
139.3   Wound me *not with* thine eye but with thy toung

Sprung rhyme

45.6   In tender Embassie of loue to *thee*
45.8   Sinkes downe to death, opprest with melancho*lie*
         (I count this instance as one unmetrical foot)

Some of these examples, by some rule interpreting, stress shifting,
and in other ways, might be brought under the rules; but all could not,
without some crude forcing; and a fair number of feet read as metrical
could be read as unmetrical (some examples were given in my discussion of Rule 5, above). There are, then, some but not many metrical
occurences in Shakespeare's sonnets which do not fit the normal and
normative practice of his sonnets.

The sonnets have 10,761 feet, by the following calculation:

151 sonnets of 14 five-foot lines	10,570
1 sonnet (No. 99) of 15 five-foot lines	75
1 sonnet (No. 126) of 12 five-foot lines	60
1 sonnet (No. 145) of 14 four-foot lines	56
	10,761

I count twenty-one unmetrical feet out of a total of 10,761, that is, .2 of 1%.[17] Some occur for special effects; some are metrical extensions; some occur from aesthetic error or carelessness. All in all, considering Shakespeare's rapid and restless energy, the amount he wrote, and his strong desire to explore wide ranges of the possibilities inherent in any form of convention, the surprise is that such lines are so few.

Feminine Endings

Feminine endings are light extra syllables at the end of iambic lines,[18] widely used in English iambics. Feminine endings are often considered extrametrical, and the concept is lumpish by the standard of Ockham's Razor, but describing such syllables by other means leads to about as many complications.

One can call the pattern $x/x/x/x/x/x$ five iambs with a feminine ending or four iambs and an amphibrach.[19] Since the latter description accounts for all the relevant metrical data within the notion of feet, it appears superior by the principle of simplicity for any given line. However, the amphibrach is an unfamiliar concept and leads to its own complications. It obscures iambic pattern since in $x/x/x/x/x/x$ the pattern $x/$ does occur five consecutive times, and the description iiiib mentions only four of those occurrences. Statements of Shakespeare's disyllabism would require qualification, since the amphibrach is a trisyllabic foot, and further qualification for some special cases, for instance a strong trochee in the fifth foot followed by a feminine ending, of which line 42.6 is an example if the "I" takes rhetorical stress, "Thou doost loue her because thou knowst *I* loue her," in which the fifth foot is a dactyl with strong second syllable if the concept of feminine ending is not used. Hence it is perhaps justifiable to stick with the more familiar concept, and I shall normally do so.

Counting feminine endings requires minimum and maximum counts, because of ambiguity of syllables.[20] Within the line one can be reasonably sure of the syllabification by the foot pattern, but not at

line end when an ambiguity occurs. Thus line 16.5, "Now stand you on
the top of happie houres," rhyming with "flowers" in line 16.7, can be
scanned iiiii or iiiii <.

By my count, in the 151 regular sonnets, 140 definite feminine
endings occur, plus 119 possible ones, making a minimum of 140 and a
maximum of 259, out of the 2,114 lines. The minimum percentage of
feminine endings is 7%, the maximum 12%, figures which will be later
discussed in relation to Daniel's *Delia*.

Rhyme

My study of Shakespeare's rhyme in the sonnets led to three
surprises (which come to one): (1) the amount of internal rhyme; (2)
the number of sonnets in which fewer than seven rhymes occur; (3) the
frequency of sound-links beyond rhyme, for instance, the number of
times all four rhymes in a quatrain have the same vowel sound. All
three show Shakespeare's fondness for heavy sound linkage; the "eye I
eyde" of line 104.2 is only a particularly notorious example. The
Elizabethans liked their sound-linkage thicker than any twentieth-
century poet does, including Vachel Lindsay. I think only of Edith
Sitwell and a few spots in Wallace Stevens, usually in him self-ironic,
which are comparable.

Over two dozen of the sonnets have fewer than seven rhymes,
Sonnet 135 having the fewest, four. In Sonnet 135 the effect is comic,
but many of the poems with fewer than seven rhymes are serious.

Many off-rhymes occur. Differences in Elizabethan and modern
pronunciation (which for rhymes is difficult and sometimes impossible
to determine) will regularize some but not all. A number of off-rhymes
are distinctly off.

One of the most unusual rhymes, which I shall call sprung rhyme, is
the rhyme of lines 45.6&8, "thee" & "melancholie," the "thee" being a
masculine ending and the "-lie" apparently a feminine ending.[21]

Rhyme with Terminal Consonantal Discrepancies

Some off-rhymes or nonrhymes require emendation, for instance,
25.9&11, "worth" & "quite," usually and probably correctly emended
to "fight" & "quite" (the error is discussed in Chapter Three); and

69.1&3, "view" and "end," usually and probably correctly emended to "view" and "due." Some other off-rhymes are emended, perhaps wrongly, four related examples being 19.5&7, "fleet'st" and "'sweets'"; 55.1&3, "monument" & "contents"; 144.6&8, "sight" & "pride"; and 153.13&14, "lies" & "eye." The normal emendations are from "fleet'st" to "fleets," "monument" to "monuments," "sight" to "side," and "eye" to "eyes." Any of these emendations is possible (144.6&8 is the most complicated instance), but none are necessary; to emend them on principle is a mistake, since the principle is based on a demonstrably false assumption: that Elizabethan poets did not rhyme pairs of words with terminal consonantal discrepancies.

The occurrence in the sonnets of four such rhymes should in itself offer a caution to emenders. Furthermore, Elizabethan poets did use such rhymes. The following example[22] is an unambiguous metrically as atrocious aesthetically, idiom and syntax requiring "streets" and "greet."

> Renouned Essex as hee pas'd the streets
> Would vaile his Bonnett to an oyster wife
> And with a kinde of louely humble greete
> The vulgar sort that did admire his life.

The following example of final consonantal variation is also unambiguous, though sometimes emended. It occurs in *A Lover's Complaint,* printed in the 1609 quarto of Shakespeare's sonnets.

> Religious loue put out religions eye:
> Not to be tempted would she be enur'd,
> And now to tempt all liberty procure.
>   (sig. Llv, lines 250-252)

I paraphrase lines 251-252 as follows: "She (a nun) would be inured (habituated to the monastic life) in order not to be tempted, but, having fallen in love with a young man, would, in order to tempt him and herself, procure all liberty." An emendation of "procure" to "procured" requires a clumsy ellipsis since *would procured* is not English, and goes beyond the story: we are not told that she ran off, only that she yearned for such freedom.

To those of us who think *A Lover's Complaint* is Shakespeare's,[23] that example is unambiguous evidence in the same book as the sonnets that Shakespeare used such rhymes. To anyone who doubts the authenticity of *A Lover's Complaint,* that example is unambiguous evidence that such rhymes were allowed in contemporary practice.

Another manuscript example occurs in a poem beginning "I loue thee not cause thou art faire," lines 9-10 being "Shee that would Cheerish my desires/ must feede my flames w[i]th equall fier."[24] Here an -*s* could have been dropped or added; but there is good reason to believe, and each example strengthens the belief, that Elizabethans were not so fussy about consonants in rhymes as we are.[25]

Such rhymes (the repetition of such sounds in rhyming places) certainly did not offend Shakespeare's ear, since they happen in sequence. Thus the following relevant runs of rhyme words occur: "die," "memory," "eyes," "lies" (lines 1.2,4,5,7); "lye," "eyes," "deny," "lyes" (lines 46.5-8); "pride," "beside," "write," "quite" (lines 103.2,4,5,7); "sight," "aside," "might," "bide" (lines 139.5-8). The first two runs compare to rhyme 153.13&14, "lies" & "eye"; the last two runs compare to rhyme 144.6&8, "sight" & "pride." In those runs there are no off-rhymes of this special sort, but the sounds of such rhymes precisely happen.

The rhyme 61.1&3, "open" & "broken,"[26] has the same kind of consonantal variation in the stressed syllables. The rhyme of lines 120.9&11, "remembred" & "tendred," has double consonantal variation in the stressed syllables. Those two sets of rhymes are normally not emended, because the feminine ending hides the off-rhyme slightly and because, if a cynical word may intrude, no handy emendation jumps to mind. But if the other four such rhymes are to be emended on principle, so should these two.

In the four examples normally emended, even if the burden of proof were not on the emender, one can make a reasonable (I do not say conclusive) case for the 1609 text in each instance. In line 19.5, "fleets" is a possible, second-person present verb form,[27] but less common and hence less likely than "fleet'st."

In line 55.1, "monuments" makes the more evident idiom, but "monument" parallels both "marble" (line 55.1) and "stone" (line 55.4) and has a metaphysical temptingness about it, Shakespeare being fond of the essential singular.

> Not marble, nor the guilded monument,
> Of Princes shall out-liue this powrefull rime,
> But you shall shine more bright in these contents
> Then vnswept stone, besmeer'd with sluttish time.
> (55.1-4)

Lines 124.5-8 are twice apposite:

No it [the speaker's love] was buylded far from accident,
It suffers not in smilinge pomp, nor falls
Vnder the blow of thralled discontent,
Whereto th'inuiting time our fashion calls.

The "accident" is a sort of metaphysical abstraction Shakespeare has a propensity for, and "the blow" is an abstraction standing for blows; Shakespeare is not thinking of a specific blow but of the kind of violence that the time calls out. "Accident" parallels "monument" in its abstraction; and "the blow" is like "the monument," an abstract singular standing for plural occasions.

Emending the rhyme of lines 144.6&8, "sight" & "pride," to "side" & "pride" is supported by an idiom in *Othello*, "Yea, curse his better angel from his side" (V. ii. 208), but gains no clarity, loses some meaning ("from my side" means merely "from me") and fails even to escape the "objectionable" rhyme, since the rhyme speaks out twice nearby, as though in protest at the emender:

Two loues I haue of comfort and dispaire,
Which like two spirits do sugiest me still,
The better angell is a man *right* faire:
The worser spirit [*sprite*] a woman collour'd ill.
(144.1-4)

In 153.13&14, "lies" & "eye," the referent of "my mistres eye" is the singular "my mistres eie" (line 153.9). In Sonnet 152, Shakespeare offers an unusual rhyme, the identical rhyme 152.10&12, "constancie" & "see," to be shortly discussed; then the rhyme in the couplet of Sonnet 152, "eye" & "lie"; then the variant of the same rhyme in the couplet of Sonnet 153. The collocation might be a highly freakish accident, but it is much more plausible that it is evidence for the intended order, the authenticity of Sonnet 153, and the off-rhyme "lies" & "eye."

Identical Rhyme

At least eight identical rhymes (allowed, and fairly common in Elizabethan poetry) occur in Shakespeare's sonnets, 10.2&4, "vnprouident" & "euident"; 34.10&12, "losse" & "losse"; 66.9&11, "authoritie" & Simplicitie"; 69.2&4 "mend" & "commend"; 89.2&4, "offence" & "defence"; 108.1&3, "character" & "register" (one could argue that that is not quite identical since "register" can be pronounced regis-ster); 124.9&11, "*Heriticke*" & "pollitick" (italics in text); 152.10&12, "constancie" & "see." The rhyme of lines 34.10&12, "losse" & "losse," is usually and probably correctly emended, the others never.

I did not count those identical rhymes which occur when more than two words rhyme, as in 133.2&4&13&14, "*me*" & "be" & "thee" & "*me*"; 135.1&3&9&11&13&14 "*Will*" & "*still*" & "*still*" & "*Will*" & "kill" & "*Will*" (italics of text ignored).

Internal Rhyme

The amount of internal rhyme in the sonnets is astonishing, even after some considerations. Our language has much vowel repetition, since there are few vowels and many words. Whenever a stressed vowel at word end happens to recur within a few words, it makes an internal rhyme, as in the words *see* and *free*. Thus much internal rhyme in prose and hence in poetry is accidental. Shakespeare liked to repeat words, and whenever a word is repeated within a line and at the end of a line, the word in the line rhymes with the rhyme-word of its repetition. Thus in line 70.11, "Yet this thy praise cannot be soe thy praise," each "praise" rhymes with "daies" of line 70.9; hence one can say that the first "praise" (70.11) is an internal rhyme rhyming with "daies" (70.9). Shakespeare also frequently clusters brief words such as *O, so,* and *no; I, my,* and *thy; me* and *thee* and rhyming words (for instance, in lines 62.3-6; lines 109.1-9,12-14; and lines 22.5,7-10 respectively). In lines 40.1-9, *my* occurs six times, *thy* twice, *I* twice (and *mine* and *thine* once) in a context of heavy repetition, *love(s)* occurring eight times. Count-ing each of the *I* and *thy* occurrences as rhyming separately with each of the *my* occurrences yields twenty-four internal rhymes, the four rhymes of *I* and *thy* with each other making twenty-eight internal rhymes in nine lines.

Counting internal rhyme, though, is an impossible task even as metrical counting goes. One does not need combed divisions and sub-divisions and cross counts to make the general point: there are prob-ably thousands and surely hundreds of occurrences of internal rhyme in the sonnets, sometimes in thickets, as in the example just given or the following example:

> Then can I greeue at greeuances *fore*-*gon*,
>
> And heauily from *woe* to *woe* tell *ore*
>
> The sad account of *fore-bemoned* *mone*,
>
> Which I new pay, as if not payd *before*.
>
> But if the while I thinke on thee (deare friend)
>
> All losses are *restord*, and *sorrowes* end.
>   (30.9-14)

Not only is there the massing of rhyme with internal rhyme, but also the marked groups of rhyme all have the same vowel sound. Such rhyming is one feature of the heavy sound-repetition and is largely caused by the penchant for repetition as such, but is heard in itself also and thus is in a real sense deliberate rhyme. It moves in a web of sound of which it is not the least part, sharing in Sonnet 30 the virtual onomatopoeia of moaning and woe.

In Sonnet 24 sound-linking, including heavy internal rhyme, is directly expressive of relation: the *mine* and *thine* and the *me* and *thee* turn about and upon each other, supported by context of meaning and sound. I note the vowel repetitions, including and extending beyond internal rhyme, in the sestet.

> Now *see* what good-turnes *eyes* for *eies* haue done,
>
> *Mine eyes* haue drawne *thy* shape, and *thine* for *me*
>
> Are windowes to *my* brest, where-through the Sun
>
> De*li*ghts to *peepe*, to gaze therein on *thee*
>
> Yet *eyes* this cunning want to grace their art
>
> They draw but what they *see*, know not the hart.

The "good-turnes" of reciprocity are subject and performance. The art is willfully and proudly visible.

No simple aesthetic conclusion follows. In Sonnet 24, as in the Will Sonnets 135-136 with their heavy punning and sound-repetition, the effect is self-applauding, ingenious, amusing, a little repellent. Yet Sonnet 30, whose effects are as thickened as those of Sonnet 24, is a deeply moving poem. I was more moved by Sonnet 30 before I saw how visibly rich the sound linkage is, and I suspect the judgment implicit in that change is right; but richness of sound is consonant with and no small cause of the range and complexity of the sonnets.

In lines 80.1-5 the internal rhyme and related sound-linkage are impudently comic, yet frightened.

O how *I* faint when *I* of you do *write*,

Knowing a better spirit [*sprite*] doth vse your name,

And in the praise thereof spends all his *might*,

To make me toung-*tide* speaking of your fame.

But since your worth (*wide* as the Ocean is)

The humble as the proudest saile doth beare,

My sawsie barke (inferior farre to his)

On your broad maine doth wilfully appeare.

(80.1-8)

In the sestet of a profound and noble poem, Sonnet 146, the internal rhymes are entirely sober. Internal rhymes are numbered and words and parts of words linking to those internal rhymes are italicized.

Then soule liue *th*ou vpon *thy* seruants losse,

And let *that pine* to aggrauat *thy* store;

Buy tearmes *diuine* in selling houres of *d*rosse:

Within be *fed*, without be rich no more,

So shalt thou *feed* on *dea*th, that *feeds* on men,

And *death* once *dead*, ther's no more *dy*ing *then*.

A similar fondness for density appears, also startlingly dense, in runs of end-rhymes with linkage, primarily vowel linkage, between sets of rhymes, as in the following examples, in which repeated vowels are italicized and other linkages numbered.

m*a*de d*a*y sh*a*de st*a*y (43.9-12)

f*i*re ab*i*de des*i*re sl*i*de (45.1-4)

s*i*ght right l*y*e *ey*es den*y* l*y*es (46.2,4-8)

s*a*y fr*a*me th*ey* s*a*me d*ai*es pr*ai*se (59.9-14)

Qu*ee*ne est*ee*m'd s*ee*ne d*ee*m'd (96.5-8)

r*a*ng'd ag*ai*ne exch*a*ng'd st*ai*ne r*ai*gn'd st*ai*n'd (109.5-8,9,11)

Sonnet 64 has the same vowel sound in ten rhymes: "defaced," "age," "rased," "rage," "gaine," "maine," "state," "decay," "ruminate," "away" (64.1-5,7,9-12). The poem has many other rich sound workings, and the effect is not exhibitionism but power.

Some Metrical Statistics

Metrical statistics are problematical in various ways, including several already discussed. Statistics for feminine endings are firm but double; few puzzling instances occur, but feminine endings must be divided into distinct (line 87.3, "The Charter of thy worth giues thee releasing") and distinctly ambiguous (line 16.5, "Now stand you on the top of happie houres" — "houres" can be one or two syllables), yielding a minimum and a maximum count.

Counting trochees leads to a single but less reliable count, since the distinction between strong trochees and strong iambs and spondees is at times thin to vanishing; since alternate correct ways of speaking lines exist; since metrically incorrect texts may sometimes be emended more than one way; and since, among other reasons, we do not know how far Elizabethan phrasal stressing differed from ours or how far Elizabethans bent speech idiom to fit meter.

Other countings, other problems. Verse-pauses admit the difficulty of definition already discussed, and sometimes admit to a different count within a single line. In line 6.6, "Which happies those that pay the willing lone," one can count no verse-pause or a verse-pause after "those." In the line 62.12 "Selfe, so selfe louing were iniquity," whether a verse-pause occurs after the first "selfe" in the line depends on how one reads the embroiled syntax of the line in its context:

> But when my glasse shewes me my selfe indeed
> Beated and chopt with tand antiquitie,
> Mine owne selfe loue quite contrary I read
> Selfe, so selfe louing were iniquity.
>
>   (62.9-12)

If one reads the first "selfe" of line 62.12 as a vocative, as the 1609 punctuation, which is some if imperfect evidence, suggests, then a verse-pause follows the first syllable of the line and "so selfe louing" is the peculiar subject of the sentence. If one takes the line to mean, "A self so-self-loving were iniquity," then no verse-pause occurs after the first syllable. In general, nonetheless, I hazard that counting verse-pauses is less problematical than counting trochees.

Since the regularities in iambics are few and the variety literally infinite, endless metrical statistics are possible, especially with the laboratory equipment available to record individual differences in reading. One could do statistics on pitch, juncture, quantity, fine degrees of stress, word counts, sound-repetition counts and patterns (alliteration, internal assonance, and on and on), and interrelationships between these and other features of meter and language. How far such studies might be useful, with the aid of computers, in determining authorship or chronology or in illuminating stylistics, is hard to tell in advance; that they might obstruct aesthetic and human understanding, while heaping up compilations, is easy for the suspicious-minded reader to suspect. The statistics I have put together are comparatively modest, whether obstructive or not.

I have compared in Tables 1-8 Daniel's *Delia* (1592) and Shakespeare's sonnets. Tables 1-3 show for Shakespeare and Tables 4-6 for Daniel counts of trochees, verse-pauses, and feminine endings respectively, and Tables 7-8 show the comparisons. Tables 9-11 make some metrical comparisons of groups within Shakespeare's sonnets.

The differences between *Delia* and Shakespeare's sonnets are distinct and all go one way. In respect to trochees and verse-pause,

Shakespeare is further from Gascoigne than Daniel is.[28] English verse in the 1570s and in many poets in the 1580s had few substitutions and a regular caesura, a verse-pause after syllable 4. The metrical advance was toward freer handling of substitution and verse-pause; in each category Shakespeare goes further than Daniel.

One unexpected result of the comparison between *Delia* and Shakespeare's sonnets is a likeness between the order of frequency in respect to both trochees and verse-pauses, the pattern of verse-pauses affecting the pattern of trochees. In both *Delia* and the sonnets, trochees occur in feet in the following order of decreasing frequency: 1, 3, 4, 2, 5. One would expect the most trochees in the first foot and the fewest in the fifth foot, but not that a pattern would hold for the other three feet.

In both *Delia* and the sonnets, verse-pauses occur after syllables in decreasing order of frequency for the first five steps: 4, 6, 5, 7, 2 (that is, there are the most verse-pauses after syllable 4, the next most after syllable 6, and so on). In both *Delia* and the sonnets, the fewest verse-pauses occur after syllable 9. One would expect the most verse-pauses after syllable 4, the fewest after syllable 9, and more medial than non-medial verse-pauses, but not the close concurrence.

Whether those trochaic and verse-pause patterns of concurrence are more widely typical of English poets or of Daniel and Shakespeare in other work would require further looking.

The patterns of change between *Delia* and the sonnets go, as I have said, in one direction; the internal comparisons of the sonnets go helter-skelter. The lack of pattern leads to a definite conclusion, that at least in these respects Shakespeare's sonnets are very homogeneous in metrical style. One can account for this truth in at least the following ways, the fifth being my preference.

(1) Shakespeare's sonnet style did not change over a period of many years.

(2) The order of the sonnets is scrambled, so such comparisons are out of court. (A rearranger who, rearranging on distinctly other grounds, produced an order which showed clear directions of metrical change, would have something, a something I predict will not occur.)

(3) Shakespeare's sonnet style changed but in ways not caught by these nets.

(4) The procedure is invalid. (It worked for *Delia* and Shakespeare's sonnets.)

(5) The sonnets were written in a comparatively short period of time (about three years, as I believe).

The Iambic Pattern

The basic rule of the sonnets is evident but not thereby trivial: one writes five iambs to a line, with exceptions. The exceptions are exceptional. Only 5% of the feet are trochees, a percentage that the six pyrrhics and three spondees leaves at 5% for substitutions. (It literally raises 5.0% to 5.1%, but I rounded off because one's conclusions cannot be more accurate than one's data.) If one counts the feminine endings as parts of amphibrachic feet, then the percentage of substitutions of feet would be 6% minimum, 8% maximum. At the least, then, 92% of the feet are iambs, and by the normal method of scanning in which a feminine ending does not occasion a substitution, 95% of the feet are iambs. In the prose sample I discussed above in the section "Metricality," 53% of the feet were iambs. In other prose samples I have found 50-60% iambs. This shows that our language does have a strong iambic tendency (the other 40-50% of the feet being divided among trochees, anapests, pyrrhics, and spondees), and that the chief feature of iambics is simply its high preponderance of iambs. We get softer and louder when we talk, more so when we recite iambic poems.

Since most features of language are free in verse of metrical restriction, variations on iambic rhythm are indefinitely possible. Degree of stress within the iambic framework is the most important freedom; but quantity, verse-pause, timbre, speed, timing, sound repetitions other than rhyme, and other linguistic features are free to go as the author wishes within the wide variety possible of speech idiom and rhythm. The freedom is great and Shakespeare greatly uses it.

The tendency of timing, quantity, and stress is to reinforce the basic iambic pattern, and how far in practice the pattern is reinforced or worked against determines much about the rhythm. When reinforcement is strong, one comes close to a basic norm of *ta tum, ta tum, ta tum, ta tum, ta tum.* In such a pattern, metrically unstressed syllables are light and short, metrically stressed syllables are heavy and long, pauses occur after each foot, and timing approaches equality. One hears variation against this norm and some others, and variation and norms together constitute expressive rhythm. All rhythms except the most basic consist of an interplay between regularity and variations.

The norm described is sometimes shown off by poets, as in the following Elizabethan examples,[29] one of them from Shakespeare's sonnets.

> Of hand, of foote, of lip, of eye, of brow
> *Shake-speares Sonnets* (106.6)

> I see, I hear, I feel, I know, I rue
> My fate, my fame, my pain, my loss, my fall
> ....
> To cross, to shame, bewitch, deceive, and kill.
> Bartholomew Griffin,
> *Fidessa* (1596) (47.1-2,5)

> They snuf, they snort, they bounce, they rage, they rore
> Spenser, *Faerie Queene* (V.2.15.6)

> To spin, to card, to sew, to wash, to wring
> Spenser, *Faerie Queene* (V.4.31.6)

> He stroke, he soust, he foynd, he hewd, he lasht
> Spenser, *Faerie Queene* (IV.3.25.6)

A less showy, more powerful line in Shakespeare's sonnets which approaches that norm is "Since brasse, nor stone, nor earth, nor boundlesse sea" (65.1).

Another major norm is the line in which the iambic movement is reinforced by degree of stress, quantity, and timing, but with strong motion through the line with one medial pause. One of the best examples of such a norm is "Increasing store with losse, and losse with store" (64.8). Three other good examples, slightly less reinforced by quantity than line 64.8, are "And time that gaue, doth now his gift confound" (60.8), "But doe thy worst to steale thy selfe away" (92.1) and "The teeming Autumne big with ritch increase" (97.6).

Lines consisting of five iambs in the sonnets have as few as three actually strong stresses or as many as eight, with one possible instance of ten strong stresses.

Sonnet 64 has one line with three actual strong stresses, "adVANTage on the KINGdome of the SHOARE" (64.6), and one with seven, "the RICH PROUD COST of OUTWORNE BURied AGE" (64.2), though each of these lines scans as five iambs. Line 140.14 deserves in my listening ten decisive blows of accent, though it too scans as five iambs: "BEARE THINE EYES STRAIGHT, THOUGH THY PROUD HEART GOE WIDE." The only syllables which might take lowered stress are "though" and "goe" so at least eight strong stresses occur in the line. A line with seven strong stresses, which again scans as five iambs, is line 104.7, one of the richest and warmest lines ever penned: "THREE APrill PERFUMES in THREE HOT IUNES BURN'D."

Within such extremes occur many lines of five iambs, of which I list a few to demonstrate the remarkable variety and expressiveness of sound, a sound more meaningful in context than out. Even out of context these lines show Shakespeare the master listener of poets.

But thou contracted to thine owne bright eyes (1.5)

When your sweet issue your sweet forme should beare (13.8)

And barren rage of deaths eternall cold (13.12)

And in fresh numbers number all your graces (17.6)

Ore-charg'd with burthen of mine owne loues might (23.8)

And mone th'expence of many a vannisht sight (30.8)

My selfe corrupting saluing thy amisse (35.7)

Or what strong hand can hold his swift foote back (65.11)

And lace it selfe with his societie (67.4)

When yellow leaues, or none, or few doe hange (73.2)

Possessing or pursuing no delight (75.11)

Now all is done, haue what shall haue no end (110.9)

To cryttick and to flatterer stopped are (112.11)

Th'expence of Spirit in a waste of shame (129.1)

My loue is as a feauer longing still (147.1)

And frantick madde with euer-more vnrest (147.10)

Canst thou O cruell, say I loue thee not (149.1)

Commanded by the motion of thine eyes (149.12)

And his loue-kindling fire did quickly steepe (153.3)

Q.E.D.

Summary

Shakespeare's rules of metrical practice in the sonnets, as inferred in this chapter and Appendix A, are the following.

(1) Shakespeare in the sonnets wrote strict iambics. The normal pattern of the line is five iambs, with no extra syllables allowed except unstressed syllables at the ends of lines. The only poem without five feet in a line is Sonnet 145, in tetrameter.

(2) Feminine endings are allowed. An alternate description is that amphibrachic substitutions in the fifth foot are allowed.

(3) Only justified trochees are allowed. There are five rules for justifying trochees: (1) trochees are allowed after verse-pauses; (2) trochees are allowed in the first foot; (3) trochees with internal verse-pause, when the trochee is preceded by a strong syllable, are allowed; (4) trochees are allowed in a pyrrhic-spondaic situation; (5) reconciled trochees, as defined above, are allowed.

Other trochees occur, and are classified in this book as unmetrical.

The principle underlying the rules for justification of trochees is that iambic flow may not be disrupted.

(4) Real pyrrhics and spondees are allowed, but are rare. Pyrrhics and near pyrrhics are not allowed in the fifth foot. Near pyrrhics and near spondees are frequent, often with the near pyrrhic immediately preceding the near spondee.

(5) Successive trochees occur, as many as three in a row, and in one possible instance, five in a row. Most but not all such trochees are justified by the rules.

(6) Trochees occur in the following feet in decreasing order of frequency (most trochees in first foot, fewest in fifth foot): 1,3,4,2,5. This order is the same in Daniel's *Delia.*

(7) Verse-pauses occur at the end of each (or almost each) line.

(8) Verse-pause is otherwise free; verse-pauses may and do appear after each syllable of the line.

(9) The fewest verse-pauses occur after syllable 9.

(10) Verse-pauses occur after the following syllables in decreasing order of frequency: 4,6,5,7,2. I give only five of the nine because the order of those five is the same as for Daniel's *Delia* and therefore of possible wider significance.

(11) The rhyme scheme required is cross-rhyming quatrains followed by a couplet. Sonnets 99 and 126 are exceptions to this rule.

(12) The same rhyme may be used in more than two lines in a sonnet, but not in such a way as to make a coherently different pattern. Six, five, and four rhymes are allowed in place of the normal seven.

(13) Sprung rhyme is allowed, one example.

(14) Identical rhyme is allowed.

(15) Off-rhymes of various kinds are allowed.

(16) Rhymes with terminal consonantal variations are allowed; hence certain common emendations are suspect.

(17) Internal rhyme is allowed, and abounds.

(18) More than one set of rhymes with the same vowel sound are allowed in a sonnet in close proximity, up to five sets of rhyme, that is, in ten lines out of fourteen.

(19) Heavy sound repetition and linkage of various kinds are allowed, and abound.

(20) The following features of verse are not allowed (some of them, for instance internal feminine endings, are allowed in Shakespeare's plays);

(a) trisyllabic feet.

(b) internal feminine endings, an unstressed extra syllable before a verse-pause within the line.

(c) truncated feet.

(d) anacrusis, an unstressed extra syllable before the first foot.

(e) Alexandrines, hexameters.

(f) short lines in pentametric contexts.

(g) caesura, a verse-pause occurring in the same place throughout the poem. In the lovely, tripping tetrametric Sonnet 145, however, verse-pauses occur only after syllables 2 or 4.

(h) word enjambment, dividing a word between two lines.

(21) The sonnets are highly homogeneous in metrical style, compared to the consistent and distinct divergence between Daniel's *Delia* and Shakespeare's sonnets.

(22) Shakespeare wrote well.

Chapter 5

Rhetoric and the Sonnets

Rhetoric was king — or at least a vocal pretender — in Renaissance education and poetry.[1] The use and abuse of persuasive eloquence; the sense of propriety to genre, style, audience, intent; the distinctions of high, middle, and low style with what was proper to each; the many figures and schemes — these were taught and retaught, misheard, half-heard, simplified, subtilized or entangled in schools and in poems. Rhetoric taught the poets the simultaneous and not always consistent love of plainness and love of richly manifested art ..nd thereby encouraged any penchant (Shakespeare's was great for both) for plain speaking or for elaboration of style.

The plain style has a typical defect: dullness. Dryden says of a would-be poet, "He affects plainness, to cover his want of imagination,"[2] a remark which has not lacked twentieth-century or earlier exemplars, but the plain style can be magnificent as in Jonson's "To Heaven" and many a line of Shakespeare's. The plain style appeals to truth as clearly seen and to our suspicion of fraud and posturing. Rich styles have as typical defects self-conscious showiness, coy artfulness (*Euphues* is the automatic illustration, but examples are numerous and Shakespeare can provide his share), obscurity, and bombast. A rich style can express more than a plain style, and the success of plainness often depends on a rhetorically and metaphysically rich context.

Renaissance rhetoric, one can safely enough say, taught some wisdom about men and about persuasion, and encouraged good things as well as some bad and dull. Since the bad and dull mostly have died their quiet deaths or quarrel on in some logical space we need not observe, we have good cause to be grateful to the flourishing of Renaissance rhetoric. Without it, Elizabethan and seventeenth-century and later literature would be a far poorer thing.

Looked at as a systematic attempt to analyze features of successful language, Renaissance rhetoric does less well. It is a theoretical hodgepodge and grew wildly. Its distinctions are repetitious, overlapping, and blurred. One of the books most useful in helping a modern student find his way in the world of Renaissance rhetoric is Richard A. Lanham's *A Handlist of Rhetorical Terms,*[3] and the need for Lanham's clearheadedness in cross-classifying and sorting out, in itself reveals the lack of a lucid intellectual structure in the rhetoric.

The grounds for distinction between trope (change of meaning) and scheme (change of arrangement) break down, since in literature all rearrangement changes meaning at least slightly and often greatly by changing response; literary meaning is total, not an abstracted paraphrase. Further, if the distinction held up, all tropes would be, as Father Ong observes, subclasses of metaphor.[4]

The subclasses of figures and schemes violate Ockham's Razor, or rather it makes confetti of them: there is no serious attempt to order the subclassifying[5] except Ramus's simplifications which violate the other edge of the Razor. The names are unsorted, with half a dozen names for the same figure or scheme, with the same name used for different figures or schemes, with overlaps, and with inconsistency of terminology.[6] The names violate another requirement of scientific and other good thinking; they sound, like a number of modern psychological, sociological, and literary terms, more technical and precise than they are.

The rhetoricians and poets at their best do not think figures are merely icing on the cake, ornaments added to substance,[7] but the temptation is there and often enough succumbed to, as in Samuel Daniel's remark, "Ornaments . . . doe but decke the house of a State."[8] Ornaments can be integral to substance. A student of mine once observed that, without ornaments, a Christmas tree is not a Christmas tree, and J. B. Leishman shrewdly observes of Othello: "Take away the hyperboles, and . . . Othello disappears."[9]

Yet Leishman's rhetoric of attack (*apodioxis,* rejecting indignantly as absurd) on rhetoric can be vivid enough, "dreary Alexandrianism," "illiterate and misconceived,"[10] though no stronger than Samuel Daniel's phrase "tyrannicall Rules of idle Rhetorique."[11] The attack on rhetoric is part of the rhetorical tradition.

The rhetorical figures are meant to cover departures from norms in syntax, idiom, word, meaning, and the like, so that one can speak of figured as against unfigured language, but plain language gets its names (*Atticism, brevitas, comma, parrhesia*) and many terms apply equally well to plain or to highly figured style (*aporia, dehortatio, exprobatio, syngnome*) or cover any possibility (clauses must be ordered according to *hypotaxis* or *parataxis*).[12] Even ordinary moves of language get named and hence there is no clear norm or departure. We can truly say that it is natural in speech to use expressive figures, metaphor, hyperbole, and the like, but the "natural" undercuts the distinction required between figured and unfigured, natural and unnatural.[13]

In some very ordinary situations, any way of saying something will be "figured."[14] If one innocently tries to make out a grocery list he is apt to become a prisoner of the Renaissance mesh.

Thus, "Please get me marmalade, oleomargarine, zucchini squash, and peanut butter" is *enumeratio* or *eutrepismus* (listing, division into parts). A gourmet might well insist that "Please get some artichokes, oranges, field peas, and Krinkles" is a *catacosmesis* (ordering from greatest to least in dignity). "And get me — oh never mind, I'll go to the store myself" is an *aposiopesis* (leaving a statement unfinished). "The Corner Market doesn't have it; try the Red Food Store" is *apocarteresis* (giving up one hope and turning to another). And so on. Two points are plain enough: Renaissance rhetoric has no way to keep the distinction between figured and unfigured language, and the figures cover a considerable assortment of disrelated kinds.

One could not, even if one wished, deal systematically with Shakespeare's use of rhetoric in the sonnets,[15] because the rhetorical "system" was highly unsystematic, and because rhetorical figures often get unexpected turns in Shakespeare. For instance, *conduplicatio* (repeating a word in successive clauses) is a common figure in the sonnets. A simple example is line 11.1, "As *fast* as thou shalt wane so *fast* thou grow'st." Lines 101.1-3 provide a double example:

> O truant Muse, what shall be thy amends
> For the neglect of *truth* in *beauty* dy'd?
> Both *truth* and *beauty* on my love depends

The grammatical relationships have shifted and the meanings are metaphysical, but the repeating itself is fairly simple. Lines 110.5-6 are twistier: "Most *true* it is, that I have look'd on *truth*/ Askance and strangely," in which the form of the word changes as we move from a statement about statements to a statement, both governed by the concept they name, truth.

In Sonnet 40 changes are rung on the word *love(s)* in several sliding meanings, especially in lines 40.1-6:

Take all my *loves*, my *love*, yea, take them all.
What has thou then more than thou hadst before?
No *love*, my *love*, that thou mayst true *love* call;
All mine was thine, before thou hadst this more.
Then if for my *love* thou my *love* receivest,
I cannot blame thee, for my *love* thou usest.

The word *love(s)* has referred at least to Shakespeare, the woman purloined, the young man, Shakespeare's earlier friends or lovers, the abstract quality, the relation to the woman, and the ideal, all in six lines, yielding seven examples of *conduplicatio*, which is *traductio* (repeating a word often) and *ploce* or *diaphora* (playing on sounds and meanings of words).

The love of repeating is Elizabethan. The twistingness of repetition is unique to Shakespeare. Spenser offers examples with as much boldness of repeating but more straightforward meaning and intent, as in the octave of Sonnet 26 of *Amoretti:*

Sweet is the Rose, but growes vpon a brere;
    Sweet is the Iunipere, but sharpe his bough;
    sweet is the Eglantine, but pricketh nere;
    sweet is the firbloome, but his braunches rough.
Sweet is the Cypresse, but his rynd is tough;
    sweet is the nut, but bitter is his pill;
    sweet is the broome-flowre, but yet sowre enough;
    and sweet is Moly, but his root is ill.

(1595)

No one who has learned from Rosemond Tuve[16] is apt to talk of these as "mere" examples; Spenser is not only offering lovely and gracefully varied examples and images, but he is excited about the truth that examples hold concepts and concepts morally applicable import; when he states in line 9 the generalization implicit in these examples, it is with logical and ontological enthusiasm: "So euery sweet with soure is tempred still." Spenser is nearer the spirit of Shakespeare's Friar in *Romeo and Juliet* gathering herbs with God-given and mysterious qualities than he is to the spirit of some purely decorative poet or that of Wordsworth's cold-blooded classifying botanist. (Actual botanists are apt to get excited about their subject in ways not unlike Spenser's.)

Spenser is making sense out of the world and finding it good to do so; Shakespeare shifts more because his intent is shiftier. In the lines in Sonnet 40 deeply felt anger and rhetorical playfulness are simultaneous. One effect of their joining, here as elsewhere in the sonnets, is self-contempt offered at the ingenious verbal sophistry required to justify rhetorically what cannot be justified emotionally or morally. Also the poet, like Hamlet, is showing contempt for himself for unpacking his heart with words rather than taking some vindictive action.

Whether engaged in sophistry and self-derision or not, Shakespeare liked to repeat words and phrases in varying patterns and sounds, to play on and off words, to turn things about or athwart. His natural delight in words was reinforced by the rhetoric he learned in school, books, and conversation.

How far he thought specifically in terms of the figures we cannot be sure. He knew the jargon and mocked it in *Love's Labor's Lost;* in the sonnets he uses logical jargon (see the next chapter) more often and technically than he uses rhetorical jargon ("ornament" [1.9 and elsewhere] and "rhetoric" [82.10] are typical); he certainly learned more from poets than rhetoricians, though, it is fair to add, from poets who had themselves learned from rhetoricians. He thought in terms of the figures at least more than a modern mind suspicious of rhetorical jargon is apt to allow. He may well have praised himself with such words as the "pretie Epanorthosis" E. K. glossed in praise of Spenser.[17] Or he may have seldom thought in such words. He did a pretty *epanorthosis* (correction of word just after using it) in line 83.3:

I never saw that you did painting need,
And therefore to your fair no painting set;
I *found* (*or thought I found*) you did exceed
The barren tender of a poet's debt.
                                        (83.1-4)

And an even prettier one in Sonnet 125, one which crosses into a world negative past nothing.

Have I not seen dwellers on form and favor
Lose *all, and more,* by paying too much rent
For compound sweet . . .
                                        (125.5-7)

Shakespeare's attitude toward rhetoric was doubtless much like what Hardin Craig[18] shows us to have been his attitude toward logic and Roland Mushat Frye[19] shows us to have been part of his attitude toward theology. He was well educated in all three subjects, he got them in his bones and fingers, he mocked pedantic examples of their

use (for instance, in Holofernes in *Love's Labor's Lost*), he did not
linger on them theoretically; he used them as he wished. He is
rhetorically overloaded, involuted, plain, magnificent.

The sonnets give plenteous examples of *anaphora* (word repetition),
offering examples or near-examples of each of the subclasses of *anaphora* listed by Peacham.[20]

Epanaphora (word repeated in the beginning of different clauses)

> Then being ask'd *where* all thy beauty lies,
> *Where* all the treasure of thy lusty days
> (2.5-6)

> *If* snow be white, why then her breasts are dun;
> *If* hairs be wires, black wires grow on her head
> (130.3-4)

Also lines 9.4-5; 12.1,3,5; 18.13-14; 46.3-4; 49.1,5,9; 66,3-12.

Epiphora (word repeated at end of clauses)

Rhyme approaches this figure, hence there are numerous near-examples in the sonnets. A literal example is the identical rhyme 34.10 &
12 (*loss* & *loss*, usually emended). Less disputable examples are the
following:

> The one by *toil*, the other to complain
> How far I *toil*, still farther off from thee
> (28.7-8)

> Thou dost *love her* because thou know'st I *love her*
> (42.6)

> Coral is far more *red* than her lips' *red*
> (130.2)

Symploce (word repeated at the beginning and another word repeated
at the end of successive clauses)

Near examples:

> *Past* reason *hunted*, and, no sooner had,
> *Past* reason *hated*, as a swallow'd bait
> (129.6-7)

> *When* I have seen by time's fell hand de*fac'd*
> The rich, proud cost of outworn buri'd age,
> *When* sometime lofty towers I see down *raz'd*
> (64.1-3)

Ploce (a proper name repeated with different significations)
Ploce is the principle of the Will Sonnets 134, 135, and 136, and also appears in Sonnet 143:

> So *will* I pray that thou may'st have thy *Will*
> (143.13)

Diaphora (a word repeated with different significations)
Peacham uses diaphora for the broader common meaning of *ploce*. Examples are frequent, including those in lines 40.1-6 already discussed and the following:

> My mistress when *she* walks treads on the ground;
> And yet by heav'n I think my love as rare
> As any *she* beli'd with false compare
> (130.12-14)

> Thy *black* is fairest in my judgment's place.
> In nothing art thou *black* save in thy deeds
> (131.12-13)

Most word repetition in Shakespeare represents some degree of *diaphora*, since his words flutter gradations of meaning even when puns are not full fledged.

Epanalepsis (same word at beginning and end of sentence)

> Sweets with sweets war not, *joy* delights in *joy*
> (8.2)

> But, ah, *thought* kills me that I am not *thought*
> (44.9)

Anadiplosis (word at end of one clause and beginning the next clause)

> Love is my sin, and thy dear virtue *hate*,
> *Hate* of my sin, grounded on sinful loving
> (142.1-2)

> Who all in *one, one* pleasing note do sing
> (8.12)

Also lines 36.14, 53.14.

Epizeuxis (word repeated with no word intervening)

> For as you were when first your *eye I ey'd*
> (104.2)

> How oft when thou my *music music* playest
> (128.1)

All examples of *anadiplosis* including those already given are also examples of *epizeuxis.*

Also lines 17.6, 43.6.

Diacope (a word repeated with one word between)

> So great a *sum of sums* yet canst not live
> (4.8)

> Strikes *each in each* by mutual ordering
> (8.10)

Also lines 8.2, 18.7, 20.7, 23.12, 24.9, 30.10, 31.14, 37.6, 37.13, 40.1 and 40.3 already discussed, 43.4, 51.12, 52.11, 56.14, 64.9-10, 123.3, 124.4 (twice), 139.4, 145.13, 150.9-10.

Traductio (a word repeated several times)

> Or *ten* times happier be it *ten* for one;
> *Ten* times thy self were happier than thou art,
> If *ten* of thine *ten* times refigur'd thee
> (6.8-10)

> Or if it were it bore not *beauty's* name;
> But now is black, *beauty's* successive heir.
> And *beauty* slander'd with a bastard shame.
> (127.2-4)

Also *world* in lines 9.4,5,9-11; *your self* in lines 13.1,2,7;*woman-women* in lines 20.1,3,4,8,9,13; *eye(s)* in lines 24.1,8,9,10,13; *love(s)* in Sonnet 40, already discussed; *eye* and *heart* in Sonnets 46 and 47; *and* as first syllable of lines 66.3-12 (already listed under *epanaphora*).

Lovers of simplicity may be a little startled at the reason Peacham gives for using *anaphora,* "to make the Oration more trimme."[21]

More complicated forms of repetition occur, for instance *chiasmus* or *antimetabole,* 1-2-2-1 grouping.

Music[1] to *hear,*[2] why *hear'st*[2] thou *music*[1] sadly?

(8.1)

But *day*[1] by *night*[2] and *night*[2] by *day*[1] oppress'd

(28.4)

Is *lust*[1] in *action;*[2] and, till *action,*[2] *lust*[1]

(129.2)

Shakespeare's sonnets, like other Renaissance poems, display examples of *anaphora* which do not fit Peacham's or other Renaissance subclassifications. The classes, elaborate as they are, fail to be exhaustive.

For instance, the chiasmic analogue to *symploce* occurs in the sonnets.

Love[1] is my sin, and thy dear virtue *hate,*[2]

Hate[2] of my sin, grounded on sinful *loving.*[1]

(142.1-2)

The classes do not cover complications caused by repeating two words together. Thus line 29.6, "Featur'd *like him, like him* with friends possess'd," is strictly two examples of *diacope* ("*like* him, *like,*" "*him, like him*"), but would be better described, outside the given classes, as an *anadiplosis* (successive repetition) of the two words taken jointly.

Nor do the classes include many other word repetitions, including those, of obvious rhetorical and metrical importance, in which the repetition is reinforced by grammatical or metrical parallelism:

O *change* thy thought, that I may *change* my mind

(10.9)

O learn to read what silent *love* hath writ!
To hear with eyes belongs to *love's* fine wit.
(23.13-14)

As subject to *time's* love or to *time's* hate
(124.3)

Mad sland'rers by *mad* ears believèd be
(140.12)

Peacham's own examples do not always fit his definitions. Thus he defines *diacope* to mean "when a worde is repeated, and but one word put betweene"[22] and exemplifies it by "thou knowest not, (foolish man) thou knowest not, what might and force vertue hath," in which three words are repeated with two words in between.

Such examples show that one could multiply (subdivide, qualify, combine, cross-classify) the rhetorical distinctions well beyond the Renaissance formularies. However, even within the Renaissance rhetoric, the possibilities for description are sufficiently extensive, as can be seen by the beginning of Shakespeare's Sonnet 8:

Music to hear, why hear'st thou music sadly?
Sweets with sweets war not, joy delights in joy.

At least the following figures are illustrated:

Alliteration (repetition of initial consonant sounds) m h s w j

Anthimera (one part of speech for another) "sweets" as noun

Asyndeton (omission of conjunction between clauses) line 8.2

Brachylogia (omission of syntactical parts) "music to hear"

Chiasmus "music . . . hear . . . hear'st . . . music"

Diacope "sweets with sweets"

Divisio (dividing into classes) "sweets" and "joy," subclasses of sympathetic response

Epiplexis (using a question for reproach)

Exempla (examples) both clauses in line 8.2

Exergasia (repeating the same thought in different ways) line 8.2

Isocolon (parallelism of clauses) line 8.2

Polyptoton (use of same word in different inflections) "hear" "hear'st"

Prosopopoeia (nonperson treated as person) "joy"

Synechdoche (part for whole) "joy" for person rejoicing

This analysis (not even exhaustive) could be seen as an example of the figure *periergia,* of which Peacham says, "when in a small matter, there is to much laboure bestowed."[23] It does however make some points clear.

First, we cannot study Shakespeare's rhetoric, even in a single sonnet, exhaustively: there are too many handles, and shadows. Second, Shakespeare sought rich rhetoric as he sought rich rhyme and sound; he loved to turn, change, involve meanings; to divide, to stress, to accord.

Analysis is endless, and love is what it is. Renaissance rhetoric supported one of Shakespeare's defects, his tendency toward the obscurely and showily elaborate; it is, though, the defect of a great virtue: his unequaled power of expression.

Shakespeare in the sonnets frequently urges the plainness of his style, against all evidence and in contradiction to the very passages in which he does so, notably in Sonnet 76.

> Why is my verse so barren of new pride?
> So far from variation or quick change?
> Why with the time do I not glance aside
> To new found methods, and to compounds strange?
> Why write I still all one, ever the same,
> And keep invention in a noted weed,
> That ev'ry word doth almost tell my name,
> Showing their birth, and where they did proceed?
> O know, sweet love, I always write of you,
> And you and love are still my argument;
> So all my best is dressing old words new,
> Spending again what is already spent.
> For as the sun is daily new and old,
> So is my love still telling what is told.

The metrical playfulness, discussed in Chapter Four, is cleverly figured, as he claims it is not. Rhetorically, he also does well what he speaks against. He begins (I shall name only a few of the figures) with a *subjectio* (rhetorical question to be answered by the speaker), which is also an *antiphora* since he is forestalling an objection. He uses the technical terms *invention* and *argument*, thus showing his deliberate consciousness of logic and rhetoric. It is by invention that the poet or rhetor finds out *topoi*, places, to build on. Shakespeare can be accused of *solecismus* (grammatical error) or at least *enallage of number* (changing from the expected grammatical form) in "their" (76.8) referring to "word" (76.7); he breaks into *apostrophe* to address his sweet love, with a pleasant *chiasmus,* "love . . . you/ . . . you . . . love" (76.9-10) and a nice mixture of *epanalepsis* (first and last word same) and *polyptoton* (same word in different forms) in "spending . . . spent" (76.12). He closes with an *epanodos* (recapitulation), a commonplace simile given a new exactitude of meaning, freshly and neatly turned, exemplifying what he is speaking about and against.

The inconsistency is itself complex.[24] Shakespeare's insistence on plain style, on the beauty of plainness, is too recurrent and emphatic to be dismissed merely as a conventional gesture or as a comfortable enough form of bragging, though it is clearly both of those. The insistence reflects the discontent he felt with himself and with his poetry (with what he most enjoyed contented least) and the feeling that however variously one's language catches or refracts the light, the truth really is as simple as sunlight; one can only spend what is seen and has been seen, what is known and is to be known. So he elaborates the simplicity of what he sees and knows, somehow — it is strange — sincerely.

The inconsistency is in the tradition too. The suspicion of rhetoric as an amoral, hence potentially wicked, instrument and as an ornamental dressing which hides the simple truth (recall the dislike of ornament displayed in Shakespeare's fierceness against cosmetics) is as old as Plato, and often repeated by Renaissance rhetoricians. To insist on plainness and on ornament is, then, to be traditional. Shakespeare is following the tradition when he proclaims plainness and when he uses the old, known, named ornaments better than anyone else. The inconsistencies are real, inwardly felt, and put to work.

The inconsistencies are part of the valuable and problematical rhetoric. One of the chief problems of such a rhetoric is that a descriptive system which would catch all the nuances and turns of writing would have to be made of very fine wire indeed; a system which could classify that finely would be too elaborated to be manageable or usable. The dilemma is, so far as I can see, insoluble. There can be no comprehensive and usable rhetoric; nor perhaps need there be. Still, a hint may be in order, a hint which I shall try to put to some use in talking about the structure of the sonnets: we might try thinking of the fundamental shapes or gestures of rhetoric as repetition, enthymeme, example, analogy. The very ambiguity of *enthymeme* [25] is here of some service. By enthymeme I mean argument, para-argument, literary assertion and its valid or persuasive supportings; by example I mean example, an astonishingly underrated literary workman; analogy includes comparison and contrast, metaphor and simile, the act of classifying, and some other things. At the least, these notions are of important use.

The main point remains: good poets write well, knowing what they know; they learn more from poets than from rhetoricians; some knowledge is fruitful. We must not forget the garden in Peacham's title: it is beauty, not theory, which is sought and sometimes found.

Shakespeare sought beauty, restlessly. He absorbed traditions, theories, verse, stories; tried what could be tried; made old and new his known. He says, what in one literal way is false, since he coined words throughout his career:

> So all my best is dressing old words new,
> Spending again what is already spent;
> For, as the sun is daily new and old,
> So is my love still telling what is told.
>   (76.11-14)

What is true in the statement is traditional, conventionally modest, and an earned if hyperbolic boast of originality. The metaphor *is* what it says, original and the most common of commonplaces. To be as traditional as the sun, is to be continuously restless, continuously new in power.

Shakespeare's emulative individuality in the sonnets and elsewhere is perpetual. I shall take the example of Sonnet 18, because it compares directly in kind to two good sonnets of good poets: Drayton's Sonnet 48 and Spenser's Sonnet 9.[26]

Drayton's Sonnet ("Amour. 48")

Who list to praise the dayes delicious lyght,
   Let him compare it to her heavenly eye:
   The sun-beames to that lustre of her sight,
   So may the learned like the similie.

The mornings Crimson, to her lyps alike,
   The sweet of *Eden*, to her breathes perfume,
   The fayre *Elizia*, to her fayrer cheeke,
   Unto her veynes, the onely Phoenix plume.

The Angels tresses, to her tressed hayre,
   The *Galixia*, to her more then white:
   Praysing the fayrest, compare it to my faire,
   Still naming her, in naming all delight.
So may he grace all these in her alone,
Superlatiue in all comparison.

Spenser's Sonnet 9

LOng while I sought to what I might compare
   those powreful eies, which lighten my dark spright,
   yet find I nought on earth to which I dare
   resemble th'ymage of their goodly light.
Not to the Sun: for they doo shine by night;
   nor to the Moone: for they are changed neuer;
nor to the Starres: for they haue purer sight;
   nor to the fire: for they consume not euer;
Nor to the lightning; for they still perseuer;
   nor to the Diamond: for they are more tender;
   nor vnto Christall: for nought may them seuer;
   nor vnto glasse; such baseness mought offend her;
Then to the Maker self they likest be,
   whose light doth lighten all that here we see.

Shakespeare's Sonnet 18

Shall I compare thee to a summer's day?
Thou art more lovely and more temperate.
Rough winds do shake the darling buds of May,
And summer's lease hath all too short a date;
Sometime too hot the eye of heaven shines
And often is his gold complexion dimm'd,
And ev'ry fair from fair sometime declines,
By chance or nature's changing course untrimm'd;
But thy eternal summer shall not fade
Nor lose possession of that fair thou ow'st,

Nor shall death brag thou wand'rest in his shade
When in eternal lines to time thou grow'st.
So long as men can breathe or eyes can see,
So long lives this, and this gives life to thee.

All three poets revel in commonplaces. The modern response to a commonplace is something like "That's commonplace, unsingular, mere generalization, trite"; the Elizabethan is more: "That's commonplace, therefore true, general-in-singular, decorous, established by good poetry, reflecting an intelligible world, recovering some glimpse of the created harmony."

All three poems use *energia* (vivid description), *ethopoeia* (description of natural propensities), *divisio,* various forms of *anaphora* (word repetition) including *epanaphora* (same word at beginning of several clauses), and *polyptoton* (repeating different forms of a word), *alliteration, exergasia* (repeating the same thought in varied figures), *isocolon* (repetition of phrases or clauses of nearly equal length and corresponding structure). In modern terms, all three poems use heavy, conscious parallelism and repetition; and lists of examples subdividing a concept. All three display rhetoric consciously and pleasedly; all three make the sun major in the argument. All three — the most evident similarity — make elaborated comparison the basis of the structure.

Drayton's variety of image, syntax, diction is for pleasantness; then he surprises us by suddenly concentrating all beauty in the loved one, her in all beauty, "still naming her, in naming all delight." Then, lest we take him too seriously, he turns back to conscious charm of rhetoric, boasting that he (through her) has been "superlatiue in all comparison."

Spenser's boldness of repetition is justified by the ontological sense of importance in his examples, creating a more serious world than Drayton's. The motion in Spenser is fixed and restless. All verse-pauses are medial; and in lines 5 through 12 each verse-pause occurs after the fourth or fifth syllable, a likeness that reinforces the highly visible likeness of the phrasing and of the structure of comparisons; yet the meter radically shifts in lines 9 through 11; either the stress must move back to "for" rather than "they," contrary to the established pattern, or the scansion of all three lines is the same; "Nor to the LIGHTning; for THEY still perSEuer," that is tiaa < as tetrameter lines, or, as pentameters tipti <, the fourth foot being unmetrical by the rules I adduced in Chapter Four for Shakespeare's sonnets. The regularity and the bold variation are both startling, both successful, Spenser's "naivete" as usual staying ahead of his reader by a transcendent pace. In the poem the Neoplatonic doctrine of beauty as a reflection of the divine is not so much a theory or a hope as an event that happens: the images catch light.

Shakespeare's poem is one of the ones best loved by readers who do not exult in subtlety; it is a lovely triumph. Yet it moves more ways, in rhetoric and meaning, than Drayton's or Spenser's poem, as well as building with more powerful steadiness to its height. Its beginning *hypophora* (question answered by the speaker) gets a deceptively modest answer, "more lovely and more temperate." It is only later the reader realizes that perfection is being claimed. The movement between particular and general is more varied than in either of the other poems; the many winds, then the single sun, then "each fair" at variance with "fair," each particular bearer of beauty being imperfect by the standard of Platonic beauty (the truly fair). The Neoplatonism seems normal, but "fair" has another way of meaning to travel.

The octave compared young man to summer; the third quatrain (here the beginning as often in Shakespeare, of a sestet) returns to the young man's eternal summer, the identification made: the "fair" the young man owns is the truly fair. He is no longer the bearer but the source and standard of the permanent and transcendent beauty. Since the poetry has won that victory, it is only just that the poem end with a double synechdoche of itself; so long lives *this* (the poem) and *this* gives life to thee, as the poem had done and is doing.

The triumph is real in feeling; the threat of lines 7-8 is subdued. Time does not waste; the poem endures.

Without the lyrical sonnet tradition and conventions, the poem could not have happened; yet its turns are unpredictable from a knowledge of the convention. Shakespeare's handling of the beloved Neoplatonic commonplaces, and of the rhetoric which embodies and permits that beauty, is deeply and gladly conventional and uniquely his own.

Some of Shakespeare's sonnets are, to be sure, more conventional in effect than others. For instance, the elaborated ingenuity of image in the eye-heart Sonnets 24, 46, and 47 seems pointless enough. But conventions seldom hold Shakespeare; he extends them or varies them within. A pleasant vale can become a minefield, and some care in travel is advised.

Sonnet 99 is a highly conventional, minor poem, a floral *effictio* (itemized description of beauties), like Spenser's Sonnet 64 in *Amoretti* and, as has been frequently noticed, much like Sonnet 9 of Book I of Henry Constable's *Diana*. But, as has not been previously observed, one passage glares with a quite unexpected rage, which reveals how Shakespearean images cluster and absorb emotion, how his rhetoric deepens to its undersongs.

> The forward violet thus did I chide,
> "Sweet thief, whence didst thou steal thy sweet that smells
> If not from my love's breath, the purple pride
> Which on thy soft cheek from complexion dwells?
> In my love's vein thou hast too grossly dy'd."
> The lily I condemnèd for thy hand
> And buds of marjoram had stol'n thy hair;
> The roses fearfully on thorns did stand,
> One blushing shame, another, white despair:
> A third, nor red nor white, had stol'n of both
> And to his robb'ry had annex'd thy breath,
> But for his theft in pride of all his growth,
> A vengeful canker ate him up to death.
> More flowers I noted, yet I none could see,
> But sweet or color it had stol'n from thee.

The rose "nor red, nor white" suffers a fate violently out of tone with the rest of the poem: "But for his theft in pride of all his growth,/ A vengeful canker ate him up to death." Where does the rage come from? From Shakespeare's soul and from incidents in his life, and also from recurrent images in his work. Some of the several parallels have been earlier commented on; the application is mine.

In *Lucrece,* written about the time of Sonnet 99 if the dating offered in Chapter Three is correct, Tarquin addresses the terrified Lucrece:

> "The color in thy face,
> That even for anger makes the lily pale,
> And the red rose blush at her own disgrace"
> (477-479)

Later in the poem the traitor Sinon's "fair . . . form" (1530) in a painting is described:

> Cheeks neither red nor pale, but mingled so
> That blushing red no guilty instance gave,
> Nor ashy pale the fear that false hearts have.
> (1510-1512)

The configurated repetition is manifest in the three passages: red-nor-pale-white-fear-blush-lily-rose-anger-shame-assault-theft. Tarquin is a rapist, a violator of hospitality, a traitor. The "perjur'd Sinon" (1521) means "devil" (1513), "false creeping craft" (1517), "black-fac'd storms" (1518), "hell-born sin" (1519). Such passion assails Lucrece that she vengefully tears Sinon in the painting with her nails, because he reminds her of Tarquin and her violation and because Sinon appears so lovely and lacking in guile. She bewails her sexual shame, her spotted beauty.

Shortly before Sonnet 99 in the sequence the poet speaks of "the shame/ Which like a canker in the fragrant rose,/ Doth spot the beauty of thy budding name" (95.1-3) and of the fair appearance which hides the secret ill, "Oh what a mansion have those vices got" (95.9). The canker that eats the rose up to death in Sonnet 99 has companions: "And loathsome canker lives in sweetest bud" (35.4), "For canker vice the sweetest buds doth love" (70.7), and closer yet in phrasing and meaning to Sonnet 99, "Full soon the canker death eats up the plant" in *Romeo and Juliet,* II. iii. 30.

The configuration is numerous, and deeply felt, near to shame, pain, sexual blame, vengeance, death.

Whether a memory, event, person (the rival poet — Marlowe, recently dead — is not an unreasonable guess),[27] or just the literary memory touched off the connection is another and not immediately relevant question. The associations underlie and enter the upsurge of rage. Shakespeare invested too much in his images and perceptions to be easily contained by any rhetorical frame, even when he tried to be contained.

Chapter 6

The Logic of
Structure

Logic makes many modern poets nervous, with some reason. Elizabethan poets were at home with logic. They were free of the widespread modern bias against abstraction and form; they learned logic in school in connection with rhetoric and poetry; they were touched by the widespread Ramist fervor for logic as a master discipline.[1] Logical invention, searching for topics, gave poems their subjects;[2] the development of poems was rightly felt to be akin to logical classifications and paradigms.[3] The Ramists, who saw the world as instinct and thriving with logic, called persons and things "arguments,"[4] an enthusiastic oddity of language picked up by Shakespeare when he calls the young man the "lovely argument" (79.5) of his poems. Shakespeare was freer than most modern poets to see and to develop the logical shapings of poems.[5]

Development within sonnets by Shakespeare depends on the structure of sentence and paragraph in any discourse, certain features of the sonnet form, Renaissance predilections for logic, and Shakespeare's sufficient individual genius.

The shapes of logical arguments are shapes and like other shapes.[6] Priorities need not here be quarreled. Is logic formal, or are forms logical? Both. Implication involves sequence. To say "A, therefore B" is to say "A connected with B and followed by B." Within our speech forms, logic is chronological: one reads the premises, then the conclusion. A poem is chronological and simultaneous.

The logic of Shakespeare's time is Aristotelian, thinned from scholastic elaborations. The Ramists simplified further without adding anything genuinely or importantly new.[7] The chief forms are the hypothetical syllogism (if-then premise), the disjunctive syllogism (either-or premise), and the categorical syllogism (class relations as premises: "all men are mortal" and such).[8]

117

The hypothetical syllogism may validly affirm the antecedent (if-statement) or deny the consequent (then-statement), but not vice versa. Thus the valid forms of the disjunctive syllogism are the following (A and B standing for statements):

If A, then B; A; therefore B.

If A, then B; not B; therefore not A.

The disjunctive syllogism has two patterns, caused by the ambiguity of the word *or*, which can signify "at least one and maybe both" or "one but not both." The weak disjunction ("at least one") has two valid forms:

Either A or B; not A; therefore B.

Either A or B; not B; therefore A.

The strong disjunction ("one but not both") has four valid forms:

Either A or B; not A; therefore B.

Either A or B; not B; therefore A.

Either A or B; A; therefore not B.

Either A or B; therefore not A.

I shall not here give the much more complex rules for the categorical syllogism, since I refer in this book only to categorical syllogisms which are obvious to common sense, as "All natural beings grow old and die; you are a natural being; therefore, you shall grow old and die." The form "If . . . , then . . . ," basic to the hypothetical syllogism, bears a close analogy to the form "When . . . , then . . . ," a form Shakespeare uses a number of times in the sonnets. Hypothetical arguments very often have a causative and chronological content, so *then* as "therefore" and as "afterward" is not merely an accidental pun. The word *consequently* carries the same ambiguity and overlap, as does the word *chronological* itself.

Poetry and paragraphing have logical and near-logical forms;

Elizabethan poetry was closer to logical training than modern poetry; and Shakespeare in the sonnets is often conscious of logic, not as a specialist or pedant but as a thoughtful man.

The first seventeen poems are one deliberate argument, an attempt to persuade the young friend to marry and have children. Sonnet 18 begins, "Shall I *compare* thee to a summer's day?" Sonnet 21 attacks literary comparison ("proud compare," 21.5) as logically invalid "hearsay" (21.13). Sonnet 35 offers a sophistry, then attacks itself for doing so: "All men make faults, and even I in this,/ Authórizing thy trespass with compare" (35.5-6). Sonnet 130 attacks, as do Sonnets 21 and 35, "false compare" (130.14). In Sonnet 42 the poet says "Loving offenders, thus I will excuse ye" (42.5), reversing the procedure of Sonnet 35 by announcing the sophistry in advance, as he does in Sonnets 51 and 139: "Thus can my love excuse the slow offence" (51.1) and "Let me excuse thee" (139.9). The term *argument* and related terms recur: "And you and love are still [always] my argument" (76.10), "thy lovely argument" (79.5, already mentioned), "both skill and argument" (100.8), "Against thy reasons making no defence" (89.4), "And on just proof surmise, accumulate" (117.10), and "with ease we prove" (136.7). These are but some of the numerous references to logic, many a *so, thus,* and *therefore* also qualifying.

The couplet of Sonnet 116 gives the hypothetical argument a clearly formal application: "If this be error and upon me prov'd,/ I never writ, nor no man ever lov'd." The implied completion is "But I have written and men have loved; so this is not error," precisely fulfilling the valid logical paradigm: If A, then B; not B, therefore not A. A sufficient proof that he has written and that men have loved is the poem itself, which verifies the claim. One may compare John 14:2, "In my Fathers house are many dwelling places; if it were not so, I wolde haue told you," which in its higher way combines logical formality with the authority of love.

If-then statements tend to be tightly woven, holding, as well as the purely logical connection, relations of many kinds, causal, chronological, contrastive, personal. Shakespeare plays with such relationships in lines 130.3-4, which I quote in context.

My mistress' eyes are nothing like the sun;
Coral is far more red than her lips' red;
If snow be white, why then her breasts are dun;
If hairs be wires, black wires grow on her head.
                    (130.1-4)

The two if-then statements both exemplify the poem's principle of negative comparing, but work their wit in different ways. "If snow be white, as it is, why then her breasts are, comparatively, dun." "If hairs be wires, as some absurd sonneteers claim, why then her hairs are wires and, worse yet, since golden hair is the ideal, black wires grow on her head."

Shakespeare's sonnets, like many poems, often depend on traditional logical paradigms as formal structure. The disjunctive argument parallels contrasts of two, including deliberations between two alternatives when choosing or rejecting. Sonnet 66 ("Tir'd with all these, for restful death I cry") offers one of the neatest examples of such a form. A possible action, suicide, is supported by eleven reasons, then refuted by one superior reason: "Tir'd with all these, from these would I be gone,/ Save that to die, I leave my love alone" (66.13-14). The choice is dramatic, and logical.

Within one side of the disjunction, that is, through most of the poem, Sonnet 66 develops by exemplification, the most important and probably the most overlooked of poetic modes of development. Exemplification is close of kin to induction, particulars leading to a general conclusion. It is also closely involved with classification, the basis of the categorical syllogism and much of our thought and perception. We name things by class names, and we see examples. If we did not *see* the class in the example when we see a cat, we would not see a cat but a blob. We could not name or recognize what we see.

Sonnet 12 ("When I do count the clock that tells the time") is close to the most classical of all categorical syllogisms. The octave gives examples of the implicit general proposition "All beings on earth are subject to time," and the sestet applies the rest of the argument: "You are a being on earth; therefore, you are subject to time's ravages." The ostensible point, that one can defeat time by having children, is tucked into a subordinate clause. The syllogistic frame carries conviction, and here as elsewhere in the sonnets the power of time is more persuasive than the briefly argued triumph over it.

Sonnet 44 ("If the dull substance of my flesh were thought") is very close to a technically invalid form of the hypothetical argument.[9] If A, then B. Not A. Therefore not B. "If flesh were thought, I would be with you. But flesh is not thought, so I am not." The premise is stated in the first quatrain, repeated and hid in negative form in the second quatrain; the third quatrain states the second premise, and the couplet adds the real point, the tears, beautifully fitting quantity and speed to meaning:

Receiving naughts by elements so sloe,
But heavy tears, badges of either's woe.

Sonnet 86 ("Was it the proud full sail of his great verse") comes very close to a strong disjunctive argument extended to three alternatives: Either A or B or C, but not more than one. Not A and not B. Hence C. What, the poem asks, is the cause of Shakespeare's failure to write poems to the friend while the rival poet is addressing poems to the friend? Is it the overwhelming beauty of the rival poet's verse? No. Is it the rival poet's "familiar ghost" (86.9)? No. Is it the friend's presence in the rival poet's poems which leaves Shakespeare's poems blank? Yes.

Sonnet 124 takes the form of a hypothetical statement combined with a disjunction.

If my dear love were but the child of state,
It might for fortune's bastard be unfather'd
As subject to time's love or to time's hate,
Weeds among weeds, or flow'rs with flowers gather'd.
(124.1-4)

"*If* my love were only the child of state, it *then* might be rejected as subject *either* to time's love *or* to time's hate." The poem rejects all parts of the compound: "No! It was builded far from accident" (124.5), neither the child of state nor subject to time. The couplet brings in a different sort of enthymeme, proof by testimony: "To this I witness call the fools of time,/ Which die for goodness, who have lived for crime."

Sonnet 49 ("Against that time, if ever that time come") offers in the quatrains a hypothetical statement: "If ever the time come when you shall reject me, I in foreboding of that time now declare that my desert is such that you may justly reject me." The logical purpose is, as so often, the justification of the friend's possible and already hinted betrayal; the rhetorical purpose is to demonstrate the painfulness in the hint.

Sonnet 53 is a classifying poem. The first quatrain says that the young man is love's substance, the class from which particular beauties draw the being of their beauty.

What is your substance, whereof are you made,
That millions of strange shadows on you tend?
Since ev'ry one hath, ev'ry one, one shade,
And you, but one, can ev'ry shadow lend.

The second and third quatrains exemplify beauties taking their beauty from the young man, line 53.12 returning to the general: "And

you in ev'ry blessèd shape we know." Line 53.13, "In all external grace
you have *some* part," lessens the claim, and line 53.14 shifts to a praise
neither the poem nor the young man has earned: "But you like none,
none you, for constant heart."

The poem rebuffs the modern critical notion that particulars are
poetically exciting, general concepts poetically dull. The first quatrain
hauntingly presents the young man as the general and generating class
of beauty; the remainder of the poem fails to find examples sufficient
to the theme.

Sonnet 92 ("But do thy worst to steal thy self away") consists of a
logical form paralleling the dilemma (which is two alternatives, each
leading to trouble),[10] but leading to happy consequences either way.
Either A or B; if A, happy; if B, happy. "Either you are faithful or not;
if you are faithful, I am happy; if you are faithless, I will be happy to
die." Line 92.12 sums the situation: "Happy to have thy love, happy to
die!"

The couplet finds a third, previously unconsidered alternative which
brings grief; it goes outside of the horns of the happy-dilemma:

> But what's so blessèd fair that fears no blot!
> Thou may'st be false, and yet I know it not.

A number of sonnets have one basic logical shape; all have at least
some logical transitions or joinings; many offer a plurality of logical
schemes, Sonnet 148 being a striking example.

> O me! what eyes hath love put in my head
> Which have no correspondence with true sight?
> *Or* if they have, where is my judgment fled
> That censures falsely what they see aright?
> *If* that be fair whereon my false eyes dote,
> What means the world to say it is not so?
> *If* it be not, *then* love doth well denote
> Love's eye is not so true as all men's. No,
> How can it? O how can love's eye be true
> That is so vex'd with watching and with tears?
> No marvel then though I mistake my view:
> The sun itself sees not till heaven clears.
> O cunning love, with tears thou keep'st me blind
> Lest eyes well-seeing thy foul faults should find.

The first quatrain means the disjunction, "Either my eyes have failed
or my judgment." The second quatrain has the double hypothetical

form common in the dilemma and something of the misarrival of the dilemma: "If my lady is fair, then the world's denial of that truth is troublesome; if my lady is not fair, it is troublesome to know that love's eye sees untruly." The sestet depends on two sophistical arguments: (1) love's eye weeps causing it to see wrongly (a blurring of literal and metaphorical); and (2) since the sun cannot shine through clouds, one can hardly expect my sight to be true through tears (an argument by analogy, by "false compare").

The purpose of the poem is expressive, not logical, yet the sense of logic, of a strong mind rapidly at work, intensifies the lament, the accusation, and even the sense of confusion.

Sonnet 91 includes the technical "adjunct" (91.5) as well as "particulars" (91.7) and "general" (91.8) themselves.

> Some glory in their birth, some in their skill,
> Some in their wealth, some in their body's force,
> Some in their garments though new-fanglèd ill,
> Some in their hawks and hounds, some in their horse;
> And ev'ry humor hath his adjunct pleasure,
> Wherein it finds a joy above the rest;
> But these particulars are not my measure:
> All these I better in one gen'ral best:
> Thy love is better than high birth to me,
> Richer than wealth, prouder than garments' cost,
> Of more delight than hawks or horses be;
> And, having thee, of all men's pride I boast,
> Wretchèd in this alone, that thou may'st take
> All this away, and me most wretchèd make.

The young man is seen as higher than and the source of other glories; he is the "one general best" (91.8), that is, the singular, the class exemplar, the ideal: these three are one. The first quatrain is seven examples of things to glory in; the linguistic and rhythmical parallelism is strong, yet quick in inward variety. The pauses are medial and shifting, coming after syllables 6, 4, 5, and 6, respectively; the some-their shape holds in each of the seven examples but only "some in their skill" (91.1) and "some in their wealth" (91.2) are word for word grammatically parallel. Each of the other parallel locutions vary from these, each in a different way, the most interesting being "some in their horse" (91.4), in which "horse" is an acceptable Elizabethan plural[11] more suggestive of the class notion than "horses" would be.

The second quatrain is in two precisely balanced parts: the generalizing that defines the bond of the examples, and the contrast preferring the young man. The third quatrain compares the young man seriatim to other glories, five of the seven examples, then in line 91.12 sums up into one of the master ideas of the sonnets: that the young man rules, somehow *is* all glories.

Hence lines 91.1-12 constitute a unit divided into two groups of six, subdivided four, two; two, four; examples, generalization; generalization, examples.

The couplet turns away in a despondent direction, to a fear never far from the glorying of the sonnets' praise. The young man is beauty, yet may leave or fade. As *Venus and Adonis* better says the fear, "with him is beauty slain,/ And beauty dead, black chaos comes again" (lines 1019-1020).

This graceful sonnet shows clearly Shakespeare's consciousness of logic as development: class relations, general and particular stated as such, are so firmly related through the first three quatrains to the poem's external shape that the couplet's new venture seems adventitious as well as a little maudlin. Shakespeare in the sonnets is very good at making self-pity more attractive than it has a right to be. The attempt is less successful here than elsewhere, in part for structural reasons. Poems are made of paragraphs as well as of fire, and tears.

The form of the Shakespearean sonnet is essentially paragraphing, and inescapable. If the paragraphs fit the rhyme shape, they fit it; if they fail to, they visibly do not, and the conflict is felt as formal, whether as violation or sucess. Fitting has some but not open freedom. Thus 1-12, 13-14; 1-4, 5-8, 9-12, 13-14; 1-4, 5-8, 9-12, 13-14 and some other variants may fit well enough, but most possible arrangements would not. The unusual form of Sonnet 91 (1-4, 5-6, 7-8, 9-12, 13-14) is borderline; it could imaginably work well, but the high sense of completeness in lines 1-12, even higher than in 1-4, 5-8, 9-12, 13-14, is apt to strand the couplet. Even when lines 1-12 are not so tightly bound, the couplet is the danger spot in the form, and Shakespeare has trouble with it.

The sonnet shape is at once tidy and loose-jointed; the manifest strengths have their correspondent temptations. The triple parallelism of the quatrains tempts to the prolix, to the illusion of analogue, to mere repetition disguised by rhetorical and metrical skill. The couplet may be or approach padding (79.13-14), feebly oxymoronic (16.13-14), a contrived reversal (42.13-14), an unnecessary summary (43.13-14), a rhetorically too easy epigram (53.13-14).

The challenge of the form is to fit, while avoiding the impression of four boxes sitting side by side. The form does not allow much room: brief narrative, brisk or indirect inferences, few exemplifications, figures of brief compass. Yet it is firm enough to insist its weight against purely associative or expressionistic development. The sonnet combines such modes of order, needs to interlace and confirm them.

Rhyme is the outward structure and sustains or crosses the logical, rhetorical, and grammatical structures; coherence between outer rhyme patterning and paragraphing, while not automatic, is surprisingly high.

Three poems fail to fit the outward verse pattern. Sonnet 126 is a twelve-line poem in rhyming couplets. Sonnet 99 is a fifteen-line poem, rhyming *ababacdcdefefgg*. Sonnet 145 is in iambic tetrameter.

The remaining 151 poems have the same form: iambic pentameter, three cross-rhymed quatrains and a couplet. Since (2 × 3) + 1= 7, most of the sonnets have seven rhymes, but twenty-one sonnets have fewer than seven. Of these, eighteen sonnets have six rhymes;[12] each begins *ababcdcd,* the last six lines taking eleven different forms in relation to the octave and internally. One sonnet, Sonnet 3, has five rhymes, with *ababcdcd* followed by *dededd.* One sonnet, Sonnet 135, has only four rhymes, and is the only sonnet of the 151 regular sonnets not to begin *ababcdcd*; this truth in itself is important evidence, to be given further support later in this chapter, of Shakespeare's strong octave sense. The rhyme scheme is *ababbcbcadadaa,* the repeated rhymes being "ouerplus" & "thus" & "spatious" & "gracious" (135.2&4&5&7, 1609 ed.) and *"Will"* & "still" & "still" & *"Will"* & "kill" & *"Will"* (rhyme 135.1&3&9&11&13&14, italics in text). The "spatious" is a metrical joke discussed in Appendix A. "Will" is a pun for vagina and sexual desire in "thou whose will is large and spatious" (135.5, 1609 ed.); and the will-rhymes, punning further on the name Will and on willfulness, increase the comedy. The heavy rhyming echoes bewilderment. Sonnet 135 is the only poem in which having fewer than seven rhymes has much effect.

The sense of syntactical-metrical integrity of individual quatrains and couplets is quite strong in the sonnets. The four units, three quatrains and couplet, combine in different ways, with subdivisions and complications, but each unit is in itself normally felt as a syntactical unit as well as a metrical one.

In only eleven sonnets (20, 21, 29, 33, 63, 66, 75, 104, 114, 129, 154) does the fifth line not begin a new clause, and in most of those the syntax is such that the quatrain sense is retained. Only in Sonnets 63, 66, 104, and 154 is the quatrain sense lost.

In only six sonnets (66, 75, 89, 129, 148,[13] 151) does the ninth line not begin a new clause, Sonnets 66, 89, 148, and 151 losing the quatrain sense. Sonnet 132 begins a clause at the ninth line but nonetheless lacks the quatrain sense, since the chief break comes at the end of the ninth line.

The couplet loses its distinctness even less often. In only five sonnets (41, 44, 108, 153, 154) does the thirteenth line not begin a clause, and in three of those, especially in Sonnet 41, the couplet achieves some distinctness. Only in Sonnets 153, 154, and 35 is the couplet sense wholly lost, Sonnet 35 losing the couplet sense at least to a modern ear even though the thirteenth line begins with a correlative clause.

So few exceptions are few;[14] and the quatrain sense is reinforced in several ways. Quatrains often begin with exclamations, with shifts to imperatives, with the second of two correlatives, with conjunctions or adverbs showing contrast or denial or logical or chronological succession, with rhetorically stressed pronouns, or with repetition or near repetition of words beginning previous quatrains.

The coherence, then, between rhyme pattern and syntax and paragraphing is major and of major structural importance.

The basic shape of rhyme (1-4, 5-8, 9-12, 13-14) can also be seen as quatrains plus couplet (1-12, 13-14), the couplet, being different in form and at the poem's end, offering an almost automatic sense of closure.[15] Thus the couplet provides a normative rhetorical break at the end of the twelfth line.

The octave-sestet shape is also felt in most sonnets. I count 119 octave-sestet sonnets. Paragraph and quatrains have many ways of subdividing and of linking. Sentence-clause shaping, emotional-rhetorical shaping, and metrical shaping do not always exactly correspond, although the tendency toward correspondence is powerful. Hence counts of poems with 8-6 shapes and 12-2 shapes will vary,[16] but those two shapes are very heavily the predominant shapes of the sonnets, and often combine rather than compete, for instance in Sonnet 1.

> From fairest creatures we desire incréase,
> That thereby beauty's rose might never die,
> But as the riper should by time decease,
> His tender heir might bear his memory;

But thou, contractèd to thine own bright eyes,
Feed'st thy light's flame with self-substantial fuel,
Making a famine where abundance lies,
Thy self thy foe, to thy sweet self too cruel;
Thou that art now the world's fresh ornament
And only herald to the gaudy spring
Within thine own bud buri'st thy content
And, tender churl, mak'st waste in niggarding.
Pity the world, or else this glutton be:
To eat the world's due, by the grave and thee.

The paragraphing division and subdivision is: 1-12, 13-14; $\overline{1\text{-}4, 5\text{-}12,}$ $\overline{13\text{-}14}$. The first quatrain is a general statement about the desirability of fair creatures procreating their kind; the second and third quatrains are negative specifying of that generalization: the young man is doing the self-destroying opposite of continuing his kind; he is refusing to marry. The couplet turns to the imperative mode and urges him to marry, an urging that becomes a threat in the disjunctive "or else" (1.13).

The 12-2 paragraph shape kept me from counting this as one of the octave-sestet sonnets. Yet the octave-sestet effect is present, largely because of the new rush of metrical energy in line 1.9, "Thou that art now the world's fresh ornament," and because the couplet links to the "thou" in line 1.9. The latter link provides an argument for a grammatical as well as a metrical sestet.

Sonnet 67 has a clear 12-2 paragraph structure and a clear grammatical sestet.

Ah, wherefore with infection should he live
And with his presence grace impiety
That sin by him advantage should achieve
And lace itself with his society?
Why should false painting imitate his cheek,
And steal dead seeing of his living hue?
Why should poor beauty indirectly seek
Roses of shadow, since his rose is true?
Why should he live, now nature bankrupt is,
Beggar'd of blood to blush through lively veins?
For she hath no exchequer now but his
And, priv'd of many, lives upon his gains.
O him she stores, to show what wealth she had
In days long since, before these last so bad.

The quatrains are a series of questions answered by the couplet; therefore the 12-2 structure is unusually clear. However, the third quatrain offers a different kind of question from the first two: in the first two quatrains the questions are about others; in the third quatrain the question is about the young man himself. Hence the "him" in line 67.13 most naturally seems to refer to the previous sentence, to the "he" in line 67.9 echoed in "his" (67.11) and "his" (67.12). Furthermore, the couplet is linked to the third quatrain by the metaphor of wealth. Hence 12-2 and 8-6 structures are both very much present.

Sonnet 71 has three parallel quatrains, imperatives asking the young man to forget the speaker, with the couplet giving the reason for the request. However, the couplet is a clause grammatically subordinate to the clause or sentence (depending on one's choice of punctuation) of the third quatrain, the pronoun in the couplet refers to the pronouns in the third quatrain, and the third quatrain is given special opening impetus by the exclamatory "O" (71.9).

No longer mourn for me when I am dead
Than you shall hear the surly, sullen bell
Give warning to the world that I am fled
From this vile world with vilest worms to dwell;
Nay, if you read this line, remember not
The hand that writ it, for I love you so
That I in your sweet thoughts would be forgot
If thinking on me then should make you woe.
O if, I say, you look upon this verse
When I (perhaps) compoundèd am with clay,
Do not so much as my poor name rehearse,
But let your love ev'n with my life decay,
Lest the wise world should look into your moan
And mock you with me after I am gone.

Many of the sonnets have unambiguous 8-6 structure, for instance, Sonnets 3 and 104.

Look in thy glass and tell the face thou viewest
Now is the time that face should form another,
Whose fresh repair if now thou not renewest
Thou dost beguile the world, unbless some mother.
For where is she so fair whose unear'd womb
Disdains the tillage of thy husbandry?
Or who is he so fond will be the tomb
Of his self-love to stop posterity?
Thou art thy mother's glass and she in thee
Calls back the lovely April of her prime,
So thou through windows of thine age shalt see,
Despite of wrinkles, this thy golden time,

But if thou live rememb'rèd not to be,
Die single and thine image dies with thee.

Lines 3.9-14 are one sentence, line 3.9 has a metrical surge, and the shift from questions to declarative makes a clean turn.

In Sonnet 104, the third quatrain is a contrast to the first two quatrains, there is no clear break between the first and second quatrains, line 104.9 opens with an exclamatory "Ah yet," and lines 104.9-14 are one sentence.

To me, fair friend, you never can be old,
For as you were when first your eye I ey'd,
Such seems your beauty still: three winters' cold
Have from the forests shook three summers' pride,
Three beauteous springs to yellow autumn turn'd
In process of the seasons have I seen,
Three April pérfumes in three hot Junes burn'd,
Since first I saw you fresh which yet are green.
Ah yet doth beauty, like a dial hand,
Steal from his figure and no pace perceiv'd;
So your sweet hue, which methinks still doth stand
Hath motion, and mine eye may be deceiv'd:
For fear of which, hear this, thou age unbred:
Ere you were born was beauty's summer dead.

When the paragraphing division and subdivision of a sonnet are ambiguous, one or more of several features often work in favor of an octave-sestet reading: grammatical links, including the natural tendency to link grammatical references to the preceding sentence or clause; exclamatory[17] or other emphatic introductions to the ninth line; an octave-sestet expectation, created in part by our experience of the octave-sestet sonnets of Shakespeare, perhaps also by memory of the Petrarchan form; and various linkings including metaphorical ones between the third quatrain and the couplet. Our linguistic tendency toward alternate stress serves an octave-sestet reading. Thus if we say (louder and softer) ONE two THREE four, we feel ONE-two as a group and THREE-four as a group. If we hear climax through three stages, then a turn, it is natural to group the third, highest stage with the turn. The turn of the couplet is immediately a turn from the third quatrain. If the couplet is not a separate sentence, it always links to a clause in or including the third quatrain. One can add the third quatrain and the couplet have the plain neighborhood of succession.

The real point is not 8-6 vs. 12-2. The 8-6 and 12-2 shapes are the chief subcategories of the basic 4-4-4-2 shape and often work together. They are the secondary structural norms of the Shakespearean sonnet. The metrical and rhetorical and often logical surges are typically at the first, ninth, and thirteenth lines, an inescapably important truth in our response to sonnet's motionings.

It is not enough to treat, as Stephen Booth does, the pattern of rhyme as merely one of the various structures of the sonnets. For the rhyme pattern is *the* constitutive pattern of the sonnet, sentences and paragraphs are *the* constituents of linguistic development in poems or prose; and the relations and disrelations of rhyme pattern and subpatterns to sentence and paragraph patterns are thus major in our response to poems; such workings, intercrossing with rhythmical and rhetorical workings line by line and stanza by stanza make the frame in which poems happen.

Booth says once, wisely, "The most important thing about a sonnet is that it is a sonnet"[18] and goes on to discuss how the sonnet form is "peculiarly urgent"[19] in our experience of a sonnet; but the general tendency of his book is quite different. He writes that "the multiplicity of structural patterns in Shakespeare's sonnets is the means by which they qualify . . . [for] poetic excellence,"[20] that "sound patterns, like the other patterns I describe, are individually insignificant,"[21] that "the reader of one of Shakespeare's sonnets is presented with a great many different ordering systems, none of which can reasonably be subordinated to any other."[22] He argues against "the traditional, self-imposed requirement of arguing for one structuring principle over all others."[23]

Yet the sonnet form is the principal form because the poet chose to write sonnets. As I have noted, Booth himself once says so, though he denies that some patterns can and should be subordinated to others when he says that "We have, however, no grounds in this sonnet [Sonnet 12] or in any of the others for assuming any . . . continuing allegiance to a particular pattern of phonetic construction."[24] The describable patterns in poetry are in kind numerous and in permutation limitless. They can and do intersect and support each other; Booth nicely shows some of their interworkings,[25] and one cannot neatly number a hierarchy for their comparative importance. But distinctions can be made: for instance, sonnet form and paragraphing are more important than consonantal repetitions to the reader's sense of the structure of a poem. Else chaos is on us, and sweat we may.

The logical patterns discussed and to be discussed are not so constitutive as rhyme and paragraph patterns, but have major importance. Shakespeare's sense of logic, sharpened by the training in schools and supported by a climate favorable to logic, is very keen; and logical and near-logical patterns constitute much of the basic forming of paragraphs.

Paragraphs have several basic modes of development, which fit rather handily into three of the figures I timidly suggested in Chapter Five as rhetorically fundamental: enthymeme, example, analogy. Enthymeme would include cause-effect, chronology, and various logical forms and paradigms, including those discussed. It would overlap with example in such modes of development as exemplification, classification, and induction. Analogy includes comparison-contrast, metaphor, allegory, and the argument by analogy itself. The possibilities for interlacing such modes of development are innumerable, and most paragraphs and poems represent more than one kind of development.

A number of the better Shakespearean sonnets are simple in development: three restatements of a theme, followed by a summary or by a logically conclusive or contrasting couplet. In Sonnet 55 ("Not marble, nor the gilded monument"), the theme ("you triumph over time in my verses") is actually stated four times, with enough pithy variations to disguise the simplicity. Sonnet 53 ("What is your substance, whereof are you made"), previously discussed, repeats the theme ("you are the essence and source of other beauty") four times, once in each quatrain and once in line 53.13, then shifts from the theme in the last line. Sonnet 60 ("Like as the waves make toward the pebblèd shore") states the theme of the power of time in each of the quatrains, then offers a contrast in the couplet: "And yet to times in hope my verse shall stand/ Praising thy worth, despite his cruel hand"). Sonnet 65 ("Since brass, nor stone, nor earth, nor boundless sea") parallels exactly that structure of Sonnet 60. Sonnet 71 ("No longer mourn for me when I am dead"), Sonnet 73 ("That time of year thou may'st in me behold"), Sonnet 87 ("Farewell! thou are too dear for my possessing"), and Sonnet 147 ("My love is as a fever longing still") are almost as simple in outer development, but subtler in the development of interior feeling than the previous examples. Sonnet 87 hides under a semblance of tight logic the truth that lines 87.1-12 say the same thing ("I don't deserve you") six times. The couplet, with its beautiful pun on "matter" (87.14), is another and magnificent departure: "Thus have I had thee as a dream doth flatter:/ In sleep a king but, waking, no such matter."

Sonnet 50 combines some of the more important modes of order, some of them overtly. The associative principle is made plain in line 50.13, "For that same groan doth put this in my mind." But mediative argument links the narrative, and the associative links are minor and beautiful.

> How heavy do I journey on the way
> When what I seek, my weary travel's end,
> Doth teach that ease and that repose to say,
> "Thus far the miles are measur'd from thy friend."
> The beast that bears me, tirèd with my woe,
> Plods dully on to bear that weight in me
> As if by some instínct the wretch did know
> His rider lov'd not speed, be'ng made from thee.
> The bloody spur cannot provoke him on
> That sometimes anger thrusts into his hide,
> Which heavily he answers with a groan,
> More sharp to me than spurring to his side.
> For that same groan doth put this in my mind:
> My grief lies onward, and my joy behind.

Narrative is a fundamental form of development because it imitates human experience fundamentally, human purposes working their way through obstacles (others, self, chance, nature, supernature) toward a final cause or causes.

The first quatrain speaks of the emotion, the narration, the end. The end itself (conceived in the feelings of arrival as well as in the metaphysics of causes: an arrow does not move when embedded in a target) adds to the heaviness of the journey. In the second quatrain the narrative continues, but with an analogy between the beast and the man, heavy in pace, heavy in feeling. In the third quatrain mood and narrative intensify. The man desires the end he does not desire (he wants the unpleasant journey over), so spurs the horse onward in a perverse anger, doubly perverse because the anger is occasioned by the beast's sympathetic response to the feeling of the rider. The resultant groan catches the complex situation and the associated groan meets the exact and dignified statement of the last line.

It is a great poem. Part of its greatness is the beauty of ordering, an ordering superior to that in some of Shakespeare's even greater sonnets.

The sonnets argue much, their favorite form of argument being exemplification. Comparison is another great power, used for argument and for much else. Sonnet 18 (also discussed in Chapter Five) is directly conscious of example[26] and of comparison.

> Shall I compare thee to a summer's day?
> Thou art more lovely and more temperate.
> Rough winds do shake the darling buds of May,
> And summer's lease hath all too short a date;
> Sometime too hot the eye of heaven shines,
> And often is his gold complexion dimm'd,
> And ev'ry fair from fair sometime declines,
> By chance or nature's changing course untrimm'd;
> But thy eternal summer shall not fade
> Nor lose possession of that fair thou ow'st,
> Nor shall death brag thou wand'rest in his shade
> When in eternal lines to time thou grow'st.
> So long as men can breathe or eyes can see,
> So long lives this, and this gives life to thee.

The paragraphing of the poem is an octave subdivided 1, 2-8 against sestet subdivided 9-12, 13-14. The poem argues against the comparison by examples. The friend is compared to a summer day to show the friend superior to the day in beauty and constancy. The fidelity of the friend merges into the immortality of the verse by a kind of lovely sleight of hand. The examples of nature "prove" the generalization ("Nature is subject to time"), set against the friend who, through the very movement of the poem, moves forward into a conclusion beyond time: the immortality of the poem and of the friend. Of course the paradox is deep and, finally, unsatisfactory. Verse does not really endure always. The friend, it turned out, was unfaithful. Shakespeare's view of time is seldom so triumphant; but it is a lovely triumph of order as of phrasing, while it lasts.

Sonnet 33, one of the sonnets which continue one metaphor throughout, uses the same comparison for obverse reasons in even more beautiful order.

> Full many a glorious morning have I seen
> Flatter the mountain tops with sov'reign eye,
> Kissing with golden face the meadows green,
> Gilding pale streams with heav'nly alchemy,
> Anon permit the basest clouds to ride
> With ugly rack on his celestial face

And from the forlorn world his visage hide,
Stealing unseen to west with this disgrace;
Ev'n so my sun one early morn did shine
With all-triumphant splendor on my brow,
But, out alack, he was but one hour mine;
The region cloud hath mask'd him from me now;
Yet him for this my love no whit disdaineth;
Suns of the world may stain when heav'n's sun staineth.

Again, the octave-sestet pattern is clear. The octave is a narrative of description, divided in precise quatrains, one about good, the other about staining evil; the sestet opens with a quatrain exactly divided in two, the two parts fitting exactly the relevant parts of the analogy in the octave.

The friend's evil is "justified" by the analogy to the natural world in a closing line powerful in quantities, which as structure draws the parallels conclusively together, even though as logic it fails.[27] The analogy errs at the crucial point: the dark behavior of the friend is sinful and willful, the darkening of the sun is accidental and determined. A hint of the desperately hid truth emerges. The same elements are present when Shakespeare uses complex and perverse irony in other sonnets such as Sonnets 57 ("Being your slave, what should I do but tend"), 87 ("Farewell! thou are too dear for my possessing"), 95 ("How sweet and lovely dost thou make the shame"), 96 ("Some say thy fault is youth, some wantonness"). In all of these, and in others, the struggle is powerful, but the tendency is to push through a number of twists of anger, irony, and bitterness to end by justifying the much-loved friend. Shakespeare is and is not deceived by his own sophistries. His sense of logic and his emotions clash, and inhere, even in dark places.

MEANINGS

Chapter 7

The Logic of Hell

Logic depends on negation throughout, in that it requires selection between true and false, affirmation and denial, and specifically in paradigms such as "Either A or B; *not* B; therefore A."

Self-inconsistency tests logic and marks negation. Negation can be strange and waste; a nothing can be a powerful and fearful thing. Shakespeare says, in one of the most central images of the sonnets, that the young man "among the wastes of time must go" (12.10). Where is that? He says of the dark lady that his eyes "see not what they see" (137.2) and, in even more gorgeously tangled self-inconsistency that "when my love swears that she is made of truth,/ I do believe her though I know she lies" (138.1-2). He says in line 121.9 "I am that I am," but means in context that he is bitter and *un*true; and he cries out to the young man in line 13.1 "O that you were your self!" knowing that we are not ourselves, that privation, falsity, change, waste are working among our lives. Sophistry struggles for justifications which do not reach, and sin has a stern logic of its own: "Only my plague thus far I count my gain,/ That she that makes me sin awards me pain" (141.13-14). Hell has logics and illogics, and heaven gives the measure, "beauty making beautiful old rhyme" (106.3), "the star to ev'ry wand'ring bark" (116.7), by which reality and unreality are judged and known. In our experience reality and unreality are deceitfully tangled.

The poet says to the young man, "if you were by my unkindness shaken/ As I by yours, you've passed a hell of time" (120.5-6). A hell of time is a time of *in*fidelity, a time of being *un*true, but it also comes close to the nature of time the destroyer, whom one must resist with progeny, love, verse, fame. The resistance has its glories and, even more, its terrors. The power of time is negative and terribly real: "the stormy gusts of winter's day/ And barren rage of death's eternal cold" (13.11-12). The rage is barren — seedless, uncreative — because it is cold, which is a privation, a nothing, a lack of being in what might be in being, and eternal, time-*less*, the empty arriving non-place of time.

The rage is nothings (death, cold, barrenness), but rages no less fiercely for that. What is presented is not a comforting metaphysics.

The hell is not yet a Christian hell, not the hell which enters Shakespeare's work in flashes in the dark lady sonnets and is to dominate *Macbeth, Othello, Hamlet,* because it does not make enough sense; it is not built by justice, as Dante's hell is; but it has its connections. The love-*less* wars against love, and the "barren rage of death's eternal cold" fits Dante's Satan uncannily well. Sonnet 13 of the "barren rage" and the Christian Sonnet 146 ("Poor soul, the center of my sinful earth") are very close in a central structure of metaphor, self as house. In each the house must be upheld against decay, but the upholders, progeny and spiritual meditation, differ.

This hell, death's eternal cold, is not the hell which W. H. Auden defined as "the being of the lie,/ That we become if we deny."[1] It is the being of the un-reality we become whether or not we deny anything.

Denial is its own hell, too, and takes in-turning, negating forms as in Sonnet 1.

> From fairest creatures we desire incréase
> That thereby beauty's rose might never die,
> But as the riper should by time decease,
> His tender heir might bear his memory;
> But thou, contractèd to thine own bright eyes,
> Feed'st thy light's flame with self-substantial fuel,
> Making a famine where abundance lies,
> Thy self thy foe, to thy sweet self too cruel;
> Thou that art now the world's fresh ornament
> And only herald to the gaudy spring
> Within thine own bud buri'st thy content
> And, tender churl, mak'st waste in niggarding.
> Pity the world, or else this glutton be:
> To eat the world's due, by the grave and thee.

In the second quatrain, before the more easily oxymoronic "thy self thy foe" (1.8), occur three stranger images which define the "waste" (1.12) and lead toward the powerful, repulsive metaphor of "eat the world's due" (1.14), with its deliberately but unpleasantly harsh rhythm. Like that metaphor, they suggest a logic gnawing inward to nothing, a turning on oneself. To be contracted to one's own eyes, however bright, is to see nothing, since eyes are made to look outward and can see themselves only in an outward mirror. Self-contracted eyes are blind. The fuel is self-consuming, as in the more famous variant of this image, line 73.12, "Consum'd with that which it was nourish'd by," but is called "self-substantial" (1.6). It tries to sustain itself, falsely and briefly; its self-substantiality is a lie, the self-consumption the reality. The "famine where abundance lies" (1.7) is a more ordinary-appearing paradox but grows strange in relation to "*eat* the world's due" (1.14). To consume one's abundance is, even while one does so, as well as when all is spent, a kind of famine, an eating of nothing.

The poem fails, largely because of its mixture of incompatible styles, including the fresh and opening lilt of "Thou that art now the world's fresh ornament/ And only herald to the gaudy spring" (1.9-10), which prefigures such famous moments as "the lark at break of day arising/ From sullen earth" (29.11-12) and the passage beginning "Full many a glorious morning have I seen" (33.1-4). But some of the imagery is darkly complex, images of waste, of strong but crooked nothings.

The great rages against time in such sonnets as Sonnets 55, 60, 63, 64, and 65 have triumph, but an outweighed triumph. Sonnet 55 is the most celebratory, yet its celebration must struggle with the befouling sibilance of "unswept stone, besmear'd with sluttish time" (55.4) and the precise ferocity of "broils root out" (55.6). Sonnets 63 and 65 also offer the consolation of immortality in verse, but less convincingly and more fearfully, in line 65.13 conditionally: "O none, *unless* this miracle have might."

Sonnet 64 is one of the best of the time poems.

When I have seen by time's fell hand defac'd
The rich proud cost of outworn buri'd age,
When sometime lofty towers I see down raz'd
And brass eternal slave to mortal rage;
When I have seen the hungry ocean gain
Advantage on the kingdom of the shore
And the firm soil win of the wat'ry main,
Increasing store with loss and loss with store;
When I have seen such interchange of state
Or state itself confoundèd to decay,
Ruin hath taught me thus to ruminate,
That time will come and take my love away.
That thought is as a death which cannot choose
But weep to have that which it fears to lose.

The structure is straightforward and satisfying. Parallel exemplifications (64.1-8) lead to a summary climax of greater generality (64.9-10), to a meditation (64.11-12), to a despairing personal conclusion inferred from the meditation. The logic is a sort of rhetorical induction leading to a categorical syllogism. The various examples "prove" (that is, persuasively exemplify) the syllogism "All human things are subject to change and death; love is a human thing; therefore love is subject to change and death." The conclusion follows from the syllogism: "weep."

In line 64.10, "Or state itself confoundèd to decay," "decay" means primarily "death," and "state" (64.9 and 64.10) means "physical substance" and "high estate." Thus the poet has seen both the interchanging of state, earth and sea mixing at the water's edge, and the overthrow of "state itself," tombs and towers broken down till they are no longer tombs and towers. But "state itself" is too dignified an expression and too climactic to mean only such things as tombs and towers: the effect is metaphysical, form itself confounded, black chaos come again. The force of that "confoundèd" (64.10) has been prepared for by the "confound" of line 60.8, "And time that gave doth now his gift confound" and the "confounding" of line 63.10, "Against confounding age's cruel knife."

The "sometime lofty towers" (64.3) mock in a special way the pretensions of men. The claims men make are in truth only sometime, because in time, therefore transient, a notion which carries into the irony of the double modification of "eternal" in "And brass eternal slave to mortal rage" (64.4). The brass is eternal in claim, in truth an eternal slave to decay.

When Shakespeare says "And time that gave doth now his gifts confound" (60.8), it is hard to feel that time is rhetorically a personification. How personify, make more real, time, already more real than the people it overcomes? Time is a real and personal enemy who rules the world and wastes it, deprives it of substance. In the close of Sonnet 60, the desperation in the sonnets resisting time is self-inconsistently caught.

> And nothing stands but for his scythe to mow.
> And yet to times in hope my verse shall stand
> Praising thy worth, despite his cruel hand.
>   (60.12-14)

Nothing stands; but in hope his verse shall; the hope cannot be triumphant. "Nothing stands but for his scythe to mow" is a way of saying "All which stands shall be mowed by his scythe," but the effect is different, as though some nothing were standing in opposition to the verses' standing. What stands is nothing, mere shadow, but overpowering, the barren rage of cold.

Negatives fascinate Shakespeare;[2] he works changes on shadows,

naughts, wastes, blanks; he likes the rumble of heaped negatives as in
line 116.14, "I never writ, nor no man ever loved."[3] The negations in
the sonnets are metaphysical, the barren rage of death's eternal cold;
they are logical-rhetorical ("I never writ, nor no man ever lov'd"); they
are evil as privation (nothing, holes in being; or shadow against
substance, or the falseness of untruth).

The doctrine of evil as privation has a long tradition, going really as
far back as the first man frightened by darkness, awed by death. For
Augustine and Aquinas, it is a chief brick of their ethical metaphysics;
this doctrine is common in medieval theology[4] and is commonplace in
Shakespeare's time,[5] in religious writers, rhetoricians, and poets. Thus
Pierre Viret says in *The World Possessed with Deuils*, "Vice is want of
vertue, as sickenesse is want of health" and "It is no great maruayle if
the Diuell be contrary to him selfe . . . he is both a lyar, & also a
deceiuer."[6] Thomas Wilson says in *The Arte of Rhetorique*, "Such a
woman beeing naught of her bodie, hath caused her husband to lose
his head."[7] Here "beeing naught" means to make love,[8] as is even
clearer in *Richard III*, I. i. 98-100:

> Naught to do with Mistress Shore? I tell thee, fellow,
> He that doth naught with her (excepting one)
> Were best to do it secretly alone.

In our time the poet and Elizabethan scholar J. V. Cunningham
offers, in his poem "Ars Amoris," a similar and even more contemptu-
ous view of coition:[9]

> Do without doing!
> Love's wilful potion
> Veils the ensuing,
> And brief, commotion.

In Sidney's *Arcadia* reason is counseled to rise above "sensuall
weaknes . . . so weake an aduersary, that in it selfe is nothinge but
weaknesse."[10] Sidney gracefully states a commonplace which empow-
ers lines 23.3-4, "some fierce thing replete with too much rage,/ Whose
strength's abundance weakens his own heart."

In Sonnet 66 ("Tir'd with all these, for restful death I cry"), the
reasons advanced for suicide include "desert a beggar born/ And needy
nothing trimm'd in jollity,/ And purest faith *un*happily forsworn"
(66.2-4), negations of the true, the non-spaces between moral possibil-

ity and realization, as are the evils of "strength by limping sway disabled" (66.8) and "Folly, doctor-like, controlling skill" (66.10), that is, weakness and pretentious ignorance triumphing over strength and good sense. Folly is ballooned nothing; it needs pricking. The "simple truth miscall'd simplicity" (66.11) is the standard by which metaphysical and moral falsity is judged. To miscall such truth is, in Swift's great phrase, "to say the thing which is not": to mis-do such truth is to do a nothing, to frustrate or pervert substance. Death is in the sonnets a dreadful evil, but in Sonnet 66 these moral evils, these loud nothings, make death desirable, were it not for love, which is the standard for moral truth as for beauty and which makes life desirable.

Shakespeare is surprisingly fierce in protesting cosmetics[11] (he might say with some justice that we are silly for not protesting cosmetics more than we do); the context of evil as privation, appearance vs. reality, shows why. Cosmetics are false attempts at beauty, and since in the sonnets beauty and love are virtually identified, cosmetics sin against love: they falsify what is in the sonnets most importantly real.

To be among change and to be capable of moral failure is not truly to be. The cry in line 13.1, "O that you were your self!" is accurately glossed by A. W. Verity as "Would that you were absolute, independent of time, free from the conditions that fetter men."[12] To be a person at all, immersed in change, is to be imperfect, to be less than real, an unreality Juliet protests when she says, on hearing of Romeo's presumed death, "I am not I, if there be such an ay" (III. ii. 48).

Moral evil carries unreality and inconsistency further, to the denial of one's capacity for righteousness, to the willing of one's unbeing. Duessa in *The Faerie Queene,* whose name is her nature, says "I that do seeme not I, *Duessa* am,"[13] which is to see the principle of self-inconsistency as the principle of evil, since God Is and verifies reality. Iago says, dreadfully, "I am not what I am" (*Othello,* I. i. 65). Wholeness is other as when St. Paul says "by the grace of God, I am that I am" (1 Cor. 15:10).

Love reveals and is illumined by the twin ideals of beauty and chastity; love is immersed in becoming, imperfection, confusion, sin. The sonnets magnificently and profoundly explore these changes. The young man is praised in great praises, and yet is also seen for what he is and is not. He is sometimes blamed, sometimes confusedly justified. Sonnet 35 not only exemplifies the struggle but speaks about it, offering a false analogy and then pointing out the sophistry.

No more bee greeu'd at that which thou hast done,
Roses haue thornes, and siluer fountaines mud,
Cloudes and eclipses staine both Moone and Sunne,
And loathsome canker liues in sweetest bud.
All men make faults, and euen I in this,
Authorizing thy trespas with compare,
My selfe corrupting saluing thy amisse,
Excusing their sins more then their sins are:
For to thy sensuall fault I bring in sence,
The aduerse party is thy Aduocate,
And gainst my selfe a lawfull plea commence,
Such ciuill war is in my loue and hate,
That I an accessary needs must be,
To that sweet theefe which sourely robs from me.
                                        (1609 ed.)

Line 35.8 is one of the most difficult in the sonnets, emended or not. Assuming the sensible if less than certain emendation "Excusing thy sins more than thy sins are," I take the line either to mean that the poet accuses himself both of irrationally justifying sins and of overdramatizing them as he does so (excusing the friend's sins more than those considerable sins are sins), or else to mean that the poet accuses himself of excusing the friend's sins more than those sins are excusable. The latter reading requires even for Shakespeare, a harsh ellipsis; the former reading is therefore preferable. Either way, the line severely attacks the friend and the poet simultaneously.

Line 35.9, "For to thy sensuall fault I bring in sence," undercuts itself. Sense (reason) is normally opposed to sensuality in Shakespeare and in Elizabethan thought. To justify sin by a false analogy and then by an outlandish pun on *sense* is seen as a contemptible thing to do; the self-contempt is reflected in the very tone of the line.

The legal imagery which follows creates an astounding court of law. The poet is an accessory to the crime, the harmed party suing the friend, the advocate of the friend, the prosecutor of the friend and of himself. That is, the speaker of the poem is in a situation where self-inconsistency and its breeding confusions are inherent.

A number of poems offer such entangled states of mind. The poet is his own chief victim, but can attack, sometimes unexpectedly as in "thou dost common grow" (69.14) or "You to your beauteous blessings add a curse,/ Be'ng fond on praise, which makes your praises worse" (84.13-14), a couplet which suggests that the young man (1) hurts his

moral reputation somewhat by being fond of praise, (2) seeks out
flatterers, and (3) does evil things so he may be praised by the evil
company he keeps. The meanings are inconsistent, at least in quality
and degree, but that does not in the world of the sonnets disprove intent.
The inconsistency is stated baldly in the couplet of Sonnet 57: "So true
a fool is love, that in your Will,/ Though you do anything, he thinks no
ill."

Confusion, irony, and justification meet in so many glancing and
mixing ways in the sonnets that it is often hard to tell whether irony is
intended. Most of Sonnet 57 certainly sounds both sincere and self-
humiliating, yet the opening of that poem is easy to read as savagely
effective irony.

> Being your slave, what should I do but tend
> Upon the hours and times of your desire?
> I have no precious time at all to spend
> Nor services to do till you require.
>   (57.1-4)

Put the sarcastic taps on the right words, and these lines are a
masterpiece of resentment; yet one cannot be sure that the poem is
being satiric or, if so, in what admixture. Resentment persistently
yields to justification; it is doubtful whether Shakespeare himself could
say always just when or how much.

The struggle to justify or deny the evils of the friend was costly and
virtually continual, taking its strongest and most startling form in lines
58.11-12: "to you it doth belong,/ Your self to pardon of self-doing
crime." The friend is the standard; therefore he can do no wrong; when
he does wrong, being the source and standard of good, he may forgive
himself wrong; he may not be blamed, be he blameworthy or not. The
blasphemy and confusion of such attitudes is fundamentally thor-
oughly serious; the young man is treated with intense religious
devotion, and the contradiction of "lascivious grace" (40.13) is known
and hardly to be endured.

Shakespeare's relation to the dark lady is moody; he may be jovial,
or tender, or teasing, or bitterly angry; yet it is a simpler relation. He
does not have to justify her, as he did have to justify the unjustifiable
young man out of deep psychological and religious need. The relation
with her is for pleasure, passion, infatuation; he does not yoke it to an
ideal, and the fundamental logic is blunt: "Only my plague thus far I
count my gain,/ That she that makes me sin awards me pain" (141.13-

14). The struggle is with himself, a fevered struggle. The ironies are intended, notably in Sonnet 138, 140, 149, 152, and direct blame strikes home in Sonnets 138, 141, and 142, and others.

Sonnet 147, one of the best of the negative sonnets, turns on the dark lady in fierce un-irony in the couplet, having portrayed the struggle within Shakespeare in the first three quatrains.

> My love is as a fever longing still
> For that which longer nurseth the disease,
> Feeding on that which doth preserve the ill,
> Th'uncertain, sickly appetite to please.
> My reason, the physician to my love,
> Angry that his prescriptions are not kept,
> Hath left me, and I desp'rate now approve,
> Desire is death, which physic did except.
> Past cure I am, now reason is past care
> And frantic-mad with evermore unrest;
> My thoughts and my discourse as madmen's are,
> At random from the truth vainly express'd,
> For I have sworn thee fair, and thought thee bright,
> Who art as black as hell, as dark as night.

The poem is intensely metaphysical; it depends on traditional knowledge about the power in unreality: to leave reason is to submit to the destructive powers within and without.

In structure the poem is an *allegoria*, a single figure carried out in a narrative; the third quatrain concludes the narrative and begins the argument which is the sestet (a very pretty combining of the 12-2 and 8-6 structures). The octave asserts fever, the third quatrain madness. The third quatrain asserts the argument and the couplet proves it. Part of the argument is unstated and clear: "Only a madman would contradict plainly evident truths; but I have done so in calling you fair and bright; therefore I am mad." The couplet twists and untwists, a self-inconsistency which as such validly proves the point asserted.

In the first line "still" probably contains the meaning "yet," suggesting that he continues to struggle with love; the battle is not over yet; but mostly "still" means "always": the "longing still" is precisely damnation, endless longing, unending confusion. In the third line, to feed on what preserves the ill is evidently irrational and parallels the self-substantial, self-consuming flame of Sonnet 1 and the consuming-nourishing in Sonnet 73. In the fourth line, the "uncertain, sickly appetite" is as unpleasantly and effectively ugly in sound as in meaning. The remainder of the poem is as clear in basic meaning, writhingly angry and humiliated in tone. Reason judges unreason with a strange and severe clarity; the poet as judge is not confused by the plight of the poet as sufferer. The poem is a great poem, in the strength of the moral understanding, in the vigorously rendered suffering, in the near-perfection of form.

Shakespeare ends the poems to the dark lady savagely and appropriately: "For I have sworn thee fair! More perjur'd I/ To swear against the truth so foul a lie" (152.13-14). The fury is a fury of conscious inconsistency, the triple pun on *I* and *eye* and *aye* not playful but a barren rage of blame. It is not a pleasant way to end 152 love sonnets; it is a great way. The greatness of these poems is not always pleasant.

Shakespeare justifies the young man; he blames the dark lady; he struggles with himself, blames himself, tries to justify himself. His self-justifications do not satisfy him, as Sonnets 119, 120, and 121 deeply reveal. In Sonnet 119 he speaks of "tears" (119.1), of "limbecs foul as hell within" (119.2), of "wretchèd errors" (119.5) and "madding fever" (119.8). The sestet tries to redeem the barren rage, to explain the evil.

> O benefit of ill! Now I find true
> That better is by evil still made better
> And ruin'd love when it is built anew
> Grows fairer than at first, more strong, far greater.
> So I return rebuk'd to my content
> And gain by ills thrice more than I have spent.

These lines would transfer to romantic love a basic Christian concept, redemption as higher than innocence, but the transfer does not reach or hold. In Sonnet 120 he again strives for a redemption. The trespasses of friend and poet balance and, more, "your trespass now becomes a fee:/ Mine ransoms yours, and yours must ransom me" (120.13-14). Again he seeks a para-Christian solution and again fails. He does not believe that sins redeem, and he turns in Sonnet 121 to an even more desperate and complicated attempt at justification.[14]

> 'Tis better to be vile than vile esteemèd,
> When not to be receives reproach of being
> And the just pleasure lost, which is so deemèd
> Not by our feeling, but by others' seeing.
> For why should others' false adult'rate eyes
> Give salutation to my sportive blood?
> Or on my frailties why are frailer spies
> Which in their wills count bad what I think good?

No, I am that I am, and they that level
At my abuses, reckon up their own.
I may be straight, though they themselves be bevel.
By their rank thoughts, my deeds must not be shown,
Unless this gen'ral evil they maintain:
All men are bad, and in their badness reign.

The poet has been blamed for sins. The whole context and the tone
suggest sexual rather than other sins and the "sportive" (121.6) and the
pun in "adult'rate" (121.5) leave no doubt. The acts could have been
but were probably not homosexual, for reasons I gave in Chapter Two.

Whatever the acts, the poet defends himself in three ways, with
additional snarls, three blatantly inconsistent ways:

1. He did not do the acts he is accused of doing.
2. He did the acts he is accused of doing, but it is wrong to blame
    him: the acts are innocent and good.
3. The accusers have no authority to accuse him because they are
    wicked persons, having themselves done such vile acts.

Since he has lost the pleasure he would have received from doing the
acts, it appears that he claims he has not done the acts. One could also,
though less plausibly, read line 121.3 to mean that he has lost the *just*
pleasure: they have taken the fun out of the acts by the accusations and
insinuations of evil. There are also ambiguities in "I may be straight"
(121.11) and "By their rank thoughts, my deeds must not be shown"
(121.12). The bet is hedged a little; all he strictly says in lines 121.11
and 121.12 is that the accusers cannot tell on their evidence and that
their authority is suspect because of their own vices. But the impression
that he has not done the acts is strongly and polemically conveyed.

The "sportive blood" (121.6) and "frailties" (121.7) and "abuses"
(121.10) are admissions against interest and therefore evidence that he
is admitting to the acts, as is the context, in which he admits to
"transgression" (120.3).

The acts are vile. He says so: "vile" (121.1), "false adult'rate" (121.5),
"frailer" (121.7), "rank" (121.12), and "bevel" (121.11).

The acts are not vile. He thinks them "good" (121.8), which is as plain
as one needs.

The inconsistencies stumble on themselves, and he cannot work
loose. The couplet gives the accusers some room to strike and drives
him toward a syllogistic corner. "If evil is general, I am evil," the poet

means and the unstated qualification "but only then" is sadly faint. The poem ends on a perversely triumphant note, a world of badness reigning, a tangle of inextricable guilt. As the mutual sins of the poet and the young man in Sonnet 120 did not save the poet, neither can the sins of the accusers. Sin is a thick wood; the ways out lead back in; the tangles of negation and contradiction stay tangled.

The contradictions could not long be endured; sanity was — I imagine quite literally — threatened. Sonnet 121 is an extreme attempt to solve a problem which could not be solved in the terms offered: lascivious grace is not grace. Nor did Shakespeare attempt much longer in the sonnets to solve the problem. Sonnet 126, a farewell, was near at hand.

Chapter 8

The Theology of
a Love

The theology of love in Shakespeare's sonnets is that romantic love is all, until the persuasion fails, as it must. In between, back and forth, we have the sonnets.

Love sonnets idealize their objects; no commonplace is more banally true than that. The hyperboles may be mocked; thus Shakespeare's Sonnet 130 ("My mistress' eyes are nothing like the sun"); thus some of Donne's wit; thus in the *Arcadia* when Sidney writes of "those immoderate praises, which the foolish Louer thinkes short of his Mistres, though they reach farre beyond the heauens"[1] or, with a somewhat more sober but still smiling warning, when he asks whether "*Cupid* be a god, or that the tyranny of our own thoughts seeme as a God vnto vs."[2]

More strictly, if one idealizes the object, to the precise degree of success hyperbole is logically impossible; to idealize is to make ideal, and the ideal is as realized in a poem as it is.

Shakespeare absorbs and extends the commonplaces; in the idealization of the sonnets he claims more than other poets.[3] No Romantic poet is so romantic as Shakespeare when he says in precisely so many words, "Both truth and beauty on my love depends" (101.3). The grammar is Elizabethan[4] but, taken as modern, is still what he means. Beauty and truth are identified, hence one subject.

Shakespeare asks, in lines 108.3-4, "What's new to speak, what now to register/ That may express my love or thy dear merit?" and replies, "Nothing, sweet boy, but yet like prayers divine,/ I must each day say o'er the very same,/ Counting no old thing old, thou mine, I thine,/ Ev'n as when first I hallow'd thy fair name" (108.5-8). The unmistakable reference is to the Lord's Prayer. The poems to the young man are like prayers to God,[5] and the boy is "a god in love . . ./ . . . next my heav'n the best" (110.12-13). Thus his love reflects, and is an analogy of

149

the love of God, when as here Shakespeare qualifies so. The "next my heav'n the best" is a flash of recognition which leads beyond the sonnets. More often Shakespeare does not qualify; the analogy becomes an identity. In lines 108.9-12 he says, "Eternal love . . ./ Weighs not the dust and injury of age,/ Nor gives to necessary wrinkles place,/ But makes antiquity for aye his page." The wrinkles are necessary, certain, unavoidable, but they do not happen; they are not there. Time's waste does not happen; times do not change. The Middle Ages are now, and changeless. The self-inconsistencies are not to be explained or resolved: they are given, essential to the identity that sustains the poems. In the poems to the young man from Sonnet 100 on, when the relation is nearing its end, such statements of divine identity are made, at times assertively, at times desperately, at times merely plainly. The young man is Shakespeare's "all-the-world" (112.5); he "never can be old" (104.1); he will remain in Shakespeare's "brain" (itself then everlasting?) "beyond all date, ev'n to eternity" (122.1,4). He is the *summum bonum*, "all thy sum of good" (109.12), "sum" as height and sum, and then, as though Shakespeare wished to remove any doubt of the theological and metaphysical nature of the reference: "For nothing this wide universe I call,/ Save thou, my rose; in it thou art my all (109.13-14). The universe is nothing compared to the young man as god (really as God), transcendent of the universe.

Since to turn to the world's nothing is to leave the young man, the young man is outside the world; since the young man is "in" (109.14) the world, he is in it. Shakespeare does not say that the wide universe is nothing compared to the young man; he says that the universe is nothing except the young man in the universe. All the universe is nothing; all the universe is nothing except the young man, who is in that non-remaining remnant of the nothing-world. The knots are strange, not to untie.

After the allusion to the Lord's Prayer in lines 108.5-8 we hear of "eternal love in love's fresh case" (108.9). "Case" may mean "example," or "form," or "dress"; they come to the same meaning, since dress is frequently a metaphor for body.[6] Shakespeare does not say that the young man is like, but that the young man is, eternity incarnate in the human form. The young man is not exactly identified with Christ; he is substituted for Christ, he is offered as the real and healing incarnation of eternal love.

Any general Elizabethan Neoplatonism moves in such a direction, and Elizabethan Neoplatonism was for Shakespeare an atmosphere to breathe, not a sequence of philosophers to discriminate and codify.

Eternal beauty manifest in and through mortal forms obviously bears an analogy and a historical allegiance to the incarnate Christ. But such forms are not Christ; they are transient bearers, reflections rather than source. Shakespeare's claiming goes beyond; the young man is shown — not as a step to the divine beauty or as a reflection of it: he is that beauty and the source of other beauty. Shakespeare says so more than once, most tellingly in the first quatrain of Sonnet 53.

> What is your substance, whereof are you made,
> That millions of strange shadows on you tend?
> Since ev'ry one hath, ev'ry one, one shade,
> And you, but one, can ev'ry shadow lend.
> Describe Adonis and the counterfeit
> Is poorly imitated after you;
> On Helen's cheek all art of beauty set,
> And you in Grecian tires are painted new.
> Speak of the spring and foison of the year:
> The one doth shadow of your beauty show,
> The other as your bounty doth appear,
> And you in every blessèd shape we know.
> In all external grace you have some part,
> But you like none, none you, for constant heart.

The shadow is Platonic; the bounty Christian; or rather they meet in a certain Elizabethan religious-literary set of mind more celebratory than observing of distinctions. The young man lends beauty to all beauty, natural and human, and he is to be thanked for nature's bounty itself. The "blessèd" and "grace" of lines 53.12 and 53.13 respectively, mean the blessing of loveliness, gracefulness, but also divine grace, hardly even as puns, since the chief function of the divine in the sonnets is to provide the blessing of beauty. What gives grace is grace.

The poem also expresses a view of art typical of these sonnets, a semi-Platonic view. The young man is the source and exemplar of beauty; other beauty in nature and persons is "poorly imitated" (53.6) after him. Shakespeare's poems, which praise the young man, have beauty the young man lends the poems, yet (with enough inconsistency) are poor imitations, inept plain things. Line 53.5 speaks of poetry as well as of people, for it says "describe." The divergence of the theory diverges in the poem; in the description of Adonis, the young man is "poorly imitated" (53.6); Helen is "painted new" (53.8), beautifully and freshly described.

Since the art is a poor imitation, Shakespeare's poems are inferior. — Since the young man inspires the poems, all the great beauty of the poems comes from him. Since the poems are rude, Shakespeare must repeatedly decry them. Since the poems are immortal, the young man's name and beauty will live in them. Since the young man is all the argument of the poems, plainness of style, crudity, and dullness are justified. The inconsistencies flourish.

The conflicts are between change and the desire for permanence, corruption and the desire for purity, confusion and the desire for truth, idolatry and the desire for the divine.

The couplet of Sonnet 15 defines a basic struggle.

> And, all in war with time for love of you,
> As he takes from you, I ingraft you new.

To put severally what is present together, (1) "in truth you change; I deny that change, speaking falsehood"; (2) "in the temporal world you change; in the world of art you are in truth made permanent"; (3) "in the temporal world you change; the ideal of beauty you reflect is changeless because ideal: it is that genuine ideal my poems enshrine"; (4) "in you I discover beauty; beauty is truth; you are truly and permanently new, renewed, once-more-ingrafted-and-grown."

The struggle is a joining sometimes achieved. F. T. Prince writes that the idealism of Shakespeare's sonnets "may even appear more exalted than theirs [Dante's and Petrarch's], and it is certainly more perilous."[7]

The identification of the loved one with the divine takes other specifically Christian forms, which is to say anti-Christian forms, since love is a competing religion.

Sonnet 29 says that God disappoints and that the young man redeems.

> When in disgrace with fortune and men's eyes,
> I all alone beweep my outcast state,
> And trouble deaf heav'n with my bootless cries
> And look upon my self and curse my fate,
> Wishing me like to one more rich in hope,
> Featur'd like him, like him with friends possess'd,
> Desiring this man's art and that man's scope,
> With what I most enjoy contentèd least;
> Yet in these thoughts my self almost despising,
> Haply I think on thee, and then my state,
> Like to the lark at break of day arising
> From sullen earth, sings hymns at heaven's gate.
> For thy sweet love rememb'rèd such wealth brings,
> That then I scorn to change my state with kings.

Line 29.3 is one of the most perturbed lines in our language. Three heavily stressed syllables ("troub-," "deaf," and "heav'n") are jarringly close together; the "heav'n with" is probably the most violent example in the sonnets of a trochee without a preceding verse-pause; the strength of "boot-" is greater because of the unusual lightness of the three preceding syllables. The heaping of stress, the harsh reversal, the rush to a vivid stress — all enforce the angry anti-religious troubled cry.

Against that heaven, against God, is set the happy heaven where the lark sings hymns. The poem is a hymn, celebrating a truth declared superior to religion, against which the poet rages, and superior to politics, which in the couplet the poet scorns.

Sonnet 30 carries the theme on, finding in the friend's love that "all losses are restor'd, and sorrows end" (30.14). All losses are restored, even of death, even of the friends "hid in death's dateless night" (30.6), a restoration defined further in Sonnet 31, where the "holy" (31.5) tears of "dear religious love" (31.6) are shed over the hidden friends and where the grief is assuaged by the discovery that the young man is "the grave where buri'd love doth live" (31.9). The young man holds "all" (31.14) of the past friends and has "all the all" (31.14) of the poet.

The references, more likely deliberate allusions than echoes, are to the lives hid with Christ in God[8] and to the Crucifixion and Resurrection. The love religion competes with those doctrines, as Sonnet 34 unmistakably competes with the doctrine of the Atonement. It is the friend's tears of repentance which "ransom all ill deeds" (34.14).

In line 55.13 even the triumph of the Resurrection means for Shakespeare only the further pacing forth of the young man.

'Gainst death and all-oblivious enmity
Shall you pace forth; your praise shall still find room
Ev'n in the eyes of all posterity
That wear this world out to the ending doom.
So till the judgment that your self arise,
You live in this, and dwell in lovers' eyes.
(55.9-14)

The lovely Sonnet 54 concords rather than embattles religious and romantic themes, the continued simile of the rose, with semi-Platonic overtones, uniting the poem and the themes of beauty, truth, and immortality.

O how much more doth beauty beauteous seem
By that sweet ornament which truth doth give:
The rose looks fair, but fairer we it deem
For that sweet odor which doth in it live;
The canker blooms have full as deep a dye
As the perfumèd tincture of the roses,
Hang on such thorns and play as wantonly
When summer's breath their maskèd buds discloses;
But for their virtue only is their show,
They live unwoo'd and unrespectèd fade,
Die to themselves. Sweet roses do not so:
Of their sweet deaths are sweetest odors made;
And so of you, beauteous and lovely youth,
When that shall vade, by verse distills your truth.

The sense of unity is enhanced by the diverse, coordinated structural patterns. In relation to the simile which begins in line 54.3 and is applied in the couplet, the structure is 1-2, 3-12, 13-14. The sentence structure, as I have punctuated the poem, is 1-11a, 11b-14. The subdivision of the simile is 3-4, 5-8, 9-11a, 11b-12. Yet both the couplet sense and the octave-sestet sense are firmly present, the "but" of line 54.9 being a major turn and the couplet, linked in syntax to the third quatrain, applying the simile. The patterns flow gently together.

The crucial point thematically in the poem is that truth (troth is truth,[9] the realization of the real moral law) makes beauty more beautiful; the truth exists for the beauty. Since beauty is the standard, the objection to immorality is that it stains beauty; the praise of goodness is that it makes beauty more gloriously fair.

Sonnet 106, with beauty as arbiter and substance, offers one of Shakespeare's favored themes, the superiority of the past to the present. Yet, since the young man is the source and standard of past beauty, the past must be defective in comparison with his present, as the future was declared inferior in lines 104.13-14: "Hear this, thou age unbred:/ Ere you were born was beauty's summer dead." In the couplets of Sonnets 67 and 68 Shakespeare had ingeniously managed to unite the past's superiority and the young man's unequaled beauty: "O him she [nature] stores, to show what wealth she had/ In days long since before these last so bad" and "And him as for a map doth nature store,/ To show false art what beauty was of yore." In Sonnet 106 he unites the themes in larger ways.

When in the chronicle of wastèd time,
I see description of the fairest wights
And beauty making beautiful old rhyme

In praise of ladies dead and lovely knights,
Then in the blazon of sweet beauties' best,
Of hand, of foot, of lip, of eye, of brow,
I see their ántique pen would have express'd
Ev'n such a beauty as you master now.
So all their praises are but prophecies
Of this our time, all you prefiguring,
And, for they look'd but with divining eyes,
They had not style enough your worth to sing;
For we which now behold these present days
Have eyes to wonder but lack tongues to praise.

In line 106.3 the "beauty" is at once (not twice, since the sonnets insist on the identity) the semi-Platonic substance-ideal beauty and the specific beauty of the ladies and lords. In line 106.5, "Then in the blazon of sweet beauties best" (1609 ed.), the reference is again the substance-ideal beauty, beauty's best, and to the particular beauties of beautiful ladies. In modern punctuation, there is no way to offer both meanings. In line 106.7, "their" has no given reference; it means the poets, the blazoners of sweet beauty.

The poem offers an analogy to Christian typology. All previous beauty is but a type of the young man's beauty-to-come and the religious cast of tone becomes very apparent in the "prophecies" (106.9), "prefiguring" (106.10) and "divining" (106.11).

In Sonnet 106, the analogy is analogy and the competition is logically present but subdued. In Sonnet 105 the competition is overt, and chipper.

Let not my love be called idolatry
Nor my belovèd as an idol show,
Since all alike my songs and praises be
To one, of one, still such, and ever so.
Kind is my love today, tomorrow kind,
Still constant in a wondrous excellence;
Therefore my verse to constancie confin'd,
One thing expressing, leaves out difference.
"Fair, kind, and true" is all my argument,
"Fair, kind, and true," varying to other words,
And in this change is my invention spent,
Three themes in one, which wondrous scope affords.
Fair, kind, and true have often liv'd alone,
Which three till now never kept seat in one.

The poem combines an apology for the simplicity of the sonnets and the theme of idolatry. The poet argues that his love in not idolatry, the loved one not an idol, since the loved one is in truth a god (God), possessing the metaphysical attributes of the divine: unchangeable and perfect beauty ("fair," 105.9,10,13); grace, the overflowing of love ("kind," 105.5, 9, 10, 13); and righteousness ("true," 105.9, 10, 13), each repeated a total of three times in lines 105.9, 105.10, and 105.13. The conclusion says, most simply, that never before has a human being been entirely beautiful, gracious, and faithful, the young man being the first to be so. Yet the clear reference to the Trinity is a denial of the Trinity in the young man's favor: "three till now never kept seat in one" (105.14). Even apart from that startling stroke of wit, the poem is sufficiently and deliberately idolatrous of the young man.

The very wit and overtness of the poem prove that Shakespeare knew that he dealt in idolatry, and it was not very long after (three years at most, more likely less: see Chapter Three) that he put in Berowne's mouth an important outburst,[10] beginning in amused contempt and ending elsewhere:

> This is the lyuer veine, which makes flesh a deitie.
> A greene Goose, a Goddesse, pure pure ydotarie.
> God amende vs, God amende, we are much out a th' way.

The "ydotarie" is a Shakespearean coinage (not previously noted), combining with pungency *idolatry* and *doting*.

After Sonnet 154 in the Rosenbach copy of the 1609 quarto of the sonnets is written, in what, according to Giles Dawson, could well be a late eighteenth-century or early nineteenth-century hand, "What a heap of wretched Infidel stuff." At moments Shakespeare would have agreed.

Again and again the poems celebrate the beauty and constancy of the young man, even after other poems have exhibited the young man's corruption with weariness, or pain, or scorn. Shakespeare writes in Sonnet 110, a fully serious poem, of return "ev'n to thy pure and most most loving breast" (110.14). The statement is on the face of it patently false, denied by earlier poem after poem. It has to be explained in religious terms or not at all.

The question of line 53.1 needs to be asked once more, a little differently: what is your *substance*? *That* is unchanging, however much or unpleasantly a young man may actually change. Shakespeare has caught in and through the young man a glimpse of what does not change, and he identifies the Reality with the young man, most famously in Sonnet 116:

Let me not to the marriage of true minds
Admit impediments. Love is not love
Which alters when it alteration finds
Or bends with the remover to remove.
O no! it is an ever-fixèd mark
Which looks on tempests and is never shaken;
It is the star to ev'ry wand'ring bark
Whose worth's unknown although his height be taken.
Love's not time's fool, though rosy lips and cheeks
Within his bending sickle's compass come;
Love alters not with his brief hours and weeks,
But bears it out ev'n to the edge of doom.
If this be error and upon me prov'd,
I never writ, nor no man ever lov'd.

Is that true? It is natural to say that it would be nice if it were, that it is a way of speaking, a hyperbole of genuine feeling, a perhaps desperate longing. Yes, but also it is true, quite literally; and Shakespeare in the couplet, discussed in Chapter Six, stakes his literary and logical reputation on that truth.

The poem is true of the ideal, and the ideal is real. Of course love is not love which alters; to the degree it alters it is hate, or indifference, or something else. The ideal (and Shakespeare believed in ideals in a way and with a passion far out of keeping with much modern thought) *is* an ever-fixed mark. Otherwise one could not measure by it. Love's worth is unknown, even though his height be taken. If one could not take the altitude (height) of a star, one could not make a navigational fix, but because one has measured something does not mean that one understands it; beauty and mystery remain.

Robert Frost makes one of the greatest comments on the sonnets (and on physical science): "It was a moment for me when I saw how Shakespeare set bounds to science when he brought in the North Star, 'whose worth's unknown although his height be taken.'"[11] He adds a characteristic Frostian twist: "Of untold worth: it brings home some that should and some that shouldn't come."

As Frost's wit suggests, human beings fail.[12] The poet says in the following sonnet, "I have hoistèd sail to all the winds/ Which should transport me furthest from your sight" (117.7-8). After all, it is the star that is everlasting, not the bark. Barks wander.

Shakespeare has identified the young man with the ideal, and in that sense Sonnet 116 is not true. Love has altered, and the poems from Sonnet 100 on show the crumbling, flaring, silencing of the relation.[13]

It is ironical and sad that Sonnet 116 is in the midst of the last, vacillating sequence of poems to the young man, but what is said of the ideal is not less true for that. Shakespeare admits realities and does not end the sequence with Sonnet 116 or one of the poems claiming immortality in verse or with the Christian Sonnet 146. He ends the sequence with Sonnet 126, which begins with a claim, moves on to a fear, and ends with a stark precise accepting of the power and inevitability of time and death.

> O thou my lovely boy, who in thy power
> Dost hold time's fickle glass, his sickle hour;
> Who hast by waning grown and therein show'st
> Thy lovers with'ring as thy sweet self grow'st.
> If nature, sov'reign mistress over wrack,
> As thou go'st onward still will pluck thee back,
> She keeps thee to this purpose that her skill
> May time disgrace and wretchèd minutes kill.
> Yet fear her, O thou minion of her pleasure,
> She may detain, but not still keep her treasure!
> Her audit, though delay'd, answer'd must be,
> And her *Quietus* is to render thee.

The last line may have a veiled religious touch of hope, but it is not central. What is central is the reality of the natural account which must be paid, the truth which must be faced. Love changes; beauty passes; men die. On that note the greatest sequence of love poems in our literature comes to a close.

Chapter 9

The Faults of Greatness

The sonnets of Shakespeare have passed one of the chief tests of literary greatness: they have endured and prospered. After three hundred and fifty years, and the ups and downs of reputation, they are probably the most widely read in England and America of any love poems; they have fascinated scholars (the lesser recommendation) and pleased lovers and lovers of poetry. The sonnets must, then, speak something of love and speak it well and feelingly.

They have had, nonetheless, a long line of illustrious detractors: Samuel Johnson (aiming at all sonnets),[1] George Steevens, William Wordsworth, John Keats, T. G. Tucker, John Crowe Ransom, Yvor Winters, Douglas Bush are among the many critics who have had negative and often harsh things to say.

Complaints have been entered against conceits and forced metaphors;[2] metaphorical incoherence;[3] unevenness;[4] sensuality and coarseness;[5] dependency of character;[6] and insincere rhetorical playfulness which violates the spirit of love.[7] George Steevens puts the case most fiercely, complaining against "quaintness, obscurity, and tautology"[8] and "affectation, pedantry, circumlocution, and nonsense"[9] as well as of a superabundance of "conceit"[10] and the Procrustean destructiveness of the limiting and stretching form.[11] One can add literary exhibitionism; frivolity; unpleasant self-complaining and self-justification; and radical inconsistency and vacillation of attitude, sometimes within a single sonnet.

All the aforementioned objections have some truth descriptively and critically. The charge of tautology is undeniable, because tautology is built into the form; repetition with variety is the principle of meter, and the sonnet has more repeating and limiting of form than most genres. Shakespeare liked his repetition thick, repetition of idea, sound, imagery, syntactical patterning, rhythm.

Analysis shows that the repetition and subpatterning are indeed complex, but analysis as such does not tell us whether to praise or reprove. A remark that has haunted me for years is Thomas Gilby's "A time comes when analysis turns into frivolity";[12] I have thought of it many times when doing, and reading, analyses of the sonnets. Good poems are not written to be talked about; but to talk about them we need to know what is genuinely relevant. Judgment which is pure response dissolves into undiscussable sentiment and relativism; once judgment begins to analyze, it can become mired in its own builded complexities.

Shakespeare liked to play with metrical and rhetorical elaborations and to mock them. Analysis fascinated and repelled him. Hence the charges of affectation, frivolity, and pedantry have some substance, but not much. Shakespeare wrote richly, with some learning in his art and with a good-humored sense of the limits of artifice. No one who has read all of even several of the Elizabethan writers of sonnets is apt to deny that Shakespeare has incomparably more significant variety and more rhetorical and metrical liveliness than his nearest competitors: Daniel, Sidney, Spenser, and Drayton.

The obscurity is of an odd kind, and kinds, so that sensible critics can talk about how plain these poems are. Stephen Booth puts the problem nicely: he says that we know what Shakespeare means but cannot tell what he says.[13]

For instance, to take an example not discussed in that connection by Booth, readers have no trouble with what Shakespeare means in context, when he writes that the dark lady has "Robb'd others' beds revénues of their rents" (142.8). He means that she has committed adultery with several married men, has taken what is due (owed, like a rent) to their wives. But what does he say? Revenues and rents involve obligation and payment. Their relationship is not just redundancy, since "robbed others' beds rents of their rents" seems to make less sense. Yet a coherent reading of the metaphorical meaning is hard or impossible to reach. The metaphors are rapidly flowed together, do not unwind.

The line shares a problem with a number of lines of the sonnets: clear until peered at. Each given instance presents a critical problem not always soluble. Some examples are snarls, some subtleties, some both at once.[14]

Other examples are syntactical. Sometimes the difficulty is only in analyzing the syntax. Line 8.1, "Music to hear, why hear'st thou music sadly?" is basically clear in meaning. The question is to decide the syntax. Is "music to hear" a vocative ("you who are music to hear"), elliptical for "with music to hear" or "since there is music to hear," or is it a special sort of absolute phrase? Sometimes the syntax is garbled (two different incomplete constructions combined) in a way that makes new syntax and meaning. In lines 25.3-4, "I, whom fortune of such triumph bars,/ Unlook'd-for-joy in that I honor most," Shakespeare has made a verb from the compound epithet *unlooked-for* and the noun *joy,* so that the meaning is "I joy with unlooked-for joy." The passage, then, is not obscure though sufficiently clumsy.

Some syntactical turns are rough, and hard to analyze, though in a context which makes their general meaning clear, for instance line 62.12.

> But when my glasse shewes me my selfe indeed
> Beated and chopt with tand antiquitie,
> Mine owne selfe loue quite contrary I read
> Selfe, so selfe louing were iniquity.
>   (62.9-12, 1609 ed.)

The general meaning of line 62.12 is something like "A self loving itself in such a way would be [guilty of] iniquity," which involves a very crude ellipsis, as does "Self [vocative], so loving one's self would be iniquity," as do other possible unfoldings. The subjunctive follows unidiomatically on the indicative. "When I see how old and ugly I am, I recognize that such a self-love is iniquity" is a more natural idiom. The line is also ugly in sound and must count as a defect.

At other times the obscurity is in intent, since Shakespeare vacillates between resentful scorn of the young man's actions and idolatrous justification of what he does. Therefore, as I have shown in Chapter Seven and elsewhere, it is often hard to know in a given instance what admixture is present and what attitude prevails. This difficulty is not lessened by Shakespeare's tendency to condense and curtail syntactical and other relations. Thus, line 77.3, "The vacant leaves [of the copybook presented] thy mind's imprint will bear," becomes a splendidly and fiercely ironic insult if one stresses the "vacant" and the "thy"; but the context of meditative seriousness convinces me that that ambiguity was unintended; what is meant is that the now-vacant leaves will receive the mind's imprint and hence cease to be vacant. The compression of time misleads.

The fault can on occasion be in the beholder and the beholder's time rather than in Shakespeare. The first quatrain of Sonnet 94 occurs in a context of painful disappointment at the young man's unchastity (Sonnets 92-96), including the context of brilliant and widely admired praise of the second quatrain and the fierce dispraise of unchastity in the couplet.

> They that have power to hurt and will do none,
> That do not do the thing they most do show,
> Who, moving others, are themselves as stone,
> Unmovèd, cold, and to temptation slow;
> They rightly do inherit heaven's graces
> And husband nature's riches from expense;
> They are the lords and owners of their faces,
> Others but stewards of their excellence.
> The summer's flower is to the summer sweet,
> Though to itself it only live and die,
> But if that flower with base infection meet,
> The basest weed outbraves his dignity;
> For sweetest things turn sourest by their deeds:
> Lilies that fester smell far worse than weeds.

The first quatrain is praise of chastity (the alternative is that Shakespeare means to praise the festering and foul-smelling weeds in line 94.14), but readers do not read it as such or are puzzled by it because the praise of the coldness of chastity, an Elizabethan and Shakespearean commonplace,[15] is so foreign to our time.

I paraphrase the first quatrain as follows: "They who, by the power of beauty, have the power to hurt others, but do not hurt others; who do not do the thing [sexual activity] which they most do show [suggest to others by their beauty]; who, moving others to unchastity by their beauty, are themselves chaste, unmoved, slow to temptation, cold as snow and strong as stone."

To read otherwise or ironically is to ignore the whole context[16] and especially the surge of conviction in the "rightly" in line 94.5.

Obscurity must reckon as one of the recurrent faults of the sonnets, especially the obscurity which springs from condensation of expression, which often results from the quickness and richness of the mind at work. The obscurity is a minor defect sprung from major virtues.

The charge of affectation raises the old and new question of the artful and natural. Art is artifice relying on nature; naturalness requires art. Art and nature are both needed; the right balance and interpenetration is to be solved only in the judging of singulars. The question was a question for Shakespeare as for us, as the discussion in Chapter Five should show. Renaissance taste was richer and bolder than ours; modern poets, even traditional or flamboyant ones, seldom offer a rhetorical and sound patterning nearly so interlaced as that which Shakespeare obviously loved.

One need not go all the way or applaud rather than dislike such exhibits as "first your eye I ey'd" (104.2) to discover that Renaissance poetics, the admiration for rhetoric and commonplace, served Renaissance poetry well. Shakespeare, as we have seen in many times and ways, wears his rhetoric and commonplaces with a difference; his originality is overwhelming, even in the passages when he said and in some true sense believed that he was working in antique and plain style.

Few of the sonnets are finally, in my judgment, artificial in the bad sense, overwrought with showy elaboration or conceits which have little propriety to central meanings and feelings. The eye-heart Sonnets 24, 46, 47; perhaps Sonnet 38 ("How can my Muse want subject to invent"), which is partly redeemed by the well-turned compliment of the couplet, "If my slight Muse do please these curious days,/ The pain be mine, but thine shall be the praise"; Sonnet 45 ("The other two, slight air and purging fire"); Sonnet 83 ("I never saw that you did painting need"); Sonnet 88 ("When thou shalt be dispos'd to set me light"); and Sonnets 113 and 114, on flattery in seeing. Of these, only the eye-heart poems are seriously bothersome. In the sonnets occur patches of show, metaphorical twists which fail to come off, metrical and dictional posturings one could spare. So much, though, is plangent, charged, powerfully imaged and sounded, deeply merged with theme, as to put any serious charge of affectation out of court. The richness and ingenuity are absorbed, and directed.

As for metaphor, yes, Shakespeare entangled and abused metaphor in the sonnets, now and again. Ransom's ingenious piece of polemics (which taught me a good bit about the sonnet form) has been well answered;[17] and it is transparently clear and widely agreed that Shakespeare used metaphor in range and profundity beyond any other English poet except possibly Milton. In comparison, Donne, a great hand at metaphor, is stiff, limited in range, and more often and more troublingly than Shakespeare, over-visibly ingenious. The metaphor of the star in Sonnet 116; of disease in Sonnets 118, 140, and 147; of the mansion in Sonnets 10, 13, and 146; of the holy grave in Sonnet 31; of theft in Sonnets 40, 75, 79, and 99; of canker in Sonnets 70, 95, and 99;

of music in Sonnets 8, 73, 102; of the hen in Sonnet 143; of shadow in
Sonnet 53; of autumn in Sonnet 73; of the dial hand in Sonnet 104; and
dozens of others; show a range and skill at metaphor too superb to
need much debate or defense.

To say that is to admit that praise is largely superfluous and much
detailed criticism of his perfectly real faults almost irrelevant. Shakespeare's realized talents are of a totally different order than those of his
English competitors, except again possibly Milton. His enormous
power at metaphor and rhetoric; his incredible linguistic talent; the
genius for portraying character which is at work in the sonnets only in
lesser degree than in the plays (he has so far failed to immortalize the
young man's name but has immortalized, probably beyond intent,
some unpleasant features of the young man's character); the equally
astonishing rhythmical and structural skill, the power to lift and
release, to build poems, to vary minutely within and across ground
patterns of sound — in all of these he is alone.

The talents are often abused; the faults are there and clearly
discernible; carelessness, densities, rapid shifts occasioning confusions.
Few of these poems have the perfection, the flawlessness of certain
great lyrics of Campion, Herrick, Dryden, and Frost; but none of those
poets can compare with Shakespeare in resonance, variety, or power.

Unevenness is certainly one of Shakespeare's most important faults;
and it is pervasive, at least in the sense that in almost every poem,
including the best, there is something one would wish away. In Sonnet
104 ("To me, fair friend, you never can be old") there is "eye I ey'd"
(104.2); in Sonnet 106 ("When in the chronicle of wasted time") there is
the metrically playful, intrusive "Of hand, of foot, of lip, of eye, of
brow" (106.6); in Sonnet 73 ("That time of year thou may'st in me
behold") the best quatrain comes first; Sonnet 124 ("If my dear love
were but the child of state"), which is a great and powerful poem if
perhaps not quite a companion of the others mentioned, has a dull line
in a crucial place, "That it nor grows with heat nor drowns with
showers" (124.12).

A few poems pleasantly escape. Sonnet 145 ("Those lips that love's
own hand did make") is charming and flawless, a little masterpiece of
tone. Among poems of more eminent stature, if Sonnet 50 ("How
heavy do I journey on my way"), Sonnet 71 ("No longer mourn for me
when I am dead"), Sonnet 97 ("How like a winter hath my absence
been"), and Sonnet 140 ("Be wise are thou art cruel; do not press")
have any defects, this reader has yet to discover them.

Shakespeare's poetic powers are not in doubt; and the defense of the value of his sonnets, with however much granting of faults, has something of the gesture of tautology: these are Shakespeare's poems, and to show them forth and to listen to them is to demonstrate that they are empowered by that establishing hand and mind.

Yet that is not all to ask. The charges of faults such as nonsense, snobbery, and vacillation have not been met; and cannot be ignored even aesthetically. Aesthetic judgment does not neatly sit apart from such concerns. The Platonic and Aristotelian objections to the abuse of rhetoric are part of the rhetorical and poetic tradition Shakespeare learned and dwelled in. Skilled persuasion for bad causes can hardly be good. Moreover, the active richness of poems is consonant at every breath with what is said, with the richness of attitudes which persuade or fail to persuade. Rich and complex techniques express rich and complex attitudes, and to separate the aesthetic and the moral-psychological-social-religious is precisely to violate our experience of poems. We are moved by something, not by nothing. Nor can we call poems great love poems if they tell nothing, truly, of love.

Love is permanent, in historic shapes. The Petrarchan tradition exalts and idealizes physical beauty; even in that tradition Shakespeare approaches or reaches the unique in his celebration of such beauty. He and his tradition depart from much that is described as modern; his praise of cold chastity falls often now on cold ears; his reprehension of cosmetics would, taken to heart or face, cause some definite economic changes; yet one can neither dismiss Shakespeare's attitudes as sadly unmodern nor use them, *tout court,* to lament these days "so bad." Lovers still fall in love; vows are sworn; many marriages are permanent; religious idealism, if in some eccentric forms, is on the startling rise; and even in modern advertising and movies many of the same ideals and conflicts appear in recognizable if sometimes fantastical forms. As advertisement in a drugstore proclaiming "'Natural Wonder' CHEEK GLISSER The first see-through blush-color that's all innocence and gleam!" shares major themes of the sonnets: nature, the glory of physical beauty, innocence, the transcendent ("wonder" and "gleam"), self-justifying selfishness ("to you it doth belong/ Your self to pardon of self-doing crime" [58.11-12]), resistance to the wasting force of time. What is lacking (besides an honest style) is the clear recognition of evil in many of the sonnets. An omission of some grim importance.

The conflicts and vacillations of the sonnets make for inclusiveness;

diverse themes and hopes for love meet and jostle. The poems confess adultery and parade witty obscenities, and uphold chastity and fidelity.

Self-conflict entails confusion and weakness, explored in Chapter Seven; the self-conflicts of Shakespeare's sonnets include the failing struggle with idealization and idolatry I attempted to define in Chapter Eight. The young man is deified and proven a fragile god. The sonnets are very revealing poems; much that they reveal is unpleasant: dependency, depression, self-humiliation, self-pity, social and professional envy, spite, and rage. The moral rages against the dark lady and against lust have a justified moral severity and a hurt ferocity more personal than just.

The sonnets display and are damaged by moral weakness; therefore they have a great and permanent moral value as exhibiting with minute complexity the working of moral weakness. The moral gain is an aesthetic gain; the beauty of the poems depends on and achieves what is seen of the human soul. But these poems are not only great exhibits of moral grandeur and weakness; they — finally — understand what they say.

The sonnets say all there is to say of human love, or very nearly all.[18] They show love's power, exaltation, joy, its "madding fever," its many complications; its stops, starts, surges, hopes, infidelities, constancies. They prove love's magnificence, its cruelties, its sensual crudeness, its despair, its limits, its relation to time, changes, death, and, in memorable glances, eternity.

These poems tell of love.

Notes

Prefatory
The Problem of the Problems

1. *The Sonnets,* ed. Hyder Edward Rollins, 2 vols., New Variorum Edition of Shakespeare (Philadelphia: J. P. Lippincott, 1944), II: 42-52, esp. II: 43. This edition henceforth is cited as *Sonnets,* ed. Rollins (Variorum).

2. For instance, Philip Martin's valuable *Shakespeare's Sonnets: Self, Love, and Art* (Cambridge: Cambridge University Press, 1972).

Chapter 1
Unity of Authorship, Authenticity, and Order

1. *Sonnets,* ed. Rollins (Variorum), II: 43.

2. Francis Meres, *Palladis Tamia* (London: 1598), sigs. 2O1v-2O2 (italics in text), "hony-tongued *Shakespeare,* witnes his *Venus* and *Adonis,* his *Lucrece,* his sugred Sonnets among his priuate friends, &c." The seldom noted "&c" has an interest of its own: to what does it refer? songs in the plays? *A Lover's Complaint?* poems which appeared a little later in *The Passionate Pilgrim?* lost poems?

3. Shakespeare's Sonnet 77, though less famous than Sonnets 129 and 146, is also a spiritual sonnet and a great one. See Yvor Winter's hard-won praise for it in *Forms of Discovery* (n.p.: Alan Swallow, 1967), pp. 61-63.

4. M. P. Jackson, *Shakespeare's "A Lover's Complaint": Its Date and Authenticity* (Auckland, New Zealand: University of Auckland, 1965).

5. *Shakespeare's Sonnets,* ed. C. F. Tucker Brooke (London: Oxford University Press, 1936), pp. 2, 56; Brents Stirling, *The Shakespeare Sonnet Order* (Berkeley and Los Angeles: University of California Press, 1968), pp. 223-225.

6. Brooke gives some of the indications, *Sonnets,* ed. Brooke, pp. 25-26. See also Winifred Nowottny, "Some Features of Form and Style in Sonnets 97-126," *New Essays on Shakespeare's Sonnets,* ed. Hilton Landry (New

York: AMS Press, Inc., 1976), pp. 65–66. This book is henceforth cited as *New Essays*, ed. Landry.

7. The phrase is Douglas Bush's, in his introduction to *Shakespeare's Sonnets*, ed. Douglas Bush and Alfred Harbage (Baltimore: Penguin Books, 1961, paper), p. 9.

8. W. H. Auden, in his introduction to William Shakespeare, *The Sonnets*, ed. William Burto (New York: New American Library, 1964, paper), pp. xxi–xxii.

9. Stirling, *Sonnet Order*, p. 16.

10. *Ibid.*, pp. 18–21.

11. *Sonnets*, ed. Brooke, pp. 1–2.

12. *Ibid.*, p. 65.

13. Stirling, *Sonnet Order*, p. 293.

14. *Ibid.*, p. 280.

15. *Ibid.*, p. 292.

16. *Ibid.*, p. 304, note 6.

17. *Ibid.*, pp. 291, 283–286 (in that order).

18. *Ibid.*, pp. 21, 23.

Chapter 2
The Biographical Questions

1. For instance, when he finds that the best antibiographical arguments, combined, are only "fully as plausible as any yet presented for *a* definite individual," *Sonnets*, ed. Rollins (Variorum), II: 251.

2. For instance, Northrop Frye, in "How True a Twain," *The Riddle of Shakespeare's Sonnets*, by Edward Hubler and others (London: Routledge & Kegan Paul, 1962), pp. 25–53, after pages of scorn against biographical interpreting, admits on p. 37 that the sonnets may be biographical; W. H. Auden, in his Introduction to William Shakespeare, *The Sonnets*, ed. William Burto (New York: New American Library, 1964, paper), pp. xvii–xxxviii, also belittles biographical interpreting at length, but then writes that the sonnets make an impression of "naked autobiographical confession," pp. xxxiv, and discusses the unpleasant "impression we get of his [Shakespeare's] friend," pp. xxxiii–xxxiv; Barbara Herrnstein Smith, in the Introduction to her edition, *William Shakespeare, Sonnets* (New York: Avon Books, 1969, paper), pp. 11–43, speaks of "putative biographers" writing "sentimental novel[s]," p. 19, yet also says, "That there was a historical counterpart to the young man . . . is hard to doubt," p. 18.

3. *Sonnets*, ed. Rollins (Variorum), II: 251.

4. The argument is advanced by, among others, A. C. Bradley, *Oxford Lectures on Poetry*, 2nd ed. (London: Macmillan, 1909), p. 331, and Edward Hubler, *The Sense of Shakespeare's Sonnets* (Princeton: Princeton University Press, 1952), p. 8: "If Shakespeare had set out to tell a story, he would have told it better." Counter-arguments are offered by Rollins, *Sonnets*, ed. Rollins (Variorum), II: 146, "one might hazard the conjecture that some of the lyrics . . . , the 'broken links,' have not survived," and James Winny, *The Master-Mistress* (London: Chatto & Windus, 1968), pp. 6, 20–22. Hubler, Rollins, and Winny do not commit themselves for or against the biographical nature of the sonnets. All three hold that the aesthetic questions are of more importance. I agree, but also affirm that the aesthetic and other problems are inescapably intertwined.

5. Rowse announced her, "Revealed at Last, Shakespeare's Dark Lady," London *Times*, January 29, 1973, p. 12. Among early comments were those in the London *Times*, February 1, 1973, p. 17; February 2, p. 15 (Agatha Christie, no less); February 6, p. 15; February 14, p. 15; February 15, p. 19; February 17, p. 15; February 20, p. 15; and February 22, p. 17. Rowse claimed in the *Times* article to have reached "the definite answer" by "following rigorous historical and literary method." He reasserted his claim, with equal certainty but less evidence (dropping along the way the claims that her husband was named Will and that Simon Forman had written she was "very brown in youth") in Rowse's books, *Shakespeare the Man*, 2nd ed. (London: Macmillan, 1973), pp. 105–113, and *Sex and Society in Shakespeare's Age* (New York: Charles Scribner's Sons, 1974), pp. 99–116. Much of the case against Rowse is summed by Louis Marder in "The Dark Lady: Demise of a Theory," *Shakespeare Newsletter*, 23(1973): 24.

6. Her husband's name apparently being Alfonso rather than Will, is some evidence against her, since Sonnets 134–136, which pun on the name Will, make better sense if Will was her husband's name as well as Shakespeare's and probably the young man's. Were the evidence conclusive, it would dismiss Mrs. Lanier's claims. The evidence is not conclusive, since the pun may not apply, as name, to all three men; since her husband may have been nicknamed Will; or since Shakespeare may not have known the husband's name. Still, it is some evidence against her candidacy. A. L. Rowse took it as good evidence when he believed Will to be her husband's name (see note 5, supra), but did not use it as evidence to lessen her claim when he became convinced that her husband's name was Alfonso (*Shakespeare the Man*, p. 109; *Sex and Society*, Index, p. 312, s.v. Lanier).

7. The young man is repeatedly made the epitome of fairness, which is not merely conventional since his fairness is contrasted with the dark lady's darkness, including her black hair. The "right fair" in line 144.3 certainly sounds blond, and in Sonnet 68 Shakespeare comes very close to saying that the young man's hair was "golden." He makes the young man the model of all

past beauty ("And him as for a map doth nature store,/ To show false art what beauty was of yore" [68.13–14]), most specifically the model for "the golden tresses of the dead" (68.5), an odd thing to do if the young man's hair was dark brown or red. Compare "golden time" (3.12) in a passage speaking of the young man's appearance.

Of the two reasons given for thinking the young man's hair was dark brown, one is highly inconclusive as evidence, line 99.7, "And buds of marjoram had stol'n thy hair." The reference is more likely to scent than color, since marjoram is an herb (Cf. *All's Well that Ends Well*, IV. v. 16–19); the poem is a conventional kind (a floral *effictio*, itemization of beauties) seldom to be taken literally; and marjoram buds at different times and in the normal senses of *bud*, can be correctly described as dark purple-red, pink, dark brown, green, white, or lavender, which would make a various theft.

The other reason advanced for thinking his hair brown is the "browny locks" of the seducer in line 85 of *A Lover's Complaint*. Hints exist, including the "deep-brain'd sonnets" of line 209, that the young man of the sonnets may be a model or the model for the young man in that poem. Hence "browny" is at least a possible color. But what color? The *Oxford English Dictionary* gives only three citations for that rare word, a nineteenth-century one, the one in *A Lover's Complaint*, and a 1582 reference to a "brownye lion." Lions are a blond sort of brown. Dark brown and black, moreover, do not sufficiently contrast.

The word *golden* occasionally means red in Shakespeare, as in the "golden blood" of *Macbeth*, II. iii. 112. Hence red or brown are possible colors for the young man's hair. But blond is more likely.

8. That disguised initials were employed, for fun or self-protection, by authors of the period, is shown by Franklin B. Williams, Jr., "An Initiation into Initials," *Studies in Bibliography*, 9(1957): 163–178, in which he shows different forms of juggling, many of his examples being reversals. Hence H. W. would be the second most likely initials for the young man. Following up some of the patterns actually used, one can say that the young man might be [John] WH[istlecraft] or [Crumlo]W H[alfshank] or H[enry] W[indsore] or W[alter, Mayor of] H[arlequin] or W[hat] H[ave you]. The possibility of disguise does exist; the imputable homosexuality could be one reason for disguise. But the chance is much less than .5 to begin with, since many more initials in books were straight rather than juggled, and is reduced by the likely pun on the young man's name as Will in Sonnets 134 and 135, especially in lines 134.1–2, "So now I haue confest that he is thine,/ And I my selfe am morgag'd to thy will" (1609 ed.).

9. The possibility that Mr. W. H. was a Catholic is strengthened by the recognition that Thomas Thorpe was a Catholic and in close connection with literary Catholics, including Jonson. See Josephine Waters Bennett, "Benson's Alleged Piracy of *Shake-speares Sonnets* . . . ," *Studies in Bibliography*, 21(1968): 239, and Albert J. Loomie, *The Spanish Elizabethans* (New York: Fordham University Press, 1963), p. 50.

10. Williams, "Initials," p. 175.

11. Thus William Minto writes, in *Characteristics of English Poets* . . . , 2nd

ed. (Edinburgh: 1885), p. 217, "When we cast about for presumptions to turn the balance of probability one way or the other [that is, to Pembroke or Southampton], we . . . . " The presumption is only two candidates.

12. *The Sonnets,* ed. John Dover Wilson (Cambridge: Cambridge University Press, 1969, paper), p. xci.

13. *Shakespeare's Sonnets,* ed. C. F. Tucker Brooke (London: Oxford University Press, 1936), p. 78.

14. Quoted from *The First Folio of Shakespeare,* ed. Charlton Hinman (1623; facs. reprint, New York: W. W. Norton, 1968), sig. A2, p. 5.

15. See *Sonnets,* ed. Rollins (Variorum), II: 186.

16. Sidney Lee, *A Life of William Shakespeare,* 2nd ed. (London: 1898), p. 125, speaking with sufficient confidence: "Twenty sonnets . . . are addressed to one who is declared without periphrasis and without disguise to be a patron of the poet's verse."

17. Leslie Hotson, *Mr. W. H.* (New York: Alfred A. Knopf, 1965), p. 16, title of chapter.

18. *Ibid.,* pp. 183–186.

19. *Ibid.,* pp. 70–72.

20. *Ibid.,* pp. 72–73.

21. *Ibid.,* pp. 71–72 and 248 respectively.

22. Rollins virtually does so, *Sonnets,* ed. Rollins (Variorum), II: 239.

23. C. S. Lewis, *English Literature in the Sixteenth Century,* Oxford History of English Literature (Oxford: Clarendon Press, 1954), p. 503.

24. For instance, Marchette Chute, *Shakespeare of London* (New York: E. P. Dutton, 1950), p. 340.

25. For instance, A. L. Rowse in a note to Sonnet 86 in his edition, *Shakespeare's Sonnets* (New York: Harper & Row, 1964), p. 178.

26. For instance, Martin Seymour-Smith, in his edition. I consider his arguments later in this chapter.

27. The passage is quoted from Christopher Marlowe, *The Poems,* ed. Millar Maclure, The Revels Marlowe (London: Methuen, 1968), pp. 8–9. According to Maclure, p. 8, note to 1.61–90, no equivalent passage occurs in Marlowe's sources.

28. Quoted from J. B. Steane, *Marlowe* (Cambridge: Cambridge University Press, 1965), p. 365.

29. See Mark Eccles, *Christopher Marlowe in London* (1934; reprint ed., New York: Octagon Books, 1967), pp. 36–37; Frederick S. Boas, *Christopher Marlowe* (Oxford: Clarendon Press, 1940), pp. 251–252.

30. See Marlowe, *Poems,* ed. Maclure, p. xxi.

31. *Shakespeare's Sonnets,* ed. Martin Seymour-Smith (New York: Barnes & Noble, 1966), p. 23. Seymour-Smith offers the traditional arguments for Chapman, pp. 21–24. He dismisses Marlowe as too early, p. 21, but admits the applicability of "the proud full sail of his great verse" to Marlowe, *ibid.,* and says that Marlowe had homosexual feelings, *ibid.*

32. *Ouids Banquet of Sence* (London: 1595), sig. A2v. In "A Coronet for his Mistresse Philosophie" in the same book, he attacks love poetry in favor of philosophical verse.

33. Quoted from first edition (London: 1598), sig. B4v (italics in text), 1.225–228 in Maclure's edition and other modern editions.

34. A. L. Rowse, *Christopher Marlowe* (New York: Harper & Row, 1964), p. 185.

35. For instance, in *2 Henry IV,* II. iv. 177–181, which echoes the chariot episode in the second part of *Tamburlaine,* IV. iii. 1–4; and in the cruel twisting in *Richard II,* IV. i. 276–291, of the "topless towers" passage in *Dr. Faustus,* V. i. 99–119, an imitation which John Bakeless in *The Tragical History of Christopher Marlowe,* 2 vols. (Cambridge, Mass.: Harvard University Press, 1942), II: 43, calls with reason "derisive." The derision by Shakespeare was the more ungracious because of his flubbed attempt to imitate Marlowe's passage in *Lucrece,* lines 1520–1526.

36. For instance, in the passage including Sir Hugh Evan's drunken rendition of "Come live with me and be my love" in *The Merry Wives of Windsor,* III. i. 11–30. The botching of that lovely lyric is hardly kind to Marlowe.

37. See Boas, *Marlowe,* p. 230, and my two preceding notes.

38. See *Marlowe,* Poems, ed. Maclure, pp. xx–xxiii, for a good discussion and summary of that "cloud of hostile witnesses" (p. xx). F. P. Wilson has some excellent things to say on the problems of Marlowe's character in *Marlowe and the Early Shakespeare* (Oxford: Clarendon Press, 1953), pp. 38–56.

39. See G. K. Hunter's splendid discussion, "The Theology of Marlowe's *The Jew of Malta,*" *Journal of the Warburg and Courtauld Institutes,* 27(1964): 221–225. See also his concluding view of Marlowe as "God-haunted atheist" on p. 240. The phrase "infinite riches in a little room" occurs in *The Jew of Malta,* I. i. 37, in H. S. Bennett's edition (1931; reprint ed., New York: Gordian Press, 1966) and other modern editions.

40. See Leslie Hotson, *The Death of Christopher Marlowe* (Cambridge, Mass.: Harvard University Press, 1925) for a study of that scene and aftermath. See also Boas, *Marlowe,* pp. 265–283.

41. See Boas, *Marlowe,* p. 283 and n., who gives a brief summary of the controversy about the allusion. See also, George Chapman, *The Poems of*

George Chapman, ed. Phyllis Brooks Bartlett (1941; reprint ed., New York: Russell and Russell, 1962), p. 432, n. 9; and Hunter, "Theology," passim. In the various parallels cited it is only Shakespeare who uses the crucial word *reckoning.*

42. See H. R. D. Anders, *Shakespeare's Books* (1904; reprint ed., New York: AMS Press, Inc., 1965), pp. 92-100, esp. 96, for further resemblances of *Hero and Leander* to Shakespeare's works, including some of the sonnets.

43. Arthur Acheson, *Shakespeare and the Rival Poet* (London: John Lane, 1903) began the controversy (pp. 90-91), finding George Chapman to be the rival poet and a member of the school (pp. 90-99). Muriel C. Bradbrook's *The School of Night* (Cambridge: Cambridge University Press, 1936) sums up opinion. Walter Oakeshott, *The Queen and the Poet* (London: Faber and Faber, 1960) gathers the arguments in favor of Sir Walter Raleigh as leader. The evidence adduced in this chapter does show that some joke at some group is intended, but no evidence so far conclusively establishes what group, whether Raleigh's school of atheism (in my judgment the most likely), a group of poets, or whatever. Marlowe had diverse relationships with many people, poets, playwrights, free-thinkers, spies, publishers among them; and people have connections with people. For the school of night, connections have been drawn between Sir Walter Raleigh, Thomas Hariot, the Earl of Derby, Lord Hunsdon (remember his affair with Emilia Bassano — do dark ladies work by night?), the Duke of Northumberland, George Chapman, Christopher Marlowe, Thomas Kyd, William Warner, Matthew Roydon, Edward Blount (a friend and associate of Thomas Thorpe, which brings us back to Shakespeare's sonnets again). The trick is to limit the web.

44. J. C. Maxwell, in "'Hero and Leander' and 'Love's Labour's Lost'," *Notes & Queries,* 197(1952): 334-335, shows that Shakespeare echoes Marlowe's *Hero and Leander,* 1.49-50, in *Love's Labor's Lost,* IV. iii. 262-264. The passages respectively follow:

Therefore in signe her treasure suffred wracke,
Since *Heroes* time, hath halfe the world been blacke.
(1598; italics in text)

Duma[ine].   To looke like her are Chimnie-sweepers blake.
Long[aville.] And since her time are Colliers counted bright.
King.   And *AEthiops* of their sweet complexion crake.
(1598; italics in text)

The passage in *Love's Labor's Lost* occurs very close to the school-of-night passage. The parody is manifest and strengthens the likelihood of the echo of Marlowe in the school-of-night passage being parody. I might add, for those suspicious of ways of search and circularity, that I read Maxwell's article and thereby noted the parody of *Hero and Leander* after I had discovered the parody of *The Massacre at Paris.*

45. Quoted from Christopher Marlowe, *The Massacre at Paris* (London: n.d. [1602?]), sigs. A4-A4v, italics in text (I. ii. 1-8 in modern eds.).

Chapter 3
The Date of Composition

1. E. D., *The Prayse of Nothing* (London: 1585), sig. C1, italics in text.

2. See Leslie Hotson, *I, William Shakespeare* (London: Jonathan Cape, 1937), pp. 53–59.

3. Henry Willoughby, *Willobie His Avisa* (London: 1594), sig. L2. (The Folger copy of the 1605 edition has a memorable misprint, reading "old prayer," sig. L2v, for "old player," with more propriety for 1605 than for 1594.)

4. James McManaway writes, in a discussion of the dating sonnets, "it is unsafe to assume that . . . [an Elizabethan poet] would employ. . . [an] allusion only in the months following the event," "The Year's Contribution to Shakespearian Study: Textual Studies [1951]," *Studies in Shakespeare, Bibliography, and Theater* (New York: Shakespeare Association of America, 1969), p. 325.

5. Leslie Hotson, *Mr. W. H.* (New York: Alfred A. Knopf, 1965), pp. 84–92.

6. See John Dover Wilson's note to this line in his edition, *The Sonnets* (Cambridge: Cambridge University Press, 1969, paper), also pp. lxxxiii–lxxxiv.

7. *Ibid.*, p. lxxiv.

8. Patricia Thomson, "The Date Clue in Shakespeare's Sonnet 98," *Neophilologus*, 50(1966): 262–269.

9. See Rollins, *Sonnets* (Variorum), II: 63–65.

10. Arthur Beatty, "Shakespeare's Sonnets and Plays," in *Shakespeare Studies . . . University of Wisconsin* (Madison: University of Wisconsin, 1916), pp. 201–214, finds ten sonnets in the plays. Three sonnets occur in *Romeo and Juliet*, the prologues to Acts I and II, and I. v. 93–106; five in *Love's Labor's Lost*, I. i. 80–93, I. i. 162–175, IV. ii. 105–118, IV. iii. 25–40, IV. iii. 58–71; one in *Henry V*, the epilogue; one in *All's Well that Ends Well*, III. iv. 4–17.

11. Similarly, Shakespeare mocks a convention but especially his own use of it, in *Love's Labor's Lost*: "a hand, a foote, a face, an eye: a gate, a state, a brow, a brest, a wast, a legge, a limme" (1598, sig. Fl; IV. iii. 182–184). Elizabethan poets offered such lists in basic iambic pentametric form (see examples in Chapter Six). The parody is closer to line 106.6 of Shakespeare's sonnets, "Of hand, of foote, of lip, of eye, of brow," than to the other examples of the form. Note the sequence hand-foot-eye-brow in Shakespeare's line 106.6 and the parody.

12. Robert Tofte, *Alba* (London: 1598), sig. G5.

13. For instance, F. W. Bateson, "Elementary, My Dear Hotson," *Essays in Criticism*, 1(1951): 81–88; Alfred Harbage, "Dating Shakespeare's Sonnets," *Shakespeare Quarterly*, 1(1950): 58; C. S. Lewis, *English Literature in the*

Sixteenth Century, Oxford History of English Literature (Oxford: Clarendon Press, 1954), p. 502.

14. Lewis, *Sixteenth Century,* p. 503.

15. *Ibid.,* p. 502.

16. See H. C. Beeching, in his edition, *The Sonnets of Shakespeare* (Boston: Athenaeum Press, 1904), pp. xvi–xvii, who also connects Sebastian in *Twelfth Night* with the young man.

17. William Shakespeare, *Supplement to . . . Shakspeare's Plays Published . . . by Samuel Johnson and George Steevens,* ed. Edmond Malone (London: 1780), p. 581n. Malone puts it strongly, but I believe rightly: "In these compositions, Daniel's Sonnets, which were published in 1592, appear to me to have been the model that Shakespeare followed."

18. Claes Schaar, *An Elizabethan Sonnet Problem,* Lund Studies in English (Lund, Sweden: C. W. K. Gleerup, 1960).

19. Samuel Daniel, *Poems and a Defence of Ryme,* ed. Arthur Colby Sprague, first paper edition (Chicago: University of Chicago Press, 1965), p. 9, italics in text.

20. *Ibid.,* the sonnet beginning "WHy should I sing in verse, why should I frame," pp. 174–175; the sonnet beginning "O Whether (poore forsaken) wilt thou goe," pp. 187–188; and the sonnet beginning "AS to the Roman that would free his Land," pp. 188–189.

21. *Ibid.,* p. 23 for text and p. 179 for emendation.

22. Quoted from *The Complete Poetical Works of Spenser,* ed. R. E. Neil Dodge (Boston: Houghton Mifflin, 1908), p. 692.

23. Schaar, *Sonnet Problem,* esp. pp. 179–180.

24. See Lewis, *Sixteenth Century,* pp. 491–493; D. G. Rees, "Italian and Italianate Poetry," in *Elizabethan Poetry,* ed. John Russell Brown and Bernard Harris, Stratford-upon-Avon Studies 2 (New York: St. Martin's Press, 1960), pp. 62–63.

25. Schaar, *Sonnet Problem,* pp. 170–172.

26. *Ibid.,* pp. 173–178, the most convincing being the change in the 1602 edition of line 42.11 in the 1592 edition.

27. F. T. Prince, in "The Sonnet from Wyatt to Shakespeare," in *Elizabethan,* ed. Brown, p. 25, finds that Sonnets 30–36 in *Delia* had a strong impact on Shakespeare.

28. Frederick S. Boas, *Christopher Marlowe* (Oxford: Clarendon Press, 1940), p. 151.

29. Cf. Hallett Smith, *Elizabethan Poetry* (Cambridge, Mass.: Harvard University Press, 1952), pp. 176–177.

Chapter 4
The Metrical Rules of the Sonnets

1. Cf. Stephen Booth, *An Essay on Shakespeare's Sonnets* (New Haven and London: Yale University Press, 1969), p. 60; Winifred Nowottny, "Formal Elements in Shakespeare's Sonnets," *Essays in Criticism,* 2(1952): 76. I would add that lines 76.1 and 76.2 are the only consecutive lines in the sonnets ending with a pyrrhic-spondaic combination. The sameness is a variation and quick change.

2. Shakespeare parodies metrical jargon in *Love's Labor's Lost,* IV. ii. 119–120 and elsewhere.

3. The Razor was not Ockham's invention, going back at least to Odo Rigaldus, nor did Ockham apparently use the form "Entities must not be multiplied without necessity (*Entia non sunt multiplicanda sine necessitate*)." He preferred "Plurality is not to be posited without necessity (*Pluritatis non est ponenda sine necessitate*)," according to Philotheus Boehner, "Introduction" to William of Ockham, *Philosophical Writings* (Indianapolis: Bobbs-Merrill, 1964, paper), pp. xx–xxi. "Rigaldus's Razor" would therefore be a better term, in truth and by the Razor, but the phrase "Ockham's Razor" has stuck in the language. Borrowed razors still may shave fine.

4. Their theory can be found in developed and revised form in Morris Halle and Samuel Jay Keyser, *English Stress* (New York: Harper & Row, 1971), pp. 164–180; it is further defended in Halle and Keyser, "English III: The Iambic Pentameter," *Versification,* ed. W. K. Wimsatt (New York: New York University Press for Modern Language Association, 1972), pp. 217–237. For some of the varied criticism and comment, see *Poetics,* No. 12, ed. by Joseph C. Beaver and J. F. Ihwe (The Hague: Mouton, 1974), esp. Joseph C. Beaver, "Generative Metrics: The Present Outlook," pp. 7–28; Wolfgang Klein, "Critical Remarks on Generative Metrics," pp. 29–48; and A. Walter Bernhart, "Complexity and Metricality," pp. 113–141; including references; and some essays in *Poetics,* Vol. 4, No. 4 (No. 16). A newer system is offered by Paul Kiparsky, "The Rhythmic Structure of English Verse," *Linguistic Inquiry,* 8(Spring 1977, No. 2): 189–247. The linguists have much yet to explore and to offer, especially in describing complexity of variations within meter (note the title of Bernhart's essay mentioned earlier in this note), and I plan to have more to say on the topic. One crucial requirement is that linguists do not impose lexical-stress or other "objective" describing, but that they listen; meter and rhythm depend on actual and ideal contours within given lines and on *heard* comparative stress.

5. In *Delia* (1592), fifty sonnets, 700 lines, I count 104 trochees in the first foot and twenty internal trochees after a verse-pause. See Table 4.

6. Daniel never to my knowledge quite declares or implies that trochees are not allowed in iambic verse, but he comes very close in *A Defence of Ryme* (1603), in *Poems and a Defence of Ryme,* ed. Arthur Colby Sprague (Chicago:

University of Chicago Press, 1930), p. 150, lines 735-738, 754-761; pp. 151-152, lines 792-824) and gives no hint anywhere in the essay that they are allowed.

7. See T. S. Omond, *English Metrists* (1921; reprint ed., New York: Phaeton Press, 1968), p. 29.

8. Thomas Campion, *Observations in the Art of English Poesie* (1602) in *The Works of Thomas Campion*, ed. Walter R. Davis (Garden City, New York: Doubleday, 1967), pp. 294-295. His chiding is evidence both that trochees were used by poets and disallowed by prosodists.

9. Both Halle and Keyser, *Stress*, and Noam Chomsky and Morris Halle, *The Sound Pattern of English* (New York: Harper & Row, 1968) deal mainly with stress contours of words, compound words, and noun phrases, offering nothing to solve the question whether, for instance, line 116.1, "Let me not to the marriage of true mindes" (which I scan tti for the first three feet) had a different contour for Shakespeare than for us. If evidence exists to solve such problems, I do not know what it is (any help — here as elsewhere — would be appreciated).

10. For instance, Dorothy L. Sipe, *Shakespeare's Metrics* (New Haven: Yale University Press, 1968), p. 32, summing standard opinion; and Baastian A. P. van Dam and Cornelis Stoffel, *William Shakespeare: Prosody and Text* (Leiden: E. J. Brill, 1900), p. 199.

11. Enid Hamer, *The Metres of English Poetry*, 4th ed. (London: Methuen, 1951), p. 11; van Dam and Stoffel, *Prosody*, p. 198. Arnold Stein, "Donne and the Couplet," *Publications of the Modern Language Association*, 57(1942): 680, finds them only in Donne.

12. Campion, *Works*, ed. Davis, p. 299. So Daniel, *Poems*, ed. Sprague, p. 150.

13. In lines 22.8, 25.6, 39.3, 42.6, 42.9, 70.9, 98.5, 101.14, 108.2, 108.4, 110.3, 115.13, 116.1, 125.13, 130.2, 136.13, 140.1, 151.4.

14. Quoted from *Paradise Lost 1667* (Menston, England: Scolar Press, 1968, facs.), sig. F3v, 2.621. See the discussion of W. K. Wimsatt and Monroe Beardsley, "The Concept of Meter," *Hateful Contraries* (Lexington: University of Kentucky Press, 1965), pp. 133-134.

15. Seventeen occurrences of two successive trochees are in the first and second feet, in lines 8.2, 12.9, 19.7, 22.7, 30.12, 42.7, 62.12, 71.13, 73.11, 102.11, 107.6, 116.1, 120.3, 121.3, 121.9, 139.3, 153.4; one in the second and third feet, line 22.13; six in the third and fourth feet, in lines 59.9, 69.1, 87.5, 109.4, 136.2, 136.14; two in the fourth and fifth feet, lines 19.2, 25.7. In lines 8.2, 42.7, 62.12, 87.5, 116.1, 121.9, and 139.3, one of the two trochees is unmetrical (see the list of unmetrical feet later in this chapter); all the others are metrical.

16. *Romeo and Juliet*, II. i. 7; *King Lear*, V. iii. 309; *The Tempest*, IV. i. 143. Other examples of five successive trochees include *The Taming of the Shrew*, I. i. 48; *As You Like It*, II. vii. 145; *Timon of Athens*, IV. ii. 1. See Matthew Bayfield, *The Measures of the Poets* (Cambridge: Cambridge University Press, 1919), pp. 46, 102.

17. I count, applying the same rules as those adduced for Shakespeare, twenty-one unmetrical feet in the 474 lines of John Donne's "The First Anniversary," in *The Poems of John Donne,* ed. Herbert J. C. Grierson, 2 vols. (London: Oxford University Press, 1912), I, 231–245. Since there are 2,370 feet in the 474 lines (each line has five feet), about .9 of 1% of the feet are unmetrical, which is about 4½ times as frequent as the unmetricalities in Shakespeare's sonnets. In Donne's "Satyre I," *Ibid.,* I, 145–149, I count, applying the same rules (but not counting as unmetrical the anapests, internal feminine endings, or hexameters, which Donne allows but Shakespeare does not allow in the sonnets), forty-six unmetricalities in 112 lines (561 feet, since one line is a hexameter), a percentage of 8% unmetricalities, which is forty times as frequent as in Shakespeare's sonnets. The comparison shows a very clear difference in metrical practice. Whether Donne is being unmetrical depends on what is exactly or inexactly meant. He certainly in the Satire is allowing trochees in all five feet without rules for justification, and the sprung rhymes. Thus, in a sense, none of the unmetricalities are unmetrical, departures from the norm of his deliberate practice in this poem. Yet he knows the rules (as the count of "The First Anniversary" shows), and deliberately breaks them, or sets them aside, for rough and tumble rhythmical effects.

18. This limited definition suffices for the sonnets, since they lack internal extra syllables.

19. Hamer, *Meters,* p. 13 and elsewhere, speaks of amphibrachs rather than feminine endings.

20. So Philip Timberlake, *The Feminine Ending in English Blank Verse* (Menasha, Wis.: George Banta, 1931), pp. 3–4.

21. This sort of rhyme occurred fairly frequently in Elizabethan poetry. The earliest discussion I know of is Edwin Guest's, in *A History of English Rhythms,* 2 vols. (London: 1838), I: 147, who calls it "a serious blunder." Some of the other discussions are R. E. Neil Dodge, "An Obsolete Elizabethan Mode of Rhyming," in *Shakespeare Studies . . . University of Wisconsin* (Madison: University of Wisconsin, 1916), pp. 174–200; G. C. Moore Smith, "The Use of an Unstressed Extra-Metrical Syllable To Carry the Rime," *Modern Language Review,* 15(1920): 300–301; Helge Kökeritz, *Shakespeare's Pronunciation* (New Haven: Yale University Press, 1953), pp. 34–35.

22. Stanza 10 of Thomas Rogers's poem "The Tragedy of Sir Walter Raleigh" quoted from Folger MS X.d.241, fol. 2.

23. See Chapter One, note 4.

24. Folger MS X.d.177, fol. 8v, upside down.

25. Frederic W. Ness, *The Use of Rhyme in Shakespeare's Plays* (New Haven: Yale University Press, 1941), pp. 134–135, refers to the rhyme "they" & "days" in *2 Henry IV,* V. iii. 140&141 and comments: "Some modern editions print *day* in the singular form for the sake of the rhyme, but the *-s* did not destroy the rhyme for the Elizabethans" (italics in text). William Sidney Walker, *A Critical Examination of the Text of Shakespeare,* 3 vols. (London: 1860) gives a number

of examples in Elizabethan verse of various inexact consonantal rhyming, I: 132–143, followed by a number of examples of rhymes of one word ending in -*s* with another word which does not, I: 143–145.

26. Cf. *Venus and Adonis*, 47&48, "broken" & "open," and Daniel, *Delia* (1592), 15.6&8, "spoken" & "open." Shakespeare is probably echoing Daniel in both places.

27. E. A. Abbott, *A Shakespearian Grammar* (1870; reprint ed., New York: Dover Publications, 1966, paper), p. 242, sec. 340. W. G. Ingram and Theodore Redpath, ed., *Shakespeare's Sonnets* (London: University of London Press, 1964), p. 6, n. to this line, point out that Abbott cites this line without noting that it is an emendation. They accept the emendation, but wonder "whether the Elizabethan reader would have been troubled by the rhyme."

28. Two astute and sensitive studies of the change of metrical styles from Gascoigne to the best Elizabethans are John Thompson, *The Founding of English Meter* (London: Routledge & Kegan Paul, 1961) and Donald C. Freeman, "On the Primes of Metrical Styles," *Linguistics and Literary Style*, ed. Donald C. Freeman (New York: Holt, Rinehart and Winston, 1970, paper), pp. 448–491, esp. pp. 464–480.

29. The lines from Spenser are quoted from *Spenser's Faerie Queene*, ed. J. C. Smith, 2 vols. (Oxford: Clarendon Press, 1909).

Chapter 5
Rhetoric and the Sonnets

1. See, among others, T. W. Baldwin, *William Shakspere's Small Latine & Less Greeke* (Urbana: University of Illinois Press, 1944), esp. pp. 29–68; and Wilbur Samuel Howell, *Logic and Rhetoric in England* (Princeton: Princeton University Press, 1956), esp. pp. 12–63. Rosemond Tuve's *Elizabethan and Metaphysical Imagery* (Chicago: University of Chicago Press, 1947) remains the best study I know of the relations between Renaissance rhetoric and logic and the actual workings of poetry.

2. John Dryden, "Of Dramatic Poesy" (1668), *Of Dramatic Poesy and Other Critical Essays*, ed. George Watson, 2 vols. (London: J. M. Dent & Sons, 1962), I: 22. Cf. J. V. Cunningham's typically plain and typically laconic remark, "The difficulty with the flat style [the Elizabethan plain style], of course, is that it is flat," "Lyric Style in the 1590's," *The Problem of Style*, ed. J. V. Cunningham (Greenwich, Conn.: Fawcett Publications, 1966), p. 168.

3. Richard A. Lanham, *A Handlist of Rhetorical Terms* (Berkeley and Los Angeles: University of California Press, 1968). Lee Ann Sonnino's highly useful *A Handbook of Sixteenth-Century Rhetoric* (London: Routledge & Kegan Paul, 1968) also does considerable crossclassifying.

4. Walter J. Ong, *Ramus* (Cambridge, Mass.: Harvard University Press, 1958), p. 274. Father Ong discusses, e.g., pp. 272–274, the theoretical limi-

tations of Renaissance rhetoric, including the too neat division of scheme and trope.

5. *Ibid.*, pp. 273–274, 275–276. Sonnino, *Handbook*, pp. 243–246 and foldout, lists the major Renaissance systems for dividing rhetoric, but then significantly offers her own more extensive and usable divisions in "Descriptive Index of Tropes and Schemes," pp. 247–266. See also Sister Miriam Joseph, *Shakespeare's Use of the Arts of Language* (New York: Columbia University Press, 1947), p. 35, a page graphically illustrative of the point.

6. See Lanham, *Handlist*, pp. 101–103.

7. See Tuve, *Imagery*, who firmly defends Renaissance rhetoricians and poets on this issue, e.g., pp. 28–32, 33–38, 138–144. Note, however, her grudging concessions on pp. 38–39 and 142–143, esp. p. 39, note 17.

8. Samuel Daniel, *A Defence of Ryme* (1603), *Poems and a Defence of Ryme*, ed. Arthur Colby Sprague (Chicago: The University of Chicago Press, 1930), p. 145.

9. J. B. Leishman, *Themes and Variations in Shakespeare's Sonnets* (London: Hutchinson, 1961), p. 157.

10. *Ibid.*, pp. 153–154.

11. Daniel, *Poems*, ed. Sprague, p. 135.

12. The following definitions are from Lanham, *Handlist*:

Atticism, "a style that is the opposite of . . . ornamental" (p. 18)
brevitas, "concise expression" (p. 20)
comma, "a short phrase or dependent clause" (p. 25)
parrhesia, "candid speech" (p. 73)
aporia, "true or feigned doubt" (p. 15)
dehortatio, "dissuasion" (p. 31)
exprobatio, "reproaching someone as ungrateful or impious" (pp. 50, 69)
syngnome, "forgiveness of injuries" (p. 97)
hypotaxis, "an arrangement of clauses . . . in a . . . subordinate relationship" (p. 57)
parataxis, "clauses or phrases arranged independently" (p. 71)

13. The problem is discussed as long ago as Quintilian, *Institutio Oratorio*, 9.1.10–14. See Joseph, *Shakespeare's Use*, pp. 32–33. Quintilian notes that *figura* can apply to all language or to language changed from the ordinary, and he chooses the latter: "Ergo figura sit arte aliqua novata forma dicendi" (9.1.14, "Therefore let *figure* mean some new form of expression made by art," trans. mine), from *The Institutio Oratorio of Quintilian*, The Loeb Classical Library trans. H. E. Butler, 4 vols. (Cambridge, Mass.: Harvard University Press, 1921), III: 354. But with that definition natural figures of speech are excluded, and the problem is with us.

Cf. Robert O. Evans, *The Osier Cage* (Lexington: University of Kentucky Press, 1966), p. 4, and Ong, *Ramus*, p. 274, who speaks of "the attempt to describe and classify the unusual without being able to identify what the usual is."

14. See I. A. Richards' witty rhetorical analysis, pp. 23–24, of some discussions about rhetoric, in his essay "The Places and the Figures," *Kenyon Review*, 11(1949): 17–30. Richards wishes to play down rhetorical learning in favor of talent and critical judgment, but is talented, and learned, enough to admit that formal rhetoric did play a part in Shakespeare's development, whether necessarily or not. All in all, he underplays the importance of Shakespeare's actual rhetorical education, but has some keen remarks on the dangers of rhetorical exfoliation and side-tracking, for instance, "As with other ancillary studies — grammar, prosody, phonetics among them — what was intended to become a help became a hindrance, preventing the student from remembering the true subject of all his study," p. 30.

15. Cf. Evans, *Osier Cage*, p. 11.

16. Tuve, *Imagery*, esp. pp. 110–115, 347–349.

17. E. K., gloss to Edmund Spenser, *The Shepheardes Calender* (London: 1586), sig. A2v. E. K. is glossing a line in *"Ianuarie. Aegloga Prima"* (italics in text): "I loue thilke lasse, (alas why doe I loue?)/ And am forlorne, (alas why am I lorne?)," sig. A2, lines 61–62 in modern eds.

18. Hardin Craig, "Shakespeare and Formal Logic," in *Studies in English Philology . . . in Honor of Frederick Klaeber*, ed. Kemp Malone and Martin B. Ruud (Minneapolis: University of Minnesota Press, 1929), pp. 380–396.

19. Roland Mushat Frye, *Shakespeare and Christian Doctrine* (Princeton: Princeton University Press, 1963), esp. pp. 10–11 and context.

20. Henry Peacham, *The Garden of Eloquence* (London: 1577), sigs. H4v–14.

21. *Ibid.*, sig. I3v.

22. *Ibid.*

23. *Ibid.*, sig. G3v.

24. Cf. Hallett Smith's discussion of plainness and complexity in Sidney, *Elizabethan Poetry* (Cambridge, Mass.: Harvard University Press, 1952), pp. 150–153.

25. Aristotle, *The "Art" of Rhetoric*, trans. John Henry Freese, The Loeb Classical Library (Cambridge, Mass.: Harvard University Press, 1926), Book 2, Chapter 25, 1402b–1403a, finds that enthymemes come from four sources, probability (*eikòs*, likeness), example (*parádeigma*), necessary sign (*tekmérion*), and sign (*semeîon*). Reasoning by enthymeme can be a shortened but logically valid proof; a reasoning by probability; a reasoning by analogy; a reasoning by examples; a reasoning on traditionally accepted premises; or other nonstrict or nonfull methods of persuasion.

In Book 1, Chapter 2, 1357a, Aristotle bases his rhetoric on enthymeme and example because of their kinship to the syllogism and the induction in logic.

26. Drayton's sonnet is quoted from *Ideas Mirrour* (London: 1594), Spenser's from *Amoretti* (London: 1595).

27. If the reference is to the rival poet, then the sonnet story adds one more character: the "vengeful canker" would be Ingram Frizer, who stabbed Marlowe to death on May 30, 1593.

Chapter 6
The Logic of Structure

1. The standard work on Ramus is Walter J. Ong, *Ramus* (Cambridge, Mass.: Harvard University Press, 1958) supported by Ong's bibliographical study *Ramus and Talon Inventory* (Cambridge, Mass.: Harvard University Press, 1958). See also Perry Miller, *The New England Mind: The Seventeenth Century* (Cambridge, Mass.: Harvard University Press, 1939), esp. pp. 116–153; T. W. Baldwin, *William Shakspere's Small Latine & Lesse Greeke* (Urbana: University of Illinois Press, 1944), pp. 4–7, 56–59; Wilbur Samuel Howell, *Logic and Rhetoric in England* (Princeton: Princeton University Press, 1956), pp. 146–246; Rosemond Tuve, *Elizabethan and Metaphysical Imagery* (Chicago: University of Chicago Press, 1947), pp. 331–353; Catherine M. Dunn's edition of *The Logike . . . P. Ramus,* trans. Roland MacIlmaine (1574) (Northridge, Calif.: San Fernando Valley State College Press, 1969), introduction, pp. xi–xxii.

2. Abraham Fraunce says Ramistically that invention is "absolutely and vniuersally applicable to the inuenting of any thing, either true or fained whatsoeuer," *The Lawiers Logike* (London: 1588), sig. C2v. See also Howell, *Logic,* pp. 17–28; Tuve, *Imagery,* pp. 284–299 (on the Predicaments, which invention searched among); and Donald Lemen Clark, *John Milton and St. Paul's School* (New York: Columbia University Press, 1948), pp. 14–15, 226–230. Logic was intrinsic in and a means to imagination, not its opponent.

3. See J. V. Cunningham, "Logic and Lyric," *Tradition and Poetic Structure* (Denver: Alan Swallow, 1960), pp. 40–58; and Frank Towne, "Logic, Lyric, and Drama," *Modern Philology,* 51(1954): 265–268, who, in attempting to refute Cunningham, shows much actual use of logic within poems. See also Tuve, *Imagery,* pp. 281–330.

4. The Ramists use the term *argument* to mean consecutive argument, our normal sense, but also to mean a term usable in an argument, that is, any noun. The Latin *argumentum* has a broader band of meaning than the English *argument,* but more is involved than that. The Ramists called nouns "arguments" because they believed that individual things are arguments.

Ramus himself defines *argumentum* as "quod ad aliquid arguendum affectum est: quales sunt singulae rationis solae & per se consideratae," *Dialecticae Libro Duo* (London: 1574), sig. A7. The definition is translated by Roland McIlmaine, "An argument is that which is *naturally bent* to proue or disproue anything, such as be single reasons separately and by them selues considered." *The Logike of . . . P. Ramus Martyr* (London: 1584), sig. B1. Cf. Miller, *New England Mind,* p. 124.

Abraham Fraunce, defending Ramus for holding that "euery seuerall thing considered alone is an argument" says that anyone who takes "this word Argument, onely for a proofe or confirmation, deceaueth himselfe, and bereaueth Logike of halfe hir dignitie," *Lawiers Logike*, sig. D1v.

5. Hardin Craig says, after a convincing survey of evidence, that "Shakespeare's language is fuller of logical meaning than the language of today, closer to the subject itself, and . . . Shakespeare himself understood in some detail the subject of logic as it was taught in the grammar schools of his day," "Shakespeare and Formal Logic," in *Studies in English Philology . . . in Honor of Frederick Klaeber*, ed. Kemp Malone and Martin B. Ruud (Minneapolis: University of Minnesota Press, 1929), p. 396

6. For some apposite samples of structural shapes see Barbara Herrnstein Smith, *Poetic Closure* (Chicago: University of Chicago Press, 1968), pp. 4–29.

7. See Craig, "Logic," p. 280: Hardin Craig, *The Enchanted Glass* (New York: Oxford University Press, 1936), esp. pp. 145–146; and Ong, *Ramus*, many places including the "Decay" in the subtitle *Methods and the Decay of Dialogue*, esp. pp. 146–147, 183–187, 187–189.

8. I use the still standard terms, overlapping Elizabethan terms, which are various. Thus Thomas Wilson, *The Rule of Reason* (London: 1580) refers to the hypothetical proposition as *"Proposita-Hypothetica,"* sig. G1v (italics in text); MacIlmaine calls the hypothetical syllogism "sillogisme ioyned," *Logike of Ramus*, sig. F5v, while Dudley Fenner, *The Artes of Logike and Rhetorike* (London: 1584), calls it "double or compound," sig. B4v; MacIlmaine calls the disjunctive syllogism "disioyned," *Logike of Ramus*, sig. F6v; Fenner calls it "Disioyning or disiunctive," *Artes*, sig. C1.

9. The argument is only technically invalid. Shakespeare's thought is elliptical, since he means "If flesh were thought I would be with you, but the laws of nature make my instant return impossible." The argument can be set in valid strong disjunctive form thus: "Either flesh is thought or I cannot instantly be with you." Few arguments in poetry or out are in full syllogistic form.

10. For instance, "If I tell the truth, I'll be punished; if I don't, I'll suffer remorse." The dilemma is discussed by Wilson in *Rule*, sig. K2v. See also Craig, "Logic," p. 384.

11. E. A. Abbott, *A Shakespearian Grammar* (1870; reprint ed., New York: Dover Publications, 1966, paper), p. 356, no. 471. Abbott says that the *s* for plural is often dropped after *-se* and some other letters, and that "*horse* is the old plural" (italics in text).

12. Sonnets 4, 6, 21, 24, 28, 29, 43, 44, 45, 46, 51, 55, 90, 96, 125, 133, 134, 136.

13. Whether Sonnet 148 loses the quatrain sense depends on how one understands the transition from line 148.8 to line 148.9: "Love's eye is not so true as all men's [eyes]. No,/ How can it" or "Love's *aye* [with pun on *eye*] is not so true as all men's *no*./ How can it?" I prefer the former, largely for rhythmical reasons.

14. None of the variations strikes my ears as flawed and some show the enticing metrical possibilities in quatrain over-flow, especially lines 63.1–6, 66.1–12, 104.1–8, and the comic 151.8–10.

15. See Smith, *Closure,* esp. pp. 50–56.

16. Stephen Booth, *An Essay on Shakespeare's Sonnets* (New Haven and London: Yale University Press, 1969), p. 36, n., finds also an octave in the majority (96) of the poems, though fewer than I do, perhaps because he is less concerned than I with the sound of the sonnets. He plays down the idea of sestet, pp. 44–49, since he stresses the importance of the couplet. The chief point is that Booth and I see the rhyme-paragraph structure similarly: B. C. Southem puts the pattern clearly: "the thought . . . [is] developed within the unit of the quatrain, with a shift at line nine, . . . the final couplet serving as a conclusion," "Shakespeare's Christian Sonnet? Number 146," *Shakespeare Quarterly,* 11(1960): 69.

17. An exclamation introduces the third quatrain twenty times, in Sonnets 10, 19, 22, 23, 32, 39, 41, 44, 61, 71, 72, 76, 95, 104, 114, 115, 119, 120, 121, 125, and the second quatrain nine times, in Sonnets 38, 51, 58, 59, 71, 90, 103, 116, 124, further evidence of octave sense.

18. Booth, *Essay,* p. 29.

19. *Ibid.*

20. *Ibid.,* p. 26.

21. *Ibid.,* p. 70.

22. *Ibid.,* p. 117.

23. *Ibid.,* p. 64.

24. *Ibid.,* p. 73–74, note 7.

25. So do W. G. Ingram, "The Shakespearean Quality," *New Essays,* ed. Landry, pp. 41–63, esp. pp. 52–63; and Nowottny, "Form and Style," *New Essays,* ed. Landry, pp. 65–107, esp. pp. 70–72, pp. 83–87, pp. 98–107.

26. C. S. Lewis, *English Literature in the Sixteenth Century,* Oxford History of English Literature (Oxford: Clarendon Press, 1954), p. 507, shows how *exemplum* and generalization are "exquisitely elaborated" in the poem, especially in the octave.

27. It was in Shakespeare's time a well-known fallacy; in our time it is widespread, though less often recognized as a fallacy. Wilson, *Rule,* sig. R4 (italics in text), gives as an example of sophistry what he calls in the margin the "Libertines errour":

Whatsoeuer is naturall, that same is not euill.
To synne is a thing natural.
Ergo to synne it is not euill.

He goes on to explain what is wrong with the second premise: sin is not natural; it is fallen.

Chapter 7
The Logic of Hell

1. W. H. Auden, "New Year's Letter," *The Collected Poetry of W. H. Auden* (New York: Random House, 1945), p. 292.

2. Sister Miriam Joseph, *Shakespeare's Use of the Arts of Language* (New York: Columbia University Press, 1947), pp. 130–141, gives a number of examples from Shakespeare's plays of the power of logical denial and "logical confusion" (p. 132).

3. See Philip Martin, *Shakespeare's Sonnets: Self, Love, and Art* (Cambridge: Cambridge University Press, 1972), pp. 91–92.

4. See Etienne Gilson, *The Spirit of Mediaeval Philosophy*, trans. A. H. C. Downes (New York: Charles Scribner's Sons, 1940), pp. 111–123. A compilation of relevant texts from Aquinas occurs in *St. Thomas Aquinas*, ed. Thomas Gilby (New York: Oxford University Press, 1960), pp. 163–180. See also H. A. Oberman, *The Harvest of Medieval Theology* (Cambridge, Mass.: Harvard University Press, 1963), esp. pp. 122–123 and notes. Augustine applys the puzzle to the very concept of falsehood: "et omnia vera sunt, in quantum sunt, nec quicquam est falsitas, nisi cum putatur esse quod non est," "All things are true so far forth as they have a being; nor is falsehood anything, unless while a thing is thought to be, which is not," *St. Augustine's Confessions*, trans. William Watts, ed. W. H. D. Rouse, 2 vols., The Loeb Classical Library (New York: G. P. Putnam's Sons, 1912), Book 7, Chapter 15. What Augustine says is true, and very peculiar. Mistakes are mistakes, not realities; but a world in which mistakes are possible is vastly different from a world in which mistakes cannot happen.

5. Wit, satire, and moralizing about nothing and nobody were common in the period. Richard Simpson writes, in his introduction to the play *No-Body and Some-Body* in Simpson's anthology *The School of Shakspere*, 2 vols. (New York: 1878), I: 270 that the "joke [about nothing and nobody] . . . was of venerable age at the time the play was probably written" (about 1592, revised after 1603, according to Simpson, I: 274) and gives other references. In the play itself many of the jokes are easy puns, but some satiric power and some pity are gained when we are told that "*Nobody* giues them [the poor] mony, meate, and drinke,/ If they be naked, clothes, then come poore souldiers,/ Sick, maymd, and shot, from any forraine warres,/ *Nobody* takes them in, prouides them harbor . . . Now *Nobodie* hath entertaind againe/ Long banisht Hospitalitie" (quoted from 1606 ed., sig. B4; 1.289, lines 298–308 in Simpson's ed.) *The Prayse of Nothing* (1585) begins with an apology for its light frivolity but soon turns to serious moralizing, investing its (after all, worthy) commonplaces with dignity and some memorable phrasing, e.g., "Of like passions, may large volumes be written, though worthy of no other pen, then a black coale" (sig. C2v) and "this greedy creditor the earth" (sig. D2v). John Donne's *A Nocturnal Upon Saint Lucy's Day* offers some of the most melancholy and subtle handling of such themes, and Rochester's *Upon Nothing*, with its underroar of cynical, sullen, abusive desperation, is another great poem.

6. Pierre Viret, *The World Possessed with Devils*, trans. Thomas Stocker (London: 1583), sigs. A7(First Part) and A5(Second Part) respectively.

7. Thomas Wilson, *The Arte of Rhetorique* (London: 1585), sig. E5v.

8. This meaning of *naught* touched Shakespeare's family when in July, 1613, his daughter Susanna Hall entered an action for slander against John Lane for alleging that she had "bin naught with Rafe Smith," according to E. K. Chambers, *William Shakespeare*, 2 vols. (Oxford: Clarendon Press, 1930), II: 12–13.

9. J. V. Cunningham, *The Exclusions of a Rhyme* (Denver: Alan Swallow, 1960), p. 60.

10. Sir Philip Sidney, *The Countess of Pembroke's Arcadia*, ed. H. Oskar Sommer (1590; facs. reprint, London: 1891), 1.12.5, sig. H4.

11. See Sonnets 21, 68, 82, 127, 142, and compare Sonnet 67, which gives the fundamental grounds of objection.

12. A. W. Verity, in *The Works of William Shakespeare*, ed. Henry Irving and Frank A. Marshall, 8 vols. (London: 1888–1890), VIII: 435, n. 31.

13. Quoted from *Spenser's Faerie Queene*, ed. J. C. Smith, 2 vols. (Oxford: Clarendon Press, 1909), I.5.26.6, italics in text.

14. G. Wilson Knight's paraphrase of Sonnet 121 in *The Mutual Flame* (London: Methuen, 1955), p. 51, is largely accurate; however Knight includes without pointing out, much less lamenting, the inconsistencies. He applauds the poem because it manifests how Shakespeare "penetrated beyond good and evil" and "deploy[ed] their interaction with . . . impersonal . . . clarity," p. 52.

Knight's remarks entail a view of Shakespeare and the world I am glad not to share.

Chapter 8
The Theology of a Love

1. Sir Philip Sidney, *The Countess of Pembroke's Arcadia*, ed. H. Oskar Sommer (1590; facs. reprint, London: 1891), sig. Z4v; 2.16.1.

2. *Ibid.*, sig. Y1; 2.13.6 (italics in text).

3. See J. B. Leishman, *Themes and Variations in Shakespeare's Sonnets* (London: Hutchinson, 1961), pp. 150–151, 171.

4. See E. A. Abbott, *A Shakespearian Grammar* (1870, reprint ed., New York: Dover Publications, 1966, paper), p. 239, sec. 336, for other examples of compound subjects with verb inflected with -*s*.

5. Douglas L. Peterson, *The English Lyric from Wyatt to Donne* (Princeton: Princeton University Press, 1967), p. 247, says that in Shakespeare's sonnets "the lover addresses the Friend as a penitent might in prayer approach Christ." Cf. Martin Seymour-Smith, "Shakespeare's Sonnets 1–42," *New Essays*, ed. Landry, pp. 34 and 39.

6. T. G. Tucker, in his edition of the sonnets, *The Sonnets of Shakespeare* (1924; reprint ed., Folcroft, Pa.: Folcroft Library Editions, 1970), p. 184, in a note to line 108.9, gives an impressive argument for "external covering, vesture." In one of his examples "case" is a metaphor for body.

7. F. T. Prince, "The Sonnet from Wyatt to Shakespeare," in *Elizabethan Poetry*, ed. John Russell Brown and Bernard Harris Stratford-upon-Studies 2 (New York: St. Martin's Press, 1960), p. 27.

8. Col. 3.3.

9. Cf. John Vyvyan, *Shakespeare and Platonic Beauty* (London: Chatto & Windus, 1961), p. 7, speaking of Shakespeare's plays in the light of the "something of great constancy" of *A Midsummer Night's Dream*, V. i. 26. Vyvyan says, "But what is the thing of constancy? The brief answer, I think, is beauty. That may sound deceptively simple; for behind it lies a great part of the Neo-Platonist philosophy of the Renaissance."

10. *Loues Labors Lost* (London: 1598), sig. E3-E3v (IV. iii. 72-74).

11. Robert Frost, *Selected Prose of Robert Frost*, ed. Hyde Cox and Edward Connery Latham (New York: Holt, Rinehart, and Winston, 1966), p. 114.

12. Cf. R. N. Hallstead, "Idolatrous Love: A New Approach to Othello," *Shakespeare Quarterly*, 19(1968): 115, "All idolatry of a human being is doomed"; George Herbert Palmer, *Intimations of Immortality in the Sonnets of Shakespere* (Boston: Houghton Mifflin, 1912), esp. pp. 39–40; and Roy W. Battenhouse's exploration of the idolatry of romantic love in *Romeo and Juliet* and elsewhere, in *Shakespearean Tragedy* (Bloomington and London: Indiana University Press, 1969), esp. pp. 102–130.

13. Cf. C. P. Laurent's fine essay, "Les sonnets de Shakespeare: étude d'une désillusion," *Les langues modernes*, 61(Jan.–Feb. 1967): 46–52, esp. p. 52 (italics in text): "Le monde qu'il s'est créé, doublement polarisé entre la mort et l'eternite, la faiblesse et la vertu, le désir et l'amour, a failli . . . . Un tel équilibre est essentiellement instable . . . . Les *Sonnets* sont le constat d'échec d'une tentative passionée pour mettre le monde en ordre. Après eux, il ne pourra plus être question que du désordre."

"The world which Shakespeare made in the sonnets, balanced between death and eternity, moral weakness and virtue, desire and love, failed . . . . Such an equilibrium is essentially unstable . . . . The sonnets are the report of the failure of a passionate attempt to put the world in order. After them, there is only disorder" (trans. mine). Or, I would like to add, the long reconciliation of Shakespeare's later work.

Chapter 9
The Faults of Greatness

1. S.v. *sonnet*, "not very suitable to the English language," and *sonnetteer*, "a small poet, in contempt," *Johnson's Dictionary*, ed. E. L. McAdam, Jr. and George Milne (New York: Pantheon Books, 1963).

2. For instance, John Keats, Letter to John Hamilton Reynolds, Nov. 22, 1817, *The Letters of John Keats*, ed. Hyder Edward Rollins, 2 vols. (Cambridge, Mass.: Harvard University Press, 1958), I: 188–189, no. 44.

3. For instance, John Crowe Ransom, "Shakespeare at Sonnets," *The World's Body*, 2nd ed. (Baton Rouge: Louisiana State University Press, 1968, paper), pp. 270–303.

4. For instance, Douglas Bush, in his introduction to the edition of Shakespeare's sonnets, *Sonnets,* ed. Douglas Bush and Alfred Harbage (Baltimore: Penguin Books, 1961, paper), p. 11.

5. For instance, William Wordsworth, marginalia to Robert Anderson's *Poets of Great Britain*, in *Coleridge's Miscellaneous Criticism*, ed. Thomas Middleton Raysor (Cambridge, Mass.: Harvard University Press, 1936), p. 454.

6. For instance, Yvor Winters, *Forms of Discovery* (n.p.: Alan Swallow, 1967), pp. 52–53.

7. For instance, T. G. Tucker in the introduction to his edition, *The Sonnets of Shakespeare* (1924; reprint ed., Folcroft, Pa.: Folcroft Library Editions, 1970), p. xxix.

8. George Steevens, in *Supplement to the Edition of Shakspeare's Plays Published in 1778 by Samuel Johnson and George Steevens . . .* , ed. Edmond Malone (London: 1780), II: 682, n. Wordsworth, who severely chastised Steevens for his criticism of the sonnets, followed Steevens's language closely when objecting to the dark lady sonnets for the faults of "sameness, tediousness, quaintness, and elaborate obscurity" in the marginalia referred to in this chapter, note 5. Wordsworth's criticism of Steevens occurs in "Essay, Supplementary to the Preface," *The Poetical Works of William Wordsworth*, ed. Ernest de Selincourt, 5 vols., 2nd ed. of Vol. 2 (Oxford: Clarendon Press, 1940–1954), II: 416. Rollins's summaries and citations in *Sonnets* (Variorum), II: 336–339, 343–344, 347–348, 349–350, 352–353, 356–357, 359–360, 361–362, 363–364, 365–366 (and see index entry for Steevens, II: 520) show that Steevens's remarks were (1) notorious, (2) often agreed with.

9. Steevens, *Supplement,* II: 684, n.

10. *Ibid.,* II: 685, n.

11. *Ibid.,* II: 682, n.

12. Thomas Gilby, *Phoenix and Turtle* (London: Longmans, Green, 1950), p. 150. (Shakespeare's hand reaches far, even to titles of books on the philosophy of being.)

13. Stephen Booth, *An Essay on Shakespeare's Sonnets* (New Haven and London: Yale University Press, 1969), p. 140.

14. Hallett Smith, *Elizabethan Poetry* (Cambridge, Mass.: Harvard University Press, 1952), p. 181, n., speaks of the metaphorical richness in some of Shakespeare's syntactical tangles. See also Smith's discussion, pp. 186–187, of line 147.8.

15. In *A Lover's Complaint* when the young man there is blamed for burning "in . . . luxury" (line 314) while he "preach'd pure maid, and prais'd cold chastity" (line 315), praising cold chastity is obviously the standard, proper thing to do. In *A Midsummer Night's Dream* Queen Elizabeth is compared to the "cold moon" (II. i. 156) whose "chaste beams" (II. i. 162) quench "Cupid's fiery shaft" (II. i. 161). "Cold" there can hardly be an insult. When Othello in his extremity cries, "Cold, cold, my girl!/ Even like thy chastity" (V. ii. 275-276), the "cold . . ./ . . . chastity" is as unqualified as praise can be. These analogies do not prove that the passage in the sonnet is meant as praise, but they do prove that for Shakespeare such a use of *cold* can be praise; and the claim that the passage is wholly or even partly blame radically violates context.

16. Some of the more important commentaries on this frequently discussed sonnet are the brief but cogent notes in *Sonnets,* ed. Tucker, p. 168; William Empson, *Some Versions of Pastoral* (London: Chatto & Windus, 1935), pp. 89-101; Smith, *Elizabethan,* pp. 188-191; Albert S. Gerard, "The Stone as Lily," *Shakespeare Jahrbuch,* 96(1960): 155-160; Hilton Landry, *Interpretations in Shakespeare's Sonnets* (Berkeley and Los Angeles: University of California Press, 1963), pp. 7-27; Ann L. Hayes, "The Sonnets," *"Starre of Poets,"* Carnegie Studies in English (Pittsburgh: Carnegie Institute of Technology, 1966), pp. 4-7. When all is said, which is not apt to be soon, one cannot prove that there is no touch of unconscious resentment in the first quatrain of Sonnet 94, but, if so, it is contrary to the deliberate meaning and the general, strong drive of feeling in the poem and context.

17. Ransom, *Body,* pp. 270-303; replied to by, among others, Arthur Mizener, "The Structure of Figurative Language in Shakespeare's Sonnets," *Southern Review,* 5(1940): 730-747; Booth, *Essay,* pp. 24-28; and Hilton Landry, "In Defense of Shakespeare's Sonnets," *New Essays,* ed. Landry, pp. 129-147. See Ransom, *Body,* p. 351, for a recantation.

18. Douglas Bush writes in his introduction to the second edition of Hyder Edward Rollins's edition of *Tottel's Miscellany,* 2 vols. (Cambridge, Mass.: Harvard University Press, 1966), I: viii, that Rollins in conversation about Shakespeare's sonnets once "said, with sudden fervor, 'They seem to me to say just about everything'; and then, as if conscious of betraying emotion, . . . began quickly to speak of everyday matters."

Appendix

The Syllables of the
Sonnets

The purpose of this appendix is to try to answer the vexing question, "How many syllables occur in each foot of Shakespeare's sonnets?" The question is aesthetically minor but textually major, at least numerically, since the answer given to the more general form of the question, "Do Elizabethan poets allow light, metrically uncounted syllables?" will affect a vast number of textual choices.

The answer given here to the narrower question is "two." Put differently, the question is "How to deal with the apparent extra syllables in these poems?" I exclude the feminine endings, which are genuine extra syllables and not relevant to this discussion except for two freakish instances I shall deal with in Note 43 to this appendix. The question admits of three answers, each corresponding to a position held by scholars: (1) that they are simply syllables, to be sounded and counted metrically; (2) that they are light syllables or semisyllables, lightly sounded and not counted metrically; (3) that they do not exist: "they" are neither pronounced nor counted metrically.

The first position has been held by George Saintsbury, and by Laura Riding and Robert Graves.[1] The second is the prevalent view, held by an impressive array of scholars, including Jakob Schipper, Norman Ault, and A. W. Partridge, for Elizabethan poetry generally; C. H. Herford and Percy Simpson, for Ben Jonson;[2] and W. G. Ingram and Theodore Redpath, for the sonnets of Shakespeare in their edition, in which they state that in the 1609 edition of the sonnets the apostrophe indicates "a lightening or semi-elision of a syllable" and believe that taking such a combination as "th'expence" as "disyllabic" is "entirely false" and destructive of "many delicate rhythms."[3] The third position has been held by B. A. P. van Dam and Cornelis Stoffel for Elizabethan poetry generally and by Helge Kökeritz for Shakespeare generally, the view that two syllables metrically are two syllables linguistically and that no anapests or semielisions occur in the sonnets.[4] This appendix supports the third position for the sonnets, and strictly only for them, even though a good deal of the evidence goes beyond. One of the frustrations of trying to settle such questions is that finally one has to decide the question for a particular text by separate scrutiny; I offer that sort of scrutiny only to one book.

The positions are not so discrete as my summary may suggest. The semielision theory is really a special case of the anapest theory and could more simply be described as the "light anapest theory." What is claimed is that light extra

191

syllables are allowed, and to say that they occasion light anapests would explain them without severing metrical and linguistic reality. The very severance is telling. The semielisionist, presumably recognizing that Elizabethan prosody is strict and not wishing to admit certain reductions, has recourse to a theory that oddly separates meter and sound.

In one way, the semielision and disyllabic positions are not sharply divided because syllables in our speech are not always neatly countable; borderline instances occur. Disyllabism however explains such instances more logically than semielisionism. To say that certain syllables are borderline instances but counted by Elizabethans sonally and metrically as either one or two, makes better sense than again to divide meter and sound, to say that Elizabethans counted such instances sonally as two but metrically as one. The burden of proof is on those who divide practice from theory. What must be explained as genuinely extra? In Shakespeare's sonnets, nothing. Further, the problem arose largely because of gaps between Elizabethan orthography and nineteenth- and twentieth-century linguistic and aesthetic understanding. To show that there is no such gap in many instances of Elizabethan practice is to dissolve much of the need for a semielision theory.

Nonetheless, some variety of practice may have occurred. It is hard to show that it did not. One can show that reductions we would not expect often happened and were by prosodists and some poets deliberately intended. One cannot very well show that in the reading of poems light extra syllables were never pronounced. Unless a reader is deliberately and unremittingly careful of metrical demands (and actors are not typically the most pedantic people in the world), he would tend to pronounce variant forms variously without precise regard to the meter. If readers were as careless as spellers (poets, scribes, editors, and compositors) in showing metrical forms, then there was inconsistency in practice.

At least four considerations, however, suggest that the inconsistency was comparatively infrequent in practice, the disyllabism being formally and deliberately made plain in reading. First, the variant doublets, to be discussed, were clearly meant to exhibit sharp difference of pronunciation. Second, rhetoricians of the period discussed figures involving deliberate distortions, including syllabic change, for the sake of meter (for instance, *aphaeresis, syncope, apocope*) and for the sake of rhyme (for instance, *antisthecon*).[5] Third, the rather artificial rhyme of such rhymes as "perpetuall" & "thrall" (154.10&12), requires some forcing of stress. Fourth, Thomas Campion writes, objecting to pyrrhic (that is, pyrrhic or weak iambic) substitutions in English poems, that such substitutions weaken the "verse, which they [the poets] supply in reading with a ridiculous, unapt drawing of their speech" as in "Was it my destiny, or dismall chaunce?"[6]

The practice of poets reading their poems was, then, to pronounce in certain contexts such a word as *destiny* as three syllables with the third syllable artificially raised in stress. Alexander Gil offers supporting testimony, saying that in poetry, but not in prose, such words as *misery, constancy, destiny* often have strong stress on the last syllable.[7] Poets pronounced their lines to fit the meters, within some limits.

Van Dam and Stoffel damage their case for disyllabism by many of their ruthless and linguistically implausible reductions and by their scornful refusal to admit the existence of borderline syllables. Kökeritz hurts his case by the aesthetic circularity I shall discuss, and by the following considerable admission when his eyes were on another target than semielisionism: "In fact, we have no means of determining today the quantity of the sounds used in *I'm* and *I am*; the former might have been emotionally prolonged to [ə'ı':m] and the latter uttered very rapidly, perhaps [əiəm]"[8] If so far, then a little further or shorter to syllabic inconsistency.

Some inconsistency of practice probably occurred: that does not mean that apparent extra syllables were regularly lightly pronounced or so pronounced by deliberate aesthetic choice or semielision theory. The evidence is that a strict disyllabism was intended in the sonnets and probably in much other poetry.

The Aesthetic Argument

The danger of circularity in discussing these questions is manifest. Kökeritz brings a wide linguistic knowledge to bear on Shakespeare's pronunciation, but is circular when he discusses the matter theoretically, offering the dubious aesthetic premise that "Shakespeare was an accomplished metrist and that consequently his verse was intrinsically regular."[9] Once one assumes this, the matter is settled, and each apparent extra syllable has to be explained away. In actual practice, however, Kökeritz handles his evidence more supplely and sensibly than do Van Dan and Stoffel.

Circularity also exists on the semielisionist side, as when Partridge writes that Kökeritz shows an "insensibility to Shakespeare's skill in modulating . . . for dramatic purposes — an aesthetic gift to which systems of typography could hardly do justice."[10] Pushed to the end of its logic, that position would mean that one could ignore any evidence for disyllabism, since Shakespeare was on presumption too fine an artist to submit to such an aesthetically narrow system. Partridge is a careful observer of orthographic niceties, but the pressure of the assumption is there.

The aesthetic argument on either side is unconvincing, for two reasons. First, modern rather than Elizabethan aesthetic assumptions intrude. Of course Elizabethan and modern aesthetics overlap greatly, but the differences are for this issue crucial. Second, the difference is not aesthetically important enough to be conclusive. Kökeritz seems to be saying that rigor is the essence of good metrics; Partridge is saying that subtle modulation is essential. He speaks of "Shakespeare's subtly modulated accentual rhythms" in the later plays, as opposed to the "old Marlovian pattern"[11] and says that the "English ideal was not metrical regularity."[12]

The trouble is that both are right, that is, when exclusive, wrong. The aesthetic truth is that a firm base which allows for subtle rhythmical variety makes for a sound and beautiful poetry and that Shakespeare's poetry achieves this whether or not his elisions are reductions or slurs. He had at his disposal the firm base of the iambic pentameter, with allowable pyrrhic, spondaic, and justified-trochaic substitutions, with a great range of actual stress within the pattern of relative stress, with more variant syllabic forms than in modern English, with great freedom of syntax, and with no rules except the idioms of the language governing the variety of quantity, timbre, speed, phrasing, and pausing. Such a metrical instrument is magnificent, with or without light extra syllables. Certainly he could have used the choice of sometime-elision, sometime-semielision for delicate rhythmical effects, as Ingram and Redpath, and others, would have. Wallace Stevens in "Sunday Morning" uses a similar metrical system with light anapests profoundly and exquisitely. The question is whether Shakespeare did, on the available evidence.

The simplest course would be to say with Abbott that "it is impossible to tell" [13] whether some syllables are light or omitted, and go on to other matters. But the problem vexes, and sometimes one can tell.

I was persuaded of the semielision theory and have changed my mind on the evidence I have encountered. That in itself proves nothing, since one can change and become wrong, but at least should suggest that I have not merely bent the evidence to a prior theory. I felt that the strict disyllabic theory was crude aesthetically and unnatural linguistically, and thus am in fair position to explain the objection.

The modern feeling that elision is crude and unnatural is at least threefold: (1) forms or reductions not in present English, sound unnatural to us, but the evidence is clear that such forms and reductions often did exist in Elizabethan speech and poetry; (2) we object to poetic license, to changing or distorting speech forms for metrical purposes, yet Tudor and Elizabethan poets availed themselves of a number of licenses overtly recognized in works on prosody and rhetoric. This modern objection, which is called "naturalistic" by Chatman,[14] is accompanied by a companion not very consistent with naturalism: (3) the feeling that poetry should be formal and not indulge in colloquial contractions and reductions;[15] Elizabethan poetry uses them frequently. Poetry must be like speech, we tend to think, but it must not be like actual speech.

All poetry combines the natural and artificial, but our notion of what of artifice and nature is allowed, blocks our view of Elizabethan practice. All three of the aforementioned feelings, in strong combination, work for the semielision theory and against the disyllabic; whatever else may or may not be concluded, it is certain that Elizabethan theory and practice contradict all three. This does not automatically mean that Shakespeare's sonnets use no extra syllables or glides, but it shows that when modern critics feel that Elizabethan poetry must have used such glides, they are being unhistorical.

Syllables

What a syllable is, is even less clear than what a stress is (see the discussion of stress in Chapter Four, in the section *Some Metrical Fundamentals*). English vowels tend to diphthongization with even such a nearly pure vowel as the *i* of *it* admitting a little glide. Hence, if one seeks a pure vowel per syllable, there are no pure syllables in English. There is no clear line between a vowel and diphthong or a diphthong and two syllables. Some words occupy a border line between one and two syllables. Words of the *-our, -ower* series (*hour, power, flower,* and such) are in present English either one syllable with a complex diphthong or two syllables, and have been counted as one or two syllables metrically for centuries. Words with light final *-en* (*heaven, even,* and such) can also be counted metrically with a syllabic variant, the ending counting as one syllable or none, and representing four distinct stages: *hevn* [hɛvn], flatly one syllable; *hevn* [hɛvn], with syllabic *n*; *hevun* [hɛvən], two syllables with reduced vowel; *heven* [hévɛn], two syllables with full vowel. The first and fourth probably do not occur normally in speech, but could occur in verse, since meter puts some pressure on pronunciation. This uncertainty of boundary has been recognized for some centuries. Alexander Hume wrote in a seventeenth-century manuscript, "we in manye places soe absorb l and n behynd a consonant . . . that the ear can hardlie judge quhither their intervenes a voual or noe." [16]

Further, syllabification in English is moderately fluid. Words often lose syllables historically and much less often add them, and many simultaneous variant forms exist, words with medial *-r-* or *-er-* being one of the strongest examples. *Hatred* is two syllables in present English; *mystery* can be clearly two or clearly three syllables or something in between. Even greater freedom of syllabification existed in Elizabethan English.

Substitution

Substitution is the use of a different kind of foot than the predominant one. Thus trochees, pyrrhics, and spondees appear in iambic lines. Strict iambics I shall define, stipulatively but not randomly, as iambics which never or very rarely allow trisyllabic substitutions within the line; loose iambics are those that allow trisyllabic substitution within lines. Again, I waive feminine endings. Thus, by these definitions, the Riding's and Graves's position implies that Shakespeare wrote loose iambics, Kökeritz's position that Shakespeare wrote strict iambics, the semielision position sitting a tricky fence between.

The Evidence

What is the evidence? First, a statement by contemporaries about Shakespeare's metrical intent. Second, the more or less contemporary prosodists. Third, certain features of the 1609 text.

Heminge and Condell

Heminge and Condell, in their preface "To the Great Variety of Readers" to the First Folio, claim to offer texts as "absolute in their numbers, as he [Shakespeare] conceiued." [17] They were actors who had worked with Shakespeare and who had read verse on the stage; they were Shakespeare's contemporaries and friends. Partridge, who takes them to be supporting strict disyllabism, goes to some pains to attempt to discredit their testimony. [18] The testimony is hard to discredit, but it may be merely a general praise of Shakespeare's rhythmical powers and a claim that they represent accurately his metrical intent without specifying what his metrical intent exactly is. Still, the suggestion of strict syllabic count is there: uncountable numbers are hardly absolute.

The Prosodists

The evidence of the prosodists has its frustrations. It is troublesome to cite what a prosodist says about an issue, when in the same passage he is making bad prosodical mistakes. Late sixteenth- and early seventeenth-century prosodists were seriously confused about a number of issues, most notoriously but not exclusively about the relation of accent to quantity. None of them seem to understand Ockham's Razor, and they exclude or ignore trochaic substitution at a time when English poets were using trochaic substitution well.

"Contemporary" is not always contemporary. The year 1575 or 1580 is a long way from the 1590s metrically. The transition from Gascoigne, with his real talent but overstrict prosody (no substitutions in theory and few in practice, strongly reinforced lines, a pause normally after the fourth syllable), to Sidney and Marlowe and Shakespeare is an astonishing change of practice, one of the greatest triumphs of the poetic spirit in any nation.[19] Consequently, the casual lumping of even two decades of prosodists can mislead.

Nonetheless the evidence of the prosodists is, after granting the slipperiness of some of the evidence, firmly on the side of disyllabism.

The contoversy is an old one: it goes back at least to whenever George Puttenham (or whoever) wrote certain passages in *The Art of English Poesie,* published in 1589. Puttenham seems at moments to support in typically confused ways both the anapestic and the semielision positions.

In Book Two, Chapter Fourteen, he quotes several lines of poetry including the following from Wyatt:

> The furi ous gone in his most ra ging ire. [sigla his]

Then Puttenham writes:

> And may moe which if ye would not allow for *dactils* [by my scanning, anapests] the verse would halt vnlesse ye would seeme to helpe it contracting a sillable by vertue of the figure *Syneresis* which I thinke was neuer their meaning, nor in deede would haue bred any pleasure to the eare, but hindred the flowing of the verse.[20]

Like Ingram and Redpath, Partridge, Ault, and others, Puttenham is objecting on aesthetic grounds to cutting out a syllable. But he does admit the possibility of reduction and even seems to feel it as the ordinary explanation.

Elsewhere he wanders, for a moment, into something like the semielisionist position:

> [The] odde [extra] sillable . . . is in a maner drownd and supprest by the flat accent [i.e., is a light unaccented syllable or glide], and shrinks away as it were inaudible and by that meane the odde verse comes almost to be an euen in euery mans hearing.[21]

The evidence of Puttenham, while something, is not very much.

First, he is thinking quantitatively, about verse that was not written quantitatively, and his position exemplifies anapestism or semielisionism only insofar as he gets quantitative and accentual-syllabic confused. Remove that confusion, and what he says would be simply irrelevant, since quantitative verse allows the mixing of trisyllabic and disyllabic feet.

Second, he is puzzled and conscious that he offers an unusual explanation, rejecting the more normal explanation of syllabic reduction.

Third, none of his examples require a semielisionist or anapestic explanation; each fits a disyllabic explanation as well or better. In the immediate contexts he quotes ten lines that involve one or more extra syllables. They all are lines with feminine endings, or hexameters, or admit obvious contractions as in the three following examples (italics in text ignored):

Shed Caesars teares vpon Pompe*i*us hed

The fur*i*ous gone in his most raging ire

So is my painefull life the burd*en* of ire.

The first two can be examples of synizesis,[22] the consonantization of vowel resulting in syllabic reduction: Pom pa yus [pompeʃəs] and fur yus [fyúɹ:jas]. In the third example "burden" can be monosyllabic, light final -*en* being frequently nonsyllabic in the period.

Puttenham's explanation is aimed at explaining all such syllables and makes no sense whatever for the feminine lines or the hexameters. In several of his examples he is wildly wrong; in the others he has at the best only an equal chance of offering a correct explanation. Which is to travel on thinning odds.

Fourth, he is confused about scansion and is the most inconsistent of the Elizabethan prosodists. Put the other way, his evidence, if not much, is something. But the other evidence cuts across his momentary views.

The Count of Syllables

James writes, "zour first syllabe in the lyne be short, the second lang, the thrid short, the fourt lang, . . . and sa furth to the end of the lyne."[23] This is strictly disyllabic and despite the use of "short" and "lang," in its context essentially accentual.

George Gascoigne writes, "We [English versifiers] use none other order but a foote of two sillables";[24] Thomas Campion, "When we speake of a Poeme written in number, we consider . . . the distinct number of the sillables";[25] Samuel Daniel, "Iambique verse in our language. . . [is] the plaine ancient verse consisting of tenne sillables or fiue feetes,"[26] elsewhere admitting the one exception, "our verse of eleuen sillables, in feminine Ryme";[27] Abraham Fraunce, "Rime [rhymed verse] containeth a certaine number of sillables ending alike";[28] William Webbe, "[Verse is] measurable Speeche . . . framed in wordes contayning number or proportion of iust syllables."[29]

The Actual Reduction of Syllables

What applies to Latin verse does not necessarily apply to English verse, but the terms *elipsis* and *synaloepha* derived from Latin prosody, where the terms clearly referred to the actual dropping of a syllable. Thus John Palsgrave writes that *ellipsis* means that a vowel shall be "*lefte vnscanned or sounded,*"[30] that is, not counted metrically or pronounced.

In English verse the omission or reduction of syllables comes sometimes from the actual speech habits of Elizabethans, as Kökeritz, Dobson,[31] Partridge, and others have clearly shown. Other reductions come from the *metaplasms* discussed by the rhetoricians: changes of letters or syllables for metrical purposes. Similar changes are called "poeticall license" by Gascoigne, who gives many examples, including such examples as "*orecome* for *ouercome*" and "*tane* for *taken*" in which the spelling makes certain that an actual syllabic reduction takes place.[32]

In the very passage in which Puttenham attacks a strict disyllabism, a good piece of evidence occurs against one sort of semielision favored by Ingram and Redpath. Puttenham gives "Th'enemie" as a "dactil," thus: "Th'enemie." That is, he assumed no syllabic problem whatever in "Th'en-." It was just pronounced as one syllable.

Peacham says that in "*Synalaepha*" one vowel "is cut of[f]" and gives as an example "t'aske" for "to aske."[33] No glide, but a cutting. We are very apt to feel that a contraction we still use, such as *it's*, was a contraction, but that where we relax a vowel, as in *the enemy* or *to ask*, the Elizabethans did not contract. But the firm evidence is that they often did.

Campion includes among examples of elision "t'inchaunt," "th'inchaunter," along with "let's," "hee's," and others.[34] All are treated as contractions, as simply shortened.

Ingram and Redpath, as I have already noted, feel that it is "entirely false" to think of "th'expense" as actually "disyllabic," an assertion contradicted by Puttenham, Sidney, and Campion, and by the statement that follows.

Ben Jonson speaks plainly, "*Apostrophus* is the rejecting of a Vowell from the beginning, or ending of a Word," and gives among his examples "th'outward" and "th'inward," saying that in such cases the vowel is "cast away."[35] Jonson speaks with some authority, as poet and observer (and as Shakespeare's friend); and "rejecting" and "cast away" are expressions not easy to square with lightening or semielision. Either Jonson's theory and practice were radically inconsistent, or Herford and Simpson are in error in believing that Jonson in *Sejanus* and elsewhere intended semielision.[36] My present opinion is that such a form in Jonson as *thou' art* means "*thou'rt,* which is reduced from *thou art.*"

Variant Forms

The existence of words with variant syllabic forms in Elizabethan English is unmistakable on all sorts of evidence, will be abundantly exemplified in my discussion of the 1609 text of Shakespeare's sonnets, and is not contested.

The existence of such forms does not as such disprove the semielision theory, but tilts against it. Time and time again, forms that seem to us irreducible are reducible by a full syllable in Elizabethan speech and poetry. As the discussion that precedes and follows should show, the cases that seem strongly to work against disyllabism vanish when we look carefully at the text and at Elizabethan practice.

In any instance of variant syllabic forms for a word, it is possible that the poet intended for the longer nonmetrical form to be sounded for speculative aesthetic reasons; hence one cannot refute the semielisionists by showing forms with actual syllabic reductions. But the semielision theory offends against Ockham's Razor for such instances, and is anachronistic: no one balks at forms with actual syllabic reductions in present English being reduced to the metrical requirements in Elizabethan poems; it is the forms which lack reductions now that call forth the imagined need for light extra syllables or glides. Consequently, the existence of variant forms in each relevant instance show that the semielision theory is for that instance most probably false. But the relevant instances in the 1609 text are all the instances.

The 1609 Text

The 1609 edition of Shakespeare's sonnets is virtually the only authority we have for these poems except for the two sonnets printed in the unauthorized *The Passionate Pilgrim*, which have no independent metrical value for my purposes. The 1609 edition has a number of errors and many metrical inconsistencies. The carelessness of the printing or copy text, combined with the metrical inconsistencies common in Elizabethan books and manuscripts, actually works against semielisionism. If the text were rigorously reliable on metrical matters, then it would be likely that such lines as line 142.9, "Be it lawfull I loue thee as thou lou'st those," and line 17.9, "So should my papers (yellowed with their age)" would represent extra syllables or glides in "be it" and "yellowed," instead of being inconsistent renderings of the contraction *be't* and the reduced form *yellow'd*.

Here are some examples of apparent extra syllables in the sonnets, representing important classes. The relevant "syllables" are italicized.

With vert*uo*us wish would beare your liuing flowers (16.7)

Though yet heau*en* knowes it is but as a tombe (17.3)

Be*ing* had to tryumph, being lackt to hope (52.14)

Some fresher stampe of the time bett*er*ing dayes (82.8)

Was it his spir*it*, by spirits taught to write (86.5)

Weeds among weeds, or flow*er*s with flowers gatherd (124.4)

Since there are only a hundred or so examples of such apparent extra syllables, which is not very many out of over 10,000 feet and over 20,000 syllables, one can safely say that at the most Shakespeare uses anapests sparingly in the sonnets. One can add, from these examples and all others, that the apparent anapests are all light. The theory that Shakespeare simply allowed anapestic substitutions is wrong. The question remains, did he intend light anapests or semielisions?

Being

The word *being* is in normal pronunciation a light two syllables to begin with. In the sonnets it occurs, spelled indifferently *beeing* or *being* with no metrical significance to the spellings, in contexts where (1) by a light anapest theory it sometimes occasions light anapests and sometimes does not; or (2) by a semielision theory it is sometimes pronounced and counted as two syllables, sometimes pronounced as two syllables or as one syllable plus a glide or slur, but counted as one; or (3) by the disyllabic theory, it is sometimes two syllables and sometimes one.

Henceforth, I shall normally discuss my examples as examples of disyllabism, not for polemical suasion but to avoid such verbosities as the previous sentence. The semielisionist may interpret the evidence in his own terms. I do not think they will prove satisfactory.

I find fourteen examples of monosyllabic *being* in the sonnets. Each is in an unstressed position, a truth hard to square with the semielision position, since *being* in an unstressed position is or is virtually a monosyllable, hence can hardly be heard to display the aesthetically desirable glide the semielisionist theory requires; and since the odds are high against the occurrences all being in unstressed positions merely by chance. It is much more likely that Shakespeare intended a monosyllabic and a disyllabic form of the word.

The word *being* once occurs in a variant doublet, in the line "Being had to tryumph, being lackt to hope" (52.14). In such doublets, to be discussed, the intention was to display differences of pronunciation.

Spirit

My first exhibit is from *Zepheria* (1594), a sonnet sequence whose author history has charitably left unknown:

Loue then the spirit of a generous sprite
. . . .
The summe of life that Chaos did vnnight.
(4.9, 4.11)

This example is really enough to show that there were two forms of *spirit*, one monosyllabic and one disyllabic. We hesitate to think of *sprite* as a full synonym or monosyllabic form of *spirit*, since nowadays *sprite* has a much narrower band of meaning than *spirit*. But that was clearly not so in Elizabethan English. References, for instance, to the *Holy Sprite* were frequent. The evidence for this word is too conclusive to need much drumming. Yet modern editions of Shakespeare's sonnets, including Ingram's and Redpath's, fail to make the distinction. Claes Schaar says of line 86.5, "Was it his spirit, by spirits taught to write," that "*Spirit* can hardly be anything but disyllabic in this line." [37] It is once monosyllabic, once disyllabic, and since the two forms occur in the near context the difference was intended to be elegantly exhibited in the reading of the line, as in the passage in *Zepheria* and in the following examples.

Variant Doublets

The two forms of *being* and *spirit* in lines 52.14 and 86.5 respectively, already quoted, are examples of variant doublets, two forms of a word in near context. Several other examples occur in the sonnets. One, which does not happen to involve a syllabic change, is unambiguous evidence that such doublets were considered an aesthetic nicety and that they were to be pronounced with a distinct difference:

From this vile world with vildest wormes to dwell (71.4)

The two forms are plainly pronounced differently. Peacham in his rhetoric gives *vilde* for *vile* as an example of the orthographical scheme *paragoge*, addition of a letter or syllable.[38] Such orthographical schemes, he tells us, exist for meter "or else to make the verse more fine." [39] Shakespeare and other poets obviously felt it made the verse even finer to offer the two pronunciations of a word as companions.[40]

Other examples in the sonnets are "flattery" as three syllables in line 114.2 and "flatry" as two syllables in line 114.9 (these may be too far away to be consciously felt as a doublet), "ti's" as monosyllabic in line 24.3 and "it is" as disyllabic in line 24.4, and the monosyllabic and disyllabic *flowers* in line 124.4, "Weeds among weeds, or flowers with flowers gatherd." Another example is lines 59.11–12, with probably two occurrences intended of the shorter form.

Whether [whe'r] we are mended, or where better they,
Or whether reuolution be the same.

The "where" in the second part of line 59.11 is the common contraction for *whether*,[41] and the "whether" in the same line is probably intended to be the same contraction.

The Suffixes -est -st *and* -ed -d -t

The greater freedom in Elizabethan English for syllabic choice over modern usage includes the choice between syllabic and nonsyllabic forms of *-est* and *-st*; and *-ed, -d,* and *-t.* The suffix *-est, -st* had differing syllabic values both for the verb ending, now lost, and for the superlative, for which we retain the form but not the syllabic choice. The distinction between *-est* and *-st* is kept with consistency by the 1609 text with only a few problematic instances. Line 136.14, "And then thou louest me for my name is *Will*" (italics in text) could be "And then thou lov̀st me for my name's Will" or "And then thou lov'st me for my name is Will." A few examples resemble monosyllabic "maiest" (82.2), which was probably felt as *maie-* plus *-st* rather than *mai-* plus *-est*.

The syllabic distinction for past participial endings is also observed (the apostrophe is sometimes used with the shortened spelling, sometimes not, a mere inconsistency), but with some errors, and with a metrically significant class of possible errors.

In well over 200 instances (I count 239 but with enough problematic instances for the count to be trustworthy only in bulk), syllabic value is correctly indicated. In sixteen instances some discrepancy occurs. Of those, four are plain mistakes, to be discussed. In the other twelve instances, the full form is given when the *-ed* is either extrametrical, anapest — causing, or not pronounced: lines 17.9, 26.11, 85.6, 97.8, 97.10, 108.8, 117.12, 120.4, 120.8, 129.7, 138.14, and 143.2. I once believed that these were aesthetic niceties, with a pleasant extra glide not used in the shortened examples.

So should my papers (yellowed with their age) (17.9)

Vnlesse my Nerues were brasse or hammered steele (120.4)

Past reason hated as a swollowed bayt (129.7)

A glide works well and the sound fits the sense nicely, in these three and some other examples. But the actual explanation is, I now believe, more homely and more disyllabic.

In the text, the nonsyllabic endings for the past participle outnumber the syllabic endings by a ratio of over three to one, over 180 to just over fifty with a few ambiguous or uncertain instances. In these twelve instances, the longer form represents the shorter pronunciation; but in only one instance, line 74.12, to be discussed, does the shortened form represent the longer pronunciation. These truths concur to suggest that Elizabethan usage was already tending to the modern situation where the participial endings are nonsyllabic but represented by *-ed*. Thus in prose, I infer, the spelling *hallowed* would normally represent the pronunciation *hallow'd*. A spelling such as *totter'd* or *ask't* was often a deliberate indication of metrical choice, and it was a very easy and natural mistake for a poet, scribe, or compositor to spell *hallowed* when the pronunciation *hallow'd* was intended.

The Classes of Apparent Extra Syllables

The following list of classes of words in the Sonnets apparently having an extra syllable is in intent exhaustive. The order has no meaning except that the first six groups have instances with reduced spellings and the last seven groups do not. The classes overlap somewhat, which does not affect my argument.

1. Contractions. Contractions of two words usually appear in reduced form:

"wer't" (125.1), "tis" (121.1); but examples of unreduced forms which should be reduced also occur: "were it" (39.10), "be it" (142.9), and, already discussed, perhaps "name is" (136.14). Contracted forms of one word also occur: "greeing" (114.11) for *agreeing*, "ore" (107.12) for *over*, and the already discussed "where" (59.11) for *whether*.

2. Words with *-en* or *-n* endings. These endings are pronounced as one syllable or none, usually as none. The only reduced form of spelling which occurs is "stolne" (line 31.6 and elsewhere), always one syllable.

3. Words with a medial *-r-* or *-er-*. Spellings with *-er-* can represent full or reduced syllabic count, for instance, "flattery" in lines 114.2 and 42.14 respectively. Reduced spellings occur: "watry" (64.7), "robb'rie" (40.9). Many of these have variant syllabic forms in present English.

4. The *-our*, *-ower* group, spelled as one syllable or two, usually pronounced as one syllable: "houre" (33.11) and "hower" (52.3) are monosyllabic, "howers" (5.1) is disyllabic. These words (or syllables) count as one or two syllables in present English. Kökeritz suggests that some of these words may have had an alternative, shorter pronunciation in Elizabethan English.[41]

5. Words with medial *-n-*, *-on-*, *-en-*. Full forms can represent full or reduced pronunciation: "gluttoning" (75.14) and "prisoner" (5.10) respectively. Reduced forms occur: "darkning" (100.4). Some forms come out right in syllabic count but are ambiguous in pronunciation: "sharpned" (56.4) could be pronounced *sharpen'd* or *sharp'nèd*. Most of these words have variant syllabic forms in present English.

6. Words with *-air* or *-ayer*. Both syllabic spellings occur: "prayers" (108.5), "ayre" (21.8), "ayer" (21.12). All such words are monosyllabic in the sonnets.

7. Words in which *-e-* appears but does not represent a syllable: "maiest" (82.2), "alaied" (56.3) rhyming with "said" (56.1). "Maiest" is presumably felt as *maie-* plus *-st* rather than *mai-* plus *-est*, as I have already noted; similarly, "alaied."

8. The word or words *toward, towards,* always monosyllabic: "toward" (9.13), "towards" (51.14). This word can be monosyllabic in present English.

9. The word *spirit*, already discussed.

10. The word *being*, already discussed.

11. Words with medial *-u-* before a vowel: two-syllabled "influence" (15.4) and "vertuous" (16.7), three-syllabled "influence" (78.10). Syncopation in such words (for instance, *influ'nce*) is common in Elizabethan practice, and even without syncopation the two vowels may virtually or actually constitute a diphthong. In trisyllabic "influence" the *-e-* [ε] is a full vowel distinctly pronounced. The suffix *-ual* is monosyllabic in the sonnets, for instance "perpetual" (56.8), except once, "perpetuall" (154.10) rhyming with "thrall" (154.12).

12. Words with medial *-i-* or *-y-* before a vowel. The *-i-* can be syllabic (happier) or nonsyllabic (gracious) in present English. It is virtually always nonsyllabic in the sonnets. Occasionally it is merely a spelling error or freak: three-syllable "vnstayined" (70.8). The phrase "many a" [mɛnja], occurring in line 33.1 and elsewhere, is commonly two syllables in Elizabethan poetry. Other examples of nonsyllabic medial *-i-* are "happier" (6.8), "gratious" (62.5), "misprision" (87.11), "ouer-partiall" (137.5). These words can exemplify syn-

cope or synizesis, for instance [mɪsprízən] or [mɪ sprízjən] respectively. An example of syllabic medial -i- is "spatious" (135.5), an archaism and a joke. Shakespeare is saying that the dark lady's will (vagina) is "large and spatious" and the joke requires a spacious pronunciation.

13. Final -er. There are many examples of final syllabic -er: "neuer" (5.5), and over two dozen others; the only examples of nonsyllabic -er are "whether" (59.11), already discussed, and "either" (70.10), perhaps eith'r or just possibly e'r.[42] The suffix or final -er is not infrequently nonsyllabic in other Elizabethan poets.

That is to say, all the examples of apparent extra syllables vanish on inspection.[43] Nor do I think I am forcing their departure to a suit a theory. When I began to examine these examples I held the semielision theory; when I finished, I did not.

The Imbalance of Spelling Errors

I have attempted to discuss every class of instances in which the spelling seems to indicate an extra syllable. The following are the only five examples I find in the sonnets in which the spelling seems to indicate one syllable too few: "guil'st th'eauen" (28.12); "disabled" (66.8); "remembred" (74.12); "th'East" (132.6); "t'haue" (138.12). The first, fourth, and fifth are patent errors for "guil'st the eauen," "the East," and "to haue," and in the other two instances the -l- and -r- are syllabic but misleadingly spelled.

The truth that the longer spellings represent the shorter pronunciation much more often than vice versa, indicates that the shorter spellings are, at least frequently, deliberate means of showing shorter pronunciations to fit the meter. However, since the longer form as in present English often represents a shorter pronunciation, it was easy to use the longer spelling for the shorter pronunciation. Thus the evidence for semielisionism of apparent extra syllables (without that evidence, semielisionism would have no case) turns out to be potent evidence for disyllabism.

Summary and Conclusion

The case for light anapests or semielision consists in (1) the belief that certain spellings in Elizabethan texts seem to indicate extra syllables, combined with (2) a complex modern prejudice against demonstrable Elizabethan pronunciations that happen to exist no longer, against poetic license, and against contracted forms. I have tried to show that, at least for the sonnets, the first point is evidence for disyllabism, and that the second is contrary to what can be established as Elizabethan practice.

In addition, Heminge and Condell speak for Shakespeare's disyllabic intent, the contemporary prosodists and rhetoricians overwhelmingly support disyllabism, and the 1609 text offers no instance that requires a semielisionist or anapestic explanation and only one instance, "either" in line 70.10, which is even to me problematical.

The aesthetic arguments on either side are inconclusive and on the semielisionist side vitiated by non-Elizabethan assumptions. Though there may have been some inconsistency in practice, disyllabism was probably the prevailing practice and theory. It is remarkably hard to prove the nonexistence of the nonexistent; it is hard to show conclusively that no Elizabethan poets adopted semielisionism on aesthetic grounds. But no evidence (except a moment in Puttenham) exists to show that they did;[44] and the burden of proof is surely on the semielisionist.

More strictly, no claim here extends beyond the sonnets of Shakespeare; to settle particular problems one has to look at (decidedly!) minute particulars, and I have done that only for the sonnets. Whether in Jonson's *Sejanus* and other works, whether in Donne, whether in Shakespeare's plays, whether elsewhere, disyllabism exists or is as strict as I find it in the sonnets, are other questions which must be answered, if they are to be answered, by particular scrutiny of a number of texts. But my concern is not there, but with establishing one basis for a more exact text and more informed aesthetic criticism of Shakespeare's sonnets. I have argued, and I hope shown, that in these poems the metrical and actual disyllabism is strict.

Notes

1. George Saintsbury, *Historical Manual of English Prosody* (London: Macmillan, 1910), pp. 174–175; Laura Riding and Robert Graves, *A Survey of Modernist Poetry* (London: W. Heinemann, 1927), p. 66.

2. Jakob Schipper, *A History of English Versification* (Oxford: Clarendon Press, 1910), pp. 165–166; Norman Ault, ed., *Elizabethan Lyrics,* 3rd ed. (New York: William Sloane Associates, 1949), pp. xiv–xv; A. C. Partridge, *Orthography in Shakespeare and Elizabethan Drama* (London: Edward Arnold, 1964), esp. pp. 95–96; C. H. Herford and Percy Simpson, eds., *The Works of Ben Jonson,* 11 vols. (Oxford: Clarendon Press, 1925-1952), IV: 338–339. Herford and Simpson also admit real elisions, *Jonson,* IV: 338, n. 1.

3. W. G. Ingram and Theodore Redpath, eds., *Shakespeare's Sonnets* (London: University of London Press, 1964), p. xxxiv.

4. Baastian A. P. van Dam and Cornelis Stoffel, *William Shakespeare: Prosody and Text* (Leiden: E. J. Brill, 1900), esp. pp. 166–173, 189; Helge Kökeritz, *Shakespeare's Pronunciation* (New Haven: Yale University Press, 1953), pp. 25–31.

5. See Sister Miriam Joseph, *Shakespeare's Use of the Arts of Language* (New York: Columbia University Press, 1947), esp. pp. 293–294, in which the following definitions are offered: "aphaeresis ... the omission of a syllable from the beginning of a word," "syncope ... the omission of a letter or syllable from the middle of a word," "apocope ... the omission of the last syllable of a word," and "antisthecon ... the exchange of one sound for another for the sake of rhyme."

6. Thomas Campion, "Observations in the Art of English Poesie" (1602), *The Works of Thomas Campion*, ed. Walter R. Davis (London: Faber and Faber, 1969), p. 295.

7. Alexander Gil, *Logonomia Anglica* (1621), ed. Otto L. Jiriczek (Strasbourg: Karl J. Trübner, 1903), p. 134. Cf. E. J. Dobson, *English Pronunciation 1500-1700*, 2nd ed., 2 vols. (Oxford: Clarendon Press, 1968), II: 842-843. Dobson, who translates part of the passage in Gil, makes clear that words such as *misery* were in the period sometimes pronounced to rhyme with *see*, sometimes with *I*, and that such words normally received secondary accent on the last syllable which could be and often was raised to a strong stress in poetry. See also Kökeritz, *Pronunciation*, p. 32.

8. Kökeritz, *Pronunciation*, p. 30.

9. *Ibid.*, p. 25.

10. Partridge, *Orthography*, p. 155. Partridge also places much reliance on Evelyn H. Scholl's essay, "New Light on Seventeenth Century Pronunciation . . . ," *Publications of the Modern Language Association*, 59(1944): 398-445, which shows that some extra syllables were sung. This is irrelevant, since music does not have the syllabic requirement of a poetic foot. In a line from Campion quoted on p. 443 of Scholl's essay "t'a" of "t'adorn" is set to two notes of music, but so are each of the following single syllables in the same line: "coun-" of "counsel'st," "-sel'st" of "counsel'st," and "-dorn" of "t'adorn."

11. Partridge, *Orthography*, p. 87.

12. *Ibid.*, p. 96.

13. E. A. Abbott, *A Shakespearian Grammar* (1870; reprint ed., New York: Dover Publications, 1966, paper), p. 328, sec. 452.

14. Seymour Chatman, *A Theory of Meter* (The Hague: Mouton, 1965), p. 111.

15. This is probably more prevalent in somewhat earlier writers, for instance, Matthew A. Bayfield, *The Measures of the Poets* (Cambridge: Cambridge University Press, 1919), pp. 49-50, n., but is an important cause of the later modern prejudice against disyllabism.

16. Alexander Hume, *Of the Orthographie and Congruitie of the Briten Tongue* (ca. 1617), ed. Henry B. Wheatley, 2nd ed., Early English Text Society, (London: 1870), p. 20.

17. *The First Folio of Shakespeare*, ed. Charlton Hinman, (1623; facs. reprint, New York: W. W. Norton, 1968), sig. A3, p. 7.

18. Partridge, *Orthography*, pp. 86-87.

19. See Chapter 4, Note 28.

20. George Puttenham, *The Arte of English Poesie* (London: 1589), sig. P3, italics and sigla in his text.

21. *Ibid.*, sig. P4v.

22. See Kökeritz, *Pronunciation,* pp. 286–291.

23. James I, King of Great Britain [later], "The Reulis and Cautelis . . . in Scottis Poesie," *The Essays of a Prentise* (Edinburgh: 1584), sig. L2.

24. George Gascoigne, "Certayne Notes of Instruction . . . ," *The Posies of George Gascoigne* (London: 1575), sig. T3.

25. Campion, *Works,* p. 292.

26. Daniel, *Poems,* p. 150.

27. *Ibid.*, p. 133.

28. Abraham Fraunce, *The Arcadian Rhetorike* (1588), ed. Ethel Seaton (Oxford: Basil Blackwell, 1950), p. 26.

29. William Webbe, *A Discourse of English Poetrie* (London: 1586), sig. D2. See Dorothy L. Sipe, *Shakespeare's Metrics* (New Haven: Yale University Press, 1968), who also sums up the evidence from Elizabethan prosodists, pp. 13–15. Sipe's book comes to conclusions similar to mine about Shakespeare's metrics although, since she discusses only the plays, our work does not formally overlap.

30. [Willem de Volder], *The Comedye of Acolastus . . . ,* trans. John Palsgrave (London: 1540), sig. E3v, italics in text.

31. Dobson, *English Pronunciation,* II: 884–895.

32. Gascoigne, *Posies,* sig. U1, italics in text.

33. Henry Peacham, *The Garden of Eloquence* (London: 1577), sig. E3, italics in text.

34. Campion, *Works,* p. 314, omitting the italics in text.

35. Ben Jonson, *The English Grammar,* in *The Workes of Benjamin Jonson* (London: 1640), vol. 3, sig. I3v, italics in text regularized.

36. *Jonson,* ed. Herford and Simpson, IV: 338–339.

37. Claes Schaar, *An Elizabethan Sonnet Problem* (Lund, Sweden: C. W. K. Gleerup, 1960), p. 149, n.

38. Peacham, *Eloquence,* sig. E2.

39. *Ibid.*, sig. E1v.

40. See, for discussion and examples of such doublets, Partridge, *Orthography,* pp. 94–95; Abbott, *Grammar,* pp. 361–363, secs. 475–476; Morris Halle and Samuel Jay Keyser, "Chaucer and the Study of Prosody," *Linguistics and Literary Style,* ed. Donald C. Freeman (New York: Holt, Rinehart and Winston, 1970), pp. 412–413; John Thompson, *The Founding of English Metre* (London: Routledge & Kegan Paul, 1961), p. 79.

41. Kökeritz, *Pronunciation,* pp. 248–249.

42. *Ibid.*, p. 322; and the *Oxford English Dictionary,* s.v. *er*, conjunction, which however gives no Elizabethan example.

43. There are, in my judgment, one likely anapest and another possible one in Shakespeare's sonnets, but of peculiar sorts which do not affect the argument. In line 42.7, "And for my sake euen so doth she abuse me," the rhetorical stress on "me" creates an anapest from the iamb in the fifth foot and feminine ending. The force of the special rhyme of "thee" & "melancholie," 45.6&8, could also occasion an anapest at the close of the line.

44. One might infer, from James I's remark, "Reulis," sig. L1, that feminine endings "are eatin vp in the pronounceing, and na way is comptit as fete," that, since James can hardly mean that feminine endings are unpronounced, phrases such as "eatin vp" may on occasion mean lightly pronounced rather than dropped.

List of Tables

TABLE 1

Trochees in Shakespeare's Sonnets

	After v-p	Not after v-p	Total
In first foot	321	0	321
In second foot	1	28	29
In third foot	57	28	85
In fourth foot	48	28	76
In fifth foot	0	18	18
	427	102	529

NOTE: Irregular Sonnets 99 and 145 and nonsonnet 126 are excluded.
151 sonnets × 14 lines = 2114 lines
2114 lines × 5 feet = 10,570 feet
529 feet are trochees, which is 5%.

TABLE 2

Verse-pauses in Shakespeare's Sonnets

After syllable	1	2	3	4	5	6	7	8	9
No. of v-p	76	134	70	878	451	505	197	86	14
% of v-p	3%	6%	3%	36%	19%	21%	8%	4%	1%

NOTE: Irregular Sonnets 99 and 145 and nonsonnet 126 are excluded.
151 sonnets × 14 lines = 2114 lines
Total no. of v-p = 2411

TABLE 3

Feminine Endings in Shakespeare's Sonnets

	No.	%
Min. count	140	7%
Max. count	259	12%

NOTE: Irregular Sonnets 99 and 145 and nonsonnet 126 are excluded.
151 sonnets × 14 lines = 2114 lines, 2114 endings

TABLE 4

Trochees in Daniel's *Delia* (1592)

	After v-p	Not after v-p	Total
In first foot	104	0	104
In second foot	1	2	3
In third foot	12	2	14
In fourth foot	7	0	7
In fifth foot	0	0	0
	124	4	128

NOTE: 50 sonnets × 14 lines = 700 lines
700 lines × 5 feet = 3500 feet
128 feet are trochees, which is 4%.

TABLE 5

Verse-pauses in Daniel's *Delia* (1592)

After syllable	1	2	3	4	5	6	7	8	9
No. of v-p	5	33	14	375	124	162	43	14	0
% of v-p	1%	4%	2%	49%	16%	21%	6%	2%	0%

NOTE: 50 sonnets × 14 lines = 700 lines
Total no. of v-p = 770

TABLE 6

Feminine endings in Daniel's *Delia* (1592)

	No.	%
Min. count	146	21%
Max. count	218	31%

NOTE: 50 sonnets × 14 lines = 700 lines, 700 endings

TABLE 7

Comparisons of Daniel's *Delia* (1592) and Shakespeare's Sonnets

	Delia	Shakespeare
1. t per poem	2.6	3.5
2. % t in first foot	81	61
3. % internal t after v-p	83	56
4. v-p per poem after syll. 4	7.5	5.8
5. % v-p after syll. 4	49	36
6. medial v-p per poem	13.2	12.1
7. % medial v-p	86	76
8. % fem. end., min.	21	7
9. % fem. end., max.	31	12

NOTE: See Tables 1-6.
Internal trochee is a trochee not in first or fifth foot. Medial verse-pause is a verse-pause after syllable 4, 5, or 6. Shakespeare's sonnets are further from the metrical style of Gascoigne and his contemporaries than Daniel's sonnets in *Delia* (1592) in all these respects.

TABLE 8

Daniel's *Delia* (1592) and Shakespeare's Sonnets
Verse-pauses in Order of Decreasing Frequency

	Delia	Shakespeare
Most v-p after syll.	4	4
	6	6
	5	5
	7	7
	2	2
	8,3 (tie)	8
	8,3 (tie)	1
	1	3
Fewest v-p after syll.	9	9

TABLE 9

Comparisons within Shakespeare's Sonnets

Sonnets	1-17	18-126	1-126	127-152
1. t per poem	3.1	3.4	3.3	4.2
2. % t in first foot	67	62	63	56
3. % internal t after v-p	53	55	55	71
4. v-p per poem after syll. 4	5.5	5.9	5.9	5.6
5. % v-p after syll. 4	37	37	37	34
6. medial v-p per poem	12.5	12.0	12.1	12.6
7. % medial v-p	84	75	76	75
8. % fem. end., min.	7	7	7	3
9. % fem. end., max.	11	13	13	9

NOTE: Sonnets 18-126 are further from the metrical style of Gascoigne and his contemporaries than Sonnets 1-17 in respects 1, 2, 6, and 7, nearer to Gascoigne in respects 3, 4, 9, with no difference in respects 5 and 8. Sonnets 1-126 are further from Gascoigne than Sonnets 127-152 in respect 3 and 6 and nearer to Gascoigne in the other respects, with the differences in respects 4, 5, 6, and 7 being trivial.

TABLE 10

Further Comparisons within Shakespeare's Sonnets

Groups	A	B	C	D
1. t per poem	3.3	3.0	2.7	4.2
2. % t in first foot	64	61	67	60
3. % internal t after v-p	50	38	52	70
4. v-p per poem after syll. 4	5.6	6.0	6.2	5.7
5. % v-p after syll. 4	36	38	40	35
6. medial v-p per poem	12.5	11.9	11.8	12.3
7. % medial v-p	79	75	76	76
8. % fem. end., min.	10	5	6	8
9. % fem. end., max.	16	9	10	15

NOTE: Group A is Sonnets 1-30, Group B Sonnets 31-60, Group C Sonnets 61-90, Group D Sonnets 91-121 excluding the irregular Sonnet 99. See Table 11.

TABLE 11

Comparisons of Groups in Table 10

Respect	(Groups arranged from nearest to Gascoigne's metrical style to furthest from Gascoigne's metrical style)			
1	C	B	A	D
2	C	A	B	D
3	D	C	A	B
4	C	B	D	A
5	C	B	A	D
6	A	D	B	C
7	A	C,D (tie)	C,D (tie)	B
8	A	D	C	B
9	A	D	C	B

NOTE: The respects 1-10 are the numbers in Table 10.

Since Gascoigne and his metrical contemporaries used fewer trochaic substitutions than later poets, Group C with 2.7 trochees per poem is nearest to Gascoigne, Group B with 3.0 trochees next nearest, Group A with 3.3 trochees next nearest, and Group D with 4.2 trochees per poem is the furthest from Gascoigne. Thus in respect 1 the order is C B A D.

The lack of pattern shows high metrical homogeneity.

Bibliography

This bibliography consists of the following sections:

Bibliographies
Reference Books
Editions of the Sonnets
Shakespeare's Works Cited
Anthologies about the Sonnets
Poets
Secondary, and Other

Bibliographies
(and summaries of scholarship)

Alden, Raymond Macdonald. "Bibliography." *The Sonnets of Shakespeare.* New Variorum Edition of Shakespeare. Boston: Houghton Mifflin, 1916, pp. 485–530.
Allen, Harold B. *Linguistics and General Linguistics.* Goldentree Bibliographies. New York: Appleton-Century-Crofts, 1966, paper. Esp. Language and Philosophy, pp. 28–30; Prosody, pp. 86–87.
Bailey, Richard W., and Dolores M. Burton. *English Stylistics: A Bibliography.* Cambridge, Mass., and London: M. I. T. Press, 1968.
Bartlett, Henrietta C. *Mr. William Shakespeare: Original and Early Editions* . . . New Haven: Yale University Press, 1922.
Bergeron, David M. *Shakespeare: A Study and Research Guide.* New York: St. Martin's Press, 1975, paper.
Bevington, David. *Shakespeare.* Goldentree Bibliographies. Arlington Heights, Ill.: AHM Publishing Corporation, 1977. Sonnets, pp. 225–229.
Bose, Kalidas. "The New Problem of the Shakespeare Sonnets." In *Essays on Shakespeare.* Ed. Bhabatosh Chatterjee. Bombay: Orient Longmans, 1965, pp. 128–144.
British Museum. *Shakespeare: An Excerpt from the General Catalogue of Printed Books in the British Museum.* London: Trustees of the British Museum, 1964. Sonnets, columns 286–298.
Bush, Douglas. "Bibliography." *English Literature in the Earlier Seventeenth*

215

Century. 2nd ed., rev. Oxford History of English Literature. Oxford: Clarendon Press, 1962, pp. 461–668. Esp. Rhetorical Theory and Prose Style, pp. 469–470, and History and Criticism of Poetry, pp. 470–476.

de Sola Pinto, V. *The English Renaissance: 1510-1688.* 3rd ed., rev. London: Cresset Press, 1966. Bibliography *passim.*

Ebisch, Walther, and Leven L. Schücking. *A Shakespeare Bibliography.* 1930. Reprint. New York and London: Benjamin Blom, 1968.

Ebisch, Walther, and Leven L. Schücking. *Supplement . . . to a Shakespeare Bibliography.* 1936. Reprint. New York and London: Benjamin Blom, 1968.

Folger Shakespeare Library. *Catalog of the Shakespeare Collection.* 2 vols. Boston: G. K. Hall, 1972. Sonnets, I, 668–686.

Hayashi, Tetsumaro. *Shakespeare's Sonnets: A Record of 20th-Century Criticism.* Metuchen, N. J.: Scarecrow Press, 1972.

Helton, Tinsley. "Contemporary Trends in Shakespeare Sonnet Scholarship." *Wisconsin English Journal,* 8(1965, no. 2): 13–16.

Howard-Hill, T. H. *Shakespearian Bibliography and Textual Criticism.* Vol. 2 of *Index to British Literary Bibliography.* Oxford: Clarendon Press, 1971. Esp. Textual Criticism. The Sonnets, pp. 158–159.

Jaggard, William. *Shakespeare Bibliography.* 1911. Reprint. New York: Frederick Ungar, 1959.

Lee, Sir Sidney, ed. "Census of Copies." *Shakespeare's Sonnets.* 1609. Facs. reprint. Oxford: Clarendon Press, 1905, pp. 62–71.

Lewis, C. S. "Bibliography." *English Literature in the Sixteenth Century.* Oxford History of English Literature. Oxford: Clarendon Press, 1954, pp. 594–685.

McGuinness, Kevin. "Shakespeare and the Sonnets." *Revues des langues vivantes,* 31(1965): 287–301.

McManaway, James G., and Jeanne Addison Roberts, eds. *A Selective Bibliography of Shakespeare: Editions, Textual Studies, Commentaries.* Charlottesville: University Press of Virginia for the Folger Shakespeare Library, 1975. Sonnets, pp. 158–161.

Nager, Rae Ann. "A Selective Annotated Bibliography of Recent Work on English Prosody." In *Style,* 11(1977): 136–170.

Nejgebauer, A. "The Sonnets" in "Twentieth-Century Studies in Shakespeare's Songs, Sonnets and Poems." *Shakespeare Survey,* 15(1962): 10–18.

Rollins, Hyder Edward. "List of Books and Articles." In *The Sonnets.* 2 vols. New Variorum Edition of Shakespeare. Philadelphia: J. P. Lippincott, 1944, II, 438–463. See also I, xi–xiv, for editions.

Seymour-Smith, Martin. *Cumulative Index to the Shakespeare Quarterly: Volumes 1-15, 1950-1964.* New York and London: AMS Press, Inc., 1969.

A Shakespeare Bibliography: The Catalogue of the Birmingham Shakespeare Library. 7 vols. London: Mansell, 1971. Sonnets, I, 202–207; IV, 222–227.

Smith, Gordon Ross. *A Classified Shakespeare Bibliography 1936-1958.* University Park: Pennsylvania State University Press, 1963. Esp. Prosody, pp. 229–230; The Sonnets, pp. 764–773.

Tannenbaum, Samuel A. *Shakspere's Sonnets.* Elizabethan Bibliographies. New York: Samuel A. Tannenbaum, 1940.

Velz, John H. *Shakespeare and the Classical Tradition: . . . Commentary, 1660-1960.* Minneapolis: University of Minnesota Press, 1968. For sonnets, see in Velz's index, pp. 447-448.

Watson, George. *The English Petrarchans: A Critical Bibliography of the "Canzoniere."* Warburg Institute Surveys. London: Warburg Institute, University of London, 1967.

Watson, George, ed. *The New Cambridge Bibliography of English Literature.* 5 vols. Cambridge: Cambridge University Press, 1974-1977. Shakespeare. Prosody, I, column 1592; Sonnets, I, columns 1560-1564.

Wells, Stanley, ed. *Shakespeare: Select Bibliographical Guides.* London: Oxford University Press, 1973.

Willen, Gerald, and Victor B. Reed, eds. "Bibliography." *A Casebook on Shakespeare's Sonnets.* New York: Thomas Y. Crowell, 1964, paper, pp. 291-300.

The following periodicals and annuals contain annual or recurrent bibliographies dealing with Shakespeare, or articles summing and discussing scholarship:

English Association. *The Year's Work in English Studies.* 1919-

Modern Humanities Research Association. *Annual Bibliography of English Language and Literature.* 1920-

Modern Language Association. *MLA International Bibliography.* 1921-

Renaissance Quarterly (formerly *Renaissance News*). 1948-

Shakespeare Association of America. *Shakespeare Association Bulletin.* 1924-1949.

Shakespeare Jahrbuch. 1865-.

Shakespeare Newsletter. 1951-.

Shakespeare Project Bulletin. 1969-.

Shakespeare Quarterly. 1950-.

Shakespeare Quarterly. See Seymour-Smith, *supra.*

Shakespearean Research and Opportunities. 1965-.

Shakespeare Survey. 1948-.

Studies in English Literature 1500-1900.

Studies in Philology. 1916-1969.

Upstart Crow. 1978-.

Reference Books

Abbott, E. A. *A Shakespearian Grammar.* 1870. Reprint. New York: Dover Publications, 1966, paper.

Arber, Edward, ed. *A Transcript of the Registers of the Company of Stationers of London: 1554-1640 A.D.* 5 vols. London: 1875-1877; Birmingham: 1894.

Dawson, Giles E., and Laetitia Kennedy-Skipton. *Elizabethan Handwriting: 1500-1650.* London: Faber and Faber, 1968.

Dictionary of National Biography. Ed. Sir Leslie Stephen and Sir Sidney Lee. 22 vols. 1885-1901. Reprint. London: Oxford University Press, 1921-1922.

Donow, Herbert S. *A Concordance to the Sonnet Sequences of Daniel, Drayton, Shakespeare, Sidney, and Spenser.* Carbondale: Southern Illinois University Press, 1969.

Ellis, Alexander J. *On Early English Pronunciation: With Especial Reference to Shakspere and Chaucer.* 5 vols. London: 1869-1889.

Furness, Mrs. Horace Howard. *A Concordance to Shakespeare's Poems: An Index to Every Word* . . . 1874. Reprint. New York: AMS Press, Inc., 1972.

The Geneva Bible. 1560. Facs. reprint. Intro. Lloyd E. Berry. Madison and London: University of Wisconsin Press, 1969.

Neilson, William Allan *et al.*, ed. *Webster's Biographical Dictionary.* Springfield, Mass.: G. & C. Merriam, 1971.

Onions, C. T., ed. *The Oxford Dictionary of English Etymology.* Oxford: Clarendon Press, 1966.

Onions, C. T., ed. *A Shakespeare Glossary.* 2nd ed., rev. Oxford: Clarendon Press, 1919.

The Oxford English Dictionary. Ed. James A. H. Murray *et al.* 13 vols. and supplement. Oxford: Clarendon Press, 1933.

Partridge, A. C. *A Substantive Grammar of Shakespeare's Nondramatic Texts.* Charlottesville: University Press of Virginia for the Bibliographical Society of the University of Virginia, 1976.

Partridge, Eric. *Shakespeare's Bawdy.* 1948. Reprint. New York: E. P. Dutton, 1960, paper.

Petti, Anthony G. *English Literary Hands from Chaucer to Dryden.* Cambridge, Mass.: Harvard University Press, 1977.

Pollard, Alfred W., and G. R. Redgrave. *A Short-Title Catalogue of Books Printed in England, Scotland, & Ireland, and of English Books Printed Abroad 1475-1640.* London: Bibliographical Society, 1926.

Pollard, Alfred W., and G. R. Redgrave. *A Short-Title Catalogue of Books Printed in England, Scotland, & Ireland and of English Books Printed Abroad 1475-1640.* 2nd ed., revised & enlarged, revised by W. A. Jackson, F. S. Ferguson, and Katharine F. Pantzer. London: Bibliographical Society, 1976 for vol. 2, I–Z (vol. 1, forthcoming).

Schmidt, Alexander. *Shakespeare-Lexicon.* Rev. and enlarged by Gregor Sarrazin. 5th unchanged ed. 2 vols. Berlin: Walter de Gruyter, 1962.

Spevack, Marvin. *A Complete and Systematic Concordance to the Works of Shakespeare.* 8 vols. Hildesheim, West Germany: Georg Olms, 1968. A Concordance to the Sonnets, II, 1255–1287.

Spevack, Marvin. *The Harvard Concordance to Shakespeare.* Hildesheim, West Germany: Georg Olms, 1973.

Viëtor, Wilhelm. *Shakespeare's Pronunciation.* 2 vols. [*A Shakespeare Phonology* and *A Shakespeare Reader*] Marburg, Germany: N. G. Elwert, 1906.

Withycome, Elizabeth Gidley. *The Oxford Dictionary of English Christian Names.* 2nd ed. Oxford: Clarendon Press, 1950.

Editions of the Sonnets

Shakespeare, William. *Shake-speares Sonnets*. London: 1609. Includes *A Louers Complaint*.

The remaining entries in this section are alphabetized by editor's last name, when editor is known.

Shakespeare, William. *The Sonnets of Shakespeare*. Ed. Raymond Macdonald Alden. New Variorum Edition of Shakespeare. Boston: Houghton Mifflin, 1916.

Shakespeare, William. *The Sonnets of Shakespeare*. Ed. C. L. Barber. New York: Dell, 1960, paper.

Shakespeare, William. *The Sonnets of Shakespeare*. Ed. H. C. Beeching. Boston: Athenaeum Press, 1904.

Shakespeare, William. *Shakespeare's Sonnets*. Ed. Stephen Booth. New Haven and London: Yale University Press, 1977.

Shakespeare, William. *Shakespeare's Sonnets*. Ed. C. F. Tucker Brooke. London and New York: Oxford University Press, 1936.

Shakespeare, William. *The Sonnets*. Ed. William Burto. Intro. W. H. Auden. The Signet Classic Shakespeare. New York: New American Library, 1964, paper.

Shakespeare, William. *Shakespeare's Sonnets*. Ed. Douglas Bush and Alfred Harbage. The Pelican Shakespeare. Baltimore: Penguin Books, 1961, paper.

Shakespeare, William. *Shakespeare's Sonnets*. Dolphin Masters. Type facs. of the 1609 ed. Garden City, N. Y.: Doubleday, n.d., paper.

Hubler, Edward, *et al. The Riddle of Shakespeare's Sonnets*. London: Routledge & Kegan Paul, 1962. Includes a text — no editor given — of the sonnets.

Shakespeare, William. *Shakespeare's Songs and Poems*. Ed. Edward Hubler. New York: McGraw-Hill, 1959.

Shakespeare, William. *Shakespeare's Sonnets*. Ed. W. G. Ingram and Theodore Redpath. London: University of London Press, 1964.

Shakespeare, William. *The Works of William Shakespeare*. Ed. Henry Irving and Frank A. Marshall. The Henry Irving Shakespeare. 8 vols. London: 1888-1890. Sonnets, vol. 8. Intro. and nn. to sonnets, A. W. Verity.

Shakespeare, William. *The Sonnets*. Ed. G. L. Kittredge. Rev. Irving Ribner. The Kittredge Shakespeare. Waltham, Mass.: Blaisdell, 1968.

Shakespeare, William. *Supplement to . . . Shakspeare's Plays Published . . . by Samuel Johnson and George Steevens*. Ed. Edmond Malone. 2 vols. London: 1780. Sonnets, I, 579-706.

Shakespeare, William. *Shakespeare's Poems: A Facsimile of the Earliest Editions*. Ed. James M. Osborn, Louis L. Martz, and Eugene Waith. The Elizabethan Club Series. New Haven and London: Yale University Press, 1964.

Shakespeare, William. *The Sonnets*. Ed. Hyder Edward Rollins. 2 vols. New Variorum Edition of Shakespeare. Philadelphia: J. P. Lippincott, 1944.

Shakespeare, William. *Sonnets*. Ed. Hyder Edward Rollins. Crofts Classics. New York: Appleton-Century-Crofts, 1951, paper.

Shakespeare, William. *Shakespeare's Sonnets*. Ed. A. L. Rowse. Perennial Classics. New York: Harper & Row, 1964, paper.

Shakespeare, William. *Shakespeare's Sonnets*. Ed. Martin Seymour-Smith. New York: Barnes & Noble, 1966.

Shakespeare, William. *Sonnets*. Ed. Barbara Herrnstein Smith. New York: Avon Books, 1969, paper.

Shakespeare, William. *The Sonnets of Shakespeare*. Ed. T. G. Tucker. 1924. Reprint. Folcroft, Pa.: Folcroft Library Editions, 1970.

Shakespeare, William. *A Casebook on Shakespeare's Sonnets*. Ed. Gerald Willen and Victor B. Reed. New York: Thomas Y. Crowell, 1964, paper. Includes a type facs. of the 1609 ed.

Shakespeare, William. *The Sonnets*. Ed. John Dover Wilson. The Works of Shakespeare. Cambridge: Cambridge University Press, 1964, paper.

Shakespeare, William. *The Sonnets of William Shakespeare*. Intro. John T. Winterich. New York: Heritage Press, 1941.

Shakespeare, William. *Shakespeare's Sonnets*. Ed. Louis B. Wright and Virginia A. Lamar. Folger Library General Reader's Shakespeare. New York: Washington Square Press, 1967, paper.

Shakespeare's Works Cited

No individual references are here given to Shakespeare's plays and poems cited, when the text implied is *The Riverside Shakespeare*. See "Texts Used, and a Note on Italics."

Shakespeare, William. *The First Folio of Shakespeare*. 1623. Reprint. Ed. Charlton Hinman. The Norton Facsimile. New York: W. W. Norton, 1968.

Shakespeare, William. *The Riverside Shakespeare*. Textual ed., G. Blakemore Evans. Intro., Harry Levin *et al*. Boston: Houghton Mifflin, 1974.

Shakespeare, William. *A Louers Complaint*. In *Shake-speares Sonnets*. London: 1609.

Shakespeare, William. *Loues Labors Lost*. London: 1598.

Shakespeare, William. *Lucrece*. London: 1594.

Shakespeare, William, *et al*. *The Passionate Pilgrim*. London: 1599.

Anthologies about the Sonnets

Hubler, Edward, *et al*. *The Riddle of Shakespeare's Sonnets*. London: Routledge & Kegan Paul, 1962. Includes selections by Edward Hubler, Northrop Frye, Leslie A. Fiedler, Stephen Spender, R. P. Blackmur, and Oscar Wilde.

Landry, Hilton, ed. *New Essays on Shakespeare's Sonnets.* New York and London: AMS Press, Inc., 1976. Essays by Rodney Poisson, Martin Seymour-Smith, W. G. Ingram, Winifred Nowottny, Anton M. Pirkhofer, Hilton Landry, Marshall Lindsay, Paul Ramsey, and Theodore Redpath.

[Smith], Barbara Herrnstein, ed. *Discussions of Shakespeare's Sonnets.* Discussions of Literature. Boston: D. C. Heath, 1964, paper. Selections by John Benson, George Steevens, Samuel Taylor Coleridge, John Keats, Henry Hallam, Leslie Hotson, F. W. Bateson, Edward Hubler, Patrick Cruttwell, G. Wilson Knight, J. W. Lever, Robert Graves and Laura Riding, William Empson, Arthur Mizener, Winifred Nowottny, and C. L. Barber.

Willen, Gerald, and Victor B. Reed, eds. *A Casebook on Shakespeare's Sonnets.* New York: Thomas Y. Crowell, 1964, paper. Includes essays by Robert Graves and Laura Riding, L. C. Knights, John Crowe Ransom, Arthur Mizener, Edward Hubler, and G. Wilson Knight, and some explications of specific sonnets.

Poets

Alexander, William. *Aurora.* London: 1604.

Allott, Robert, ed. *Englands Parnassus.* London: 1600.

Auden, W. H. *The Collected Poetry of W. H. Auden.* New York: Random House, 1945.

Ault, Norman, ed. *Elizabethan Lyrics.* 3rd ed. New York: William Sloane, 1949.

Barnes, Barnabe. *A Diuine Centurie of Spirituall Sonnets.* London: 1595.

Barnes, Barnabe. *Parthenophil and Parthenophe.* London: 1593.

Barnfield, Richard. *Cynthia.* London: 1595.

Bridges, Robert. *Poetical Works of Robert Bridges.* 2nd ed. reissued with *The Testament of Beauty* added. London: Oxford University Press, 1953.

C., E.. *Emaricdulfe.* London: 1595.

Caine, T. H., ed. *Sonnets of Three Centuries.* London: 1882.

Campion, Thomas. *The Works of Thomas Campion.* Ed. Walter R. Davis. London: Faber and Faber, 1969.

Campion, Thomas. *Obseruations in the Art of English Poesie.* London: 1602.

Chapman, George. *The Poems of George Chapman.* Ed. Phyllis Brooks Bartlett. 1941. Reprint. New York: Russell & Russell, 1962.

Chapman, George. *Ouids Banquet of Sence.* London: 1595.

Chapman, George. *Skià Nuktòs: The Shadow of Night.* London: 1594.

Chapman, George. See, in this section, Homer.

Coleridge, Samuel Taylor. *Coleridge's Miscellaneous Criticism.* Ed. Thomas Middleton Raysor. Cambridge, Mass.: Harvard University Press, 1936.

Coleridge, Samuel Taylor. *The Poems of Samuel Taylor Coleridge.* Ed. Ernest Hartley Coleridge. London: Oxford University Press, 1912.

Constable, Henry. *The Poems of Henry Constable.* Ed. Joan Grundy. Liverpool: Liverpool University Press, 1960.

Constable, Henry. *Diana.* London: 1592.

Craig, Alexander. *The Amorose Songes, Sonets, and Elegies.* London: 1606.
Crow, Martha Foote, ed. *Elizabethan Sonnet Cycles.* 4 vols. London: 1896-1898.
Cunningham, J. V. *The Exclusions of a Rhyme.* Denver: Alan Swallow, 1960.
Cunningham, J. V. *Tradition and Poetic Structure.* Denver: Alan Swallow, 1960.
Cunningham, J. V., ed. *The Problem of Style.* Greenwich, Conn.: Fawcett Publications, 1966. Includes an essay by the editor.
Daniel, Samuel. *Poems and a Defence of Ryme.* Ed. Arthur Colby Sprague. Chicago: University of Chicago Press, 1930.
Daniel, Samuel. *Poems and a Defence of Ryme.* Ed. Arthur Colby Sprague. First paper ed. Chicago: University of Chicago Press, 1965.
Daniel, Samuel. *Delia.* London: 1592.
Daniel, Samuel. See, in this section, Sidney, Sir Philip, *Syr P.S.*
Davies, John. *Wittes Pilgrimage.* London: n.d. [1605?].
Dickey, James. *Poems 1957-1967.* Middletown, Conn.: Wesleyan University Press, 1967.
Donne, John. *The Poems of John Donne.* Ed. Herbert J. C. Grierson. 2 vols. London: Oxford University Press, 1912.
Drayton, Michael. *Idea The Shepheards Garland.* London: 1593.
Drayton, Michael. *Ideas Mirrour.* London: 1594.
Dryden, John. *The Poems of John Dryden.* Ed. James Kinsley. 4 vols. Oxford: Clarendon Press, 1958.
Dryden, John. *Of Dramatic Poesy and Other Critical Essays.* Ed. George Watson. 2 vols. London: J. M. Dent & Sons, 1962.
Edwards, Richard. *Damon and Pithias.* London: 1571.
Fletcher, Giles. *Licia.* London: n.d. [1593?].
Frost, Robert. *The Poetry of Robert Frost.* Ed. Edward Connery Latham. New York: Holt, Rinehart and Winston, 1969.
Frost, Robert. *Selected Prose of Robert Frost.* Ed. Hyde Cox and Edward Connery Latham. New York: Holt, Rinehart, and Winston, 1966.
Gascoigne, George. *The Posies of George Gascoigne.* London: 1575.
Googe, Barnabe. *Eglogs, Epytaphes, and Sonettes.* London: 1563.
Greville, Fulke. *Certaine Learned and Elegant Workes.* London: 1633. Includes *Caelica.*
Griffin, Bartholomew. *Fidessa.* London: 1596.
Herrick, Robert. *Hesperides.* London: 1648.
Hamer, Enid, ed. *The English Sonnet.* London: Methuen, 1936.
Homer. *The Whole Works of Homer.* Trans. George Chapman. London: 1616.
Jonson, Ben. *The Works of Ben Jonson.* Ed. C. H. Herford, Percy Simpson, and Evelyn Simpson. 11 vols. Oxford: Clarendon Press, 1925-1952.
Jonson, Ben. *The English Grammar.* In *The Workes of Benjamin Jonson.* The Second Volume. London: 1640.
Keats, John. *The Letters of John Keats.* Ed. Hyder Edward Rollins. 2 vols. Cambridge, Mass.: Harvard University Press, 1958.
Lee, Sir Sidney, ed. *Elizabethan Sonnets.* 2 vols. [London]: Constable, 1904.

Lindsay, Vachel. *Collected Poems.* Rev. ed. New York: Macmillan, 1925.

Lodge, Thomas. *Phillis.* London: 1593.

Lok, Henry. *Ecclesiastes.* London: 1597.

Lyly, John. *Euphues.* London: 1578.

Lynche, Richard. *Diella.* London: 1596.

Main, David M., ed. *A Treasury of English Sonnets.* Manchester: 1880.

Marlowe, Christopher. *The Complete Works of Christopher Marlowe.* Ed. Fredson Bowers. 2 vols. Cambridge: Cambridge University Press, 1973.

Marlowe, Christopher. *The Poems.* Ed. Miller Maclure. The Revels Marlowe. London: Methuen, 1968.

Marlowe, Christopher. *The Complete Plays of Christopher Marlowe.* Ed. Irving Ribner. New York: Odyssey Press, 1963.

Marlowe, Christopher. *Hero and Leander.* London: 1598.

Marlowe, Christopher. *Hero and Leander.* 1598. Reprint. Ed. Louis L. Martz. The Folger Facsimiles. New York: Johnson Reprint Corporation; Washington: The Folger Shakespeare Library, 1972.

Marlowe, Christopher. *The Jew of Malta.* Ed. H. S. Bennett. 1931. Reprint. New York: Gordian Press, 1966.

Marlowe, Christopher. *The Massacre at Paris.* London: n.d. [prob. between 1594 and 1602 inclusive — see Bowers, ed., Marlowe's *Works*, I, 355-357].

Marlowe, Christopher. *The Massacre at Paris.* n.d. Facs. reprint. The English Experience. Amsterdam and New York: Da Capo Press, 1971.

Milton, John. *Paradise Lost 1667.* Facs. reprint. Menston, England: The Scolar Press, 1968.

No-body and Some-body. London: [1606].

No-body and Some-body. See, in this section, Simpson, Richard.

Nugent, Richard. *Rich[ard] Nugents Cynthia.* London: 1604.

Nye, Robert, ed. *A Book of Sonnets.* New York: Oxford University Press, 1976.

Percy, William. *Sonnets to the Fairest Coelia.* London: 1594.

[Petrarch.] Petrarca, Francesco. *Le Rime.* Florence. A. Salani, 1958.

[Petrarch.] *Petrarch's Lyric Poems: The "Rime sparse" and Other Lyrics.* Trans. Robert M. Durling. Cambridge, Mass., and London: Harvard University Press, 1976.

[Petrarch.] *Sonnets & Songs.* Trans. Anna Maria Armi. Intro. Theodor E. Mommsen. 1946. Universal Library edition. New York: Grosset & Dunlap, 1968, paper.

[Petrarch.] *Selected Sonnets, Odes and Letters.* Ed. Thomas Goddard Bergin. Trans. Geoffrey Chaucer, Sir Thomas Wyatt, *et al.* Crofts Classics. Northbrook , Illinois: AHM Publishing Corporation, 1966, paper.

The Religious Tract Society. *Devotional Poetry.* London: 1846. Includes religious sonnets from a 16th- or 17th-century manuscript.

Rochester, Earl of. See, in this section, Wilmot, John.

Sidney, Sir Philip. *Poems.* Ed. William A. Ringler, Jr. Oxford: Clarendon Press, 1962.

Sidney, Sir Philip, *et al. Syr P.S. His Astrophel and Stella.* London: 1591. Includes poems by Samuel Daniel and others.

Sidney, Sir Philip. *The Countess of Pembroke's Arcadia.* 1590. Facs. reprint. Ed. H. Oskar Sommer. London: 1891.

Simpson, Richard, ed. *The School of Shakspere.* 2 vols. New York: 1878. Includes *No-Body and Some-Body.*

Sitwell, Dame Edith. *The Collected Poems of Edith Sitwell.* London: Gerald Duckworth, 1930.

[Smith, William.] *Chloris.* London: 1596.

Southern, John. *Pandora.* London: 1584.

Spenser, Edmund. *The Complete Poetical Works of Spenser.* Ed. R. E. Neil Dodge. Boston: Houghton Mifflin, 1908.

Spenser, Edmund. *Amoretti and Epithalamion.* London: 1595.

Spenser, Edmund. *The Shepheardes Calender.* London: 1586.

Spenser, Edmund. *Spenser's Faerie Queene.* Ed. J. C. Smith. 2 vols., being Vols. 2 and 3 of *The Poetical Works of Edmund Spenser.* Oxford: Clarendon Press, 1909.

Stevens, Wallace. *The Collected Poems of Wallace Stevens.* New York: Alfred A. Knopf, 1954.

Tofte, Robert. *Alba.* London: 1598.

Tofte, Robert. *Laura.* London: 1597.

Turberville, George. *Epitaphes, Epigrams, Songs and Sonets.* London: 1567.

Watson, Thomas. *The Hekatompathia or Passionate Centurie of Loue.* London: [1582].

Watson, Thomas. *The Tears of Fancie.* London: 1593.

[Willoughby, Henry.] *Willobie His Avisa.* London: 1594.

Wilmot, John. *The Complete Poems of John Wilmot, Earl of Rochester.* Ed. David M. Vieth. New Haven and London: Yale University Press, 1968.

Winters, Yvor. *Forms of Discovery.* n.p: Alan Swallow, 1967.

Winters, Yvor. "The Influence of Meter on Poetic Convention." *In Defence of Reason* (1947). First English edition. London: Routledge & Kegan Paul, 1960, pp. 103-150.

Wordsworth, William. *The Poetical Works of William Wordsworth.* Ed. Ernest de Selincourt. 5 vols. Oxford: Clarendon Press, 1940-1954.

Wyatt, Sir Thomas. *Collected Poems of Sir Thomas Wyatt.* Ed. Kenneth Muir and Patricia Thomson. Liverpool: Liverpool University Press, 1969.

Zepheria. London: 1594.

Secondary, and Other

Acheson, Arthur. *Shakespeare and the Rival Poet.* London: John Lane, 1903.

Akrigg, G. P. V. *Shakespeare and the Earl of Southampton.* Cambridge, Mass.: Harvard University Press, 1968.

Alden, Raymond Macdonald. "The Lyrical Conceit of the Elizabethans." *Studies in Philology,* 13(1916): 129-152.

Alpers, Paul J., ed. *Elizabethan Poetry: Modern Essays in Criticism.* New York: Oxford University Press, 1967, paper. Includes essays by, among others, G. K. Hunter, Rosemond Tuve, I. A. Richards, Hallett Smith, and T. S. Eliot.

Anders, H. R. D. *Shakespeare's Books.* 1904. Reprint. New York: AMS Press, Inc., 1965.

Aquinas, St. Thomas. *St. Thomas Aquinas: Philosophical Texts.* Ed. and trans. Thomas Gilby. A Galaxy Book. New York: Oxford University Press, 1960, paper.

Aristotle. *The Art of Rhetoric.* Trans. John Henry Freese. The Loeb Classical Library. Cambridge, Mass.: Harvard University Press, 1926.

[St. Augustine.] Augustinus, Aurelius. *St. Augustine's Confessions.* Trans. William Watts. Ed. W. H. D. Rouse. 2 vols. The Loeb Classical Library. New York: G. P. Putman's Sons, 1912.

Bakeless, John E. *Christopher Marlowe.* New York: William Morrow, 1937.

Baldwin, T. W. *On the Literary Genetics of Shakspere's Poems & Sonnets.* Urbana: University of Illinois Press, 1950.

Baldwin, T. W. *William Shakspere's Small Latine & Lesse Greeke.* Urbana: University of Illinois Press, 1944.

Barroll, Leeds. *Artificial Persons: The Formation of Character in the Tragedies of Shakespeare.* Columbia, S.C.: University of South Carolina Press, 1974.

Bateson, F. W. "Elementary, My Dear Hotson." *Essays in Criticism,* 1(1951): 81–88.

Battenhouse, Roy W. *Shakespearean Tragedy.* Bloomington and London: Indiana University Press, 1969.

Baum, Paull Franklin. *The Principles of English Versification.* Cambridge, Mass.: Harvard University Press, 1922.

Bayfield, Matthew A. *The Measures of the Poets.* Cambridge: Cambridge University Press, 1919.

Beaver, Joseph C. "A Grammar of Prosody." *College English,* 29(1968): 310–321.

Beaver, Joseph C. "The Rules of Stress in English Verse." *Language,* 47(1971): 586–614.

Bennett, Josephine Waters. "Benson's Alleged Piracy of *Shake-speares Sonnets.* . . ." *Studies in Bibliography,* 21(1968): 235–248.

Bernard, J. E., Jr. *Prosody of the Tudor Interlude.* New Haven: Yale University Press, 1939.

Berry, Francis. *Poet's Grammar.* London: Routledge & Kegan Paul, 1958.

Bloom, J. Harvey. *Shakespeare's Garden.* 1903. Reprint. Detroit: Tower Books, 1971.

Boas, Frederick S. *Christopher Marlowe.* Oxford: Clarendon Press, 1940.

Booth, Stephen. *An Essay on Shakespeare's Sonnets.* New Haven and London: Yale University Press, 1969.

Bradbrook, Muriel C. *The School of Night.* Cambridge: Cambridge University Press, 1936.

Bradbrook, Muriel C. *Shakespeare and Elizabethan Poetry.* London: Chatto and Windus, 1961.

Bradley, A. C. *Oxford Lectures on Poetry.* 2nd ed. London: Macmillan, 1909.

Broadbent, J. B. *Poetic Love.* London: Chatto & Windus, 1964.

Brockington, Ruth. "The Necessity of Blank Verse." *Shakespeare Review* (ed. G. K. Chesterton), 1(1928): 217–221.

Brooke, [C. F.] Tucker. "Marlowe's Versification and Style." *Studies in Philology,* 19(1922): 188–205.

Brown, John Russell, and Bernard Harris, eds. *Elizabethan Poetry.* Stratford-upon-Avon Studies. New York: St. Martin's Press, 1960.

Chambers, David Laurance. *The Metre of Macbeth.* 1903. Reprint. Folcroft, Pa.: Folcroft Library Editions, 1974.

Chambers, E. K. *Shakespearean Gleanings.* London: Oxford University Press, 1944.

Chambers, E. K. *William Shakespeare.* 2 vols. Oxford: Clarendon Press, 1930.

Chatman, Seymour. *A Theory of Meter.* The Hague: Mouton, 1965.

Chatman, Seymour, and Samuel R. Levin, eds. *Essays on the Language of Literature.* Boston: Houghton Mifflin, 1967.

Chomsky, Noam, and Morris Halle. *The Sound Pattern of English.* New York: Harper & Row, 1968.

Chute, Marchette. *Shakespeare of London.* New York: E. P. Dutton, 1950.

Ciummo, Candido. *Dualismo e funzionalità nei «Sonnets» di William Shakespeare.* Lugano, Switzerland: Cenobio, 1966.

Clark, Donald Lemen. *John Milton at St. Paul's School.* New York: Columbia University Press, 1948.

Colie, Rosalie L. *Shakespeare's Living Art.* Princeton: Princeton University Press, 1974.

Collins, John Churton. *Ephemera Critica.* Westminster: A. Constable, 1901.

Cooper, Sherod M., Jr. *The Sonnets of Astrophel and Stella.* The Hague and Paris: Mouton, 1968.

Craig, Hardin. "The Elizabethan Sonnet." *The Literature of the English Renaissance.* A History of English Literature. 1950. Reprint. New York: Collier Books, 1962, paper, pp. 111–119.

Craig, Hardin. *The Enchanted Glass.* New York: Oxford University Press, 1936.

Craig, Hardin. "Shakespeare and Formal Logic." *Studies in English Philology . . . in Honor of Frederick Klaeber.* Ed. Kemp Malone and Martin B. Ruud. Minneapolis: University of Minnesota Press, 1929, pp. 380–396.

Cruttwell, Patrick. *The English Sonnet.* Writers and Their Work. London: Longmans, Green for the British Council and the National Book League, 1966, paper.

Cruttwell, Patrick. *The Shakespearean Moment.* New York: Random House, 1960, paper.

Curtius, Ernst Robert. *European Literature and the Latin Middle Ages.* Trans. Willard R. Trask. Harper Torchbooks. New York: Harper & Row, 1963. For Shakespeare, see Index, also topics, rhetoric, *et passim* (e.g., inexpressibility, beauty, theatrical metaphors).

D., E. [probably Edward Daunce or Sir Edward Dyer.] *The Prayse of Nothing.* London: 1585.

Deneef, A. Leigh. "Epideictic Rhetoric and the Renaissance Lyric." *Journal of Medieval and Renaissance Studies,* 3(1973): 203–231.

Dobson, E. J. *English Pronunciation 1500-1700.* 2nd ed. 2 vols. Oxford: Clarendon Press, 1968.

Dronke, Peter. *Medieval Latin and the Rise of the European Love Lyric.* 2 vols. Oxford: Clarendon Press, 1965.

Eccles, Mark. *Christopher Marlowe in London.* 1934. Reprint. New York: Octagon Books, 1967.

Ellrodt, Robert. *Neoplatonism in the Poetry of Spenser.* 1960. Reprint. Folcroft, Pa.: Folcroft Press, 1969.

Emerson, Oliver Farrar. "Shakespeare's Sonneteering." *Studies in Philology,* 20(1923): 111–136.

Empson, William. *Some Versions of Pastoral.* London: Chatto & Windus, 1935.

Evans, Robert O. *The Osier Cage.* Lexington: University of Kentucky Press, 1966.

Fenner, Dudley. *The Artes of Logike and Rhetorike.* London: 1584.

Ficino, Marsilio. *De sole et lumine.* Florence: Antonio Miscomini, 1493.

Ficino, Marsilio. *Marsilio Ficino's Commentary on Plato's Symposium.* Trans. Sears R. Jayne. University of Missouri Studies. Columbia, Mo.: University of Missouri, 1944.

Fleay, F. G. "On Metrical Tests as Applied to Dramatic Poetry. Part I. Shakspere." *New Shakspere Society's Transactions,* 1(1874): 1–9.

Fraunce, Abraham. *The Arcadian Rhetorike* (1588). Ed. Ethel Seaton. Oxford: Basil Blackwell, 1950.

Fraunce, Abraham. *The Lawiers Logike.* London: 1588.

Freeman, Donald C., ed. *Linguistics and Literary Style.* New York: Holt, Rinehart and Winston, 1970, paper.

Frye, Roland Mushat. *Shakespeare and Christian Doctrine.* Princeton: Princeton University Press, 1963.

Furnivall, F. J. *The Succession of Shakspere's Works and the Use of Metrical Texts in Settling It.* London: 1874.

Fuzier, Jean. "Poésie et perplexité: réflexions sur un sonnet de Shakespeare." *Les langues modernes,* 61(Jan.-Feb. 1967): 38–45.

Gerard, Albert S. "The Stone as Lily." *Shakespeare Jahrbuch,* 96(1960): 155–160.

Gil, Alexander. *Logonomia Anglica* (1621). Ed. Otto L. Jiricsek. Strasbourg: Karl J. Trübner, 1903.

Gilbert, Allan H. "Logic in the Elizabethan Drama." *Studies in Philology,* 32(1935): 527–545.

Gilby, Thomas. *Phoenix and Turtle.* London: Longmans, Green, 1950.

Gilson, Etienne. *The Spirit of Mediaeval Philosophy.* Trans. A. H. C. Downes. New York: Charles Scribner's Sons, 1940.

Goldin, Frederick. *The Mirror of Narcissus in the Courtly Love Lyric.* Ithaca: Cornell University Press, 1967.

Goldstien, Neal L. "*Love's Labour's Lost* and the Renaissance Vision of Love." *Shakespeare Quarterly,* 25(1974): 335–350.

Grivelet, Michel. "Shakespeare's "War with Time": The Sonnets and "Richard II"." *Shakespeare Survey,* 23(1970): 69–78.

Groom, Bernard. *The Diction of Poetry from Spenser to Bridges.* Toronto: University of Toronto Press, 1955.

Grundy, Joan. "Shakespeare's Sonnets and the Elizabethan Sonneteers." *Shakespeare Survey,* 15(1962): 41–49.

Guest, Edwin. *A History of English Rhythms.* 2 vols. London: 1838.

Halle, Morris, and Samuel Jay Keyser. *English Stress.* New York: Harper & Row, 1971.

Halle, Morris, and Samuel Jay Keyser. "English III: The Iambic Pentameter." In *Versification.* Ed. W. K. Wimsatt. New York: New York University for Modern Language Association, 1972, pp. 217–237.

Hallstead, R. N. "Idolatrous Love: A New Approach to *Othello.*" *Shakespeare Quarterly,* 19(1968): 107–124.

Hamer, Enid. *The Metres of English Poetry.* 4th ed. London: Methuen, 1951.

Harbarge, Alfred. "Dating Shakespeare's Sonnets." *Shakespeare Quarterly,* 1(1950): 57–63.

Hardison, O. B., Jr. *The Enduring Monument: A Study of the Idea of Praise in Renaissance Literary Theory and Practice.* Chapel Hill: University of North Carolina Press, 1962.

Hardison, O. B. Jr. "The Orator and the Poet: The Dilemma of Humanistic Literature." *Journal of Medieval and Renaissance Studies,* 1(1971): 33–44.

Hardison, O. B., Jr. "Petrarch and Modern Lyric Poetry." In *Studies in the Continental Background of Renaissance English Literature: Essays Presented to John L. Lievsay.* Ed. Dale B. J. Randall and George Walton Williams. Durham, N. C.: Duke University Press, 1977, pp. 29–41.

Harrison, John Smith. *Platonism in English Poetry.* New York: Columbia University Press, 1903.

Hayashi, Tetsumaro. "The Concept of Nothingness in *King Lear.*" *Indiana Speech Journal,* 13(1978): 27–31. (Sonnet 146.)

Hayes, Ann L. "The Sonnets." In *Starre of Poets.* Carnegie Studies in English. Pittsburgh: Carnegie Institute of Technology, 1966, pp. 1–15.

Hemphill, George, ed. *Discussions of Poetry: Rhythm and Sound.* Boston: D. C. Heath, 1961, paper.

Hotson, Leslie. *The Death of Christopher Marlowe.* Cambridge, Mass.: Harvard University Press, 1925.

Hotson, Leslie. *I, William Shakespeare.* London: Jonathan Cape, 1937.

Hotson, Leslie. *Mr. W. H.* New York: Alfred A. Knopf, 1965.

Hotson, Leslie. *Shakespeare's Sonnets Dated.* London: Rupert Hart-Davis, 1949.

Howell, Wilbur Samuel. *Logic and Rhetoric in England.* Princeton: Princeton University Press, 1956.

Hubler, Edward. *The Sense of Shakespeare's Sonnets.* Princeton: Princeton University Press, 1952.

Hume, Alexander. *Of the Orthographie and Congruitie of the Briten Tongue.* Ed. Henry B. Wheatley. 2nd ed. Early English Text Society. London: 1870.

Hunter, G. K. "Drab and Golden Lyrics of the Renaissance." In *Forms of Lyric.* Ed. Reuben A. Brower. Selected Papers of the English Institute. New York and London: Columbia University Press, 1970, pp. 1–18.

Hunter, G. K. "The Theology of Marlowe's *The Jew of Malta.*" *Journal of the Warburg and Courtauld Institutes,* 27(1964): 211–240.

Ing, Catherine. *Elizabethan Lyrics.* London: Chatto & Windus, 1951.

Inglis, Fred. *The Elizabethan Poets.* Literature in Perspective. London: Evans Brothers, 1969, esp. pp. 112–126.

Issac, Hermann. "Die Sonett-Periode in Shakespeare's Leben." *Shakespeare Jahrbuch,* 19(1884): 176–264.

Jackson, MacD[onald]. P. *Shakespeare's "A Lover's Complaint": Its Date and Authenticity.* University of Auckland English Series. Auckland, New Zealand: University of Auckland, 1964.

Jakobson, Roman, and Lawrence G. Jones. *Shakespeare's Verbal Art in "Th' Expence of Spirit."* De Proprietatibus Litterarum, Series Practica. The Hague and Paris: Mouton, 1970.

James I, King of Great Britain [later]. "Ane Schort Treatise Conteining Some Revlis . . . in Scottis Poesie." *The Essayes of a Prentise in . . . Poesie.* Edinburgh: 1584, Sigs. K1-N1.

Jayne, Sears R. "Ficino and the Platonism of the English Renaissance." *Comparative Literature,* 4(1952): 214-238.

John, Lisle Cecil. *The Elizabethan Sonnet Sequence.* 1938. Reprint. New York: Russell & Russell, 1964.

Johnson, Samuel. *Johnson's Dictionary* [1755]: *A Modern Selection.* Ed. E. L. McAdam, Jr., and George Milne. New York: Pantheon Books, 1963.

Joseph, Sister Miriam. *Shakespeare's Use of the Arts of Language.* New York: Columbia University Press, 1947.

Kerr, Jessica. *Shakespeare's Flowers.* New York: Thomas Y. Crowell, 1969.

Kiparsky, Paul. "The Rhythmic Structure of English Verse." *Linguistic Inquiry,* 8(1977): 189-247.

Knight, G. Wilson. *The Mutual Flame.* London: Methuen, 1955.

Knights, L. C. *Explorations.* New York: New York University Press, 1964.

Knights, L. C. *Some Shakespearean Themes.* Stanford: Stanford University Press, 1960.

Kökeritz, Helge. *Shakespeare's Pronunciation.* New Haven: Yale University Press, 1953.

Koskimiës, Rafael. "The Question of Platonism in Shakespeare's Sonnets." *Neuphilologische Mitteilungen* (Helsinki), 71(1970): 260-270.

Krieger, Murray. *A Window to Criticism: Shakespeare's Sonnets and Modern Poetics.* Princeton: Princeton University Press, 1964.

Kreiger, Murray. *The Play and Place of Criticism.* Baltimore: Johns Hopkins University Press, 1967.

Kristeller, Paul Oskar. *The Classics and Renaissance Thought.* Oberlin, Ohio: Oberlin College, by Harvard University Press, 1955.

Kristeller, Paul Oskar. *The Philosophy of Marsilio Ficino.* Trans. Virginia Conant. 1943. Reprint. Gloucester, Mass.: Peter Smith, 1964.

Landry, Hilton. *Interpretations in Shakespeare's Sonnets.* Berkeley and Los Angeles: University of California Press, 1963.

Landry, Hilton. "The Marriage of True Minds." *Shakespeare Studies,* 3(1967): 98-110.

Lanham, Richard A. *A Handlist of Rhetorical Terms.* Berkeley and Los Angeles: University of California Press, 1968.

Laurent, C.-P. "Les sonnets de Shakespeare: étude d'une désillusion." *Les langues modernes,* 61(Jan.-Feb. 1967): 46-52.

Lee, Sir Sidney. *Elizabethan and Other Essays.* Ed. Frederick S. Boas. Oxford: Clarendon Press, 1929.

Lee, Sir Sidney. *A Life of William Shakespeare.* 2nd ed. London: 1898.

Leishman, J. B. *Themes and Variations in Shakespeare's Sonnets.* London: Hutchinson, 1961.

Lever, J. W. *The Elizabethan Love Sonnet.* 2nd ed. London: Methuen, 1966.

Lewis, C. S. *English Literature in the Sixteenth Century.* Oxford History of English Literature. Oxford: Clarendon Press, 1954.

Lloyd, Roger. "Love and Charity in Shakespeare." *Manchester Guardian Weekly,* 16 Feb. 1956, p. 6.

Loomie, Albert J. *The Spanish Elizabethans.* New York: Fordham University Press, 1963.

McClumpha, C. F. "Parallels between Shakespere's *Sonnets* and *A Midsummer Night's Dream.*" *Modern Language Notes,* 16(1901): 164–168.

McClumpha, C. F. "Parallels between Shakspere's *Sonnets* and *Love's Labour's Lost.*" *Modern Language Notes,* 15(1900): 168–174.

McClumpha, C. F. "Shakespeare's *Sonnets* and *Romeo and Juliet.*" *Shakespeare Jahrbuch,* 40(1904): 187–203.

Mackail, J. W. *Lectures on Poetry.* London: Longmans, Green, 1911.

McManaway, James G. *Studies in Shakespeare, Bibliography, and Theater.* New York: Shakespeare Association of America, 1969.

Mahood, M. M. "Love's Confined Doom." *Shakespeare Survey,* 15(1962): 50–61.

Mahood, M. M. *Shakespeare's Wordplay.* London: Methuen, 1957.

Malof, Joseph. *A Manual of English Meters.* Bloomington and London: Indiana University Press, 1970.

Marder, Louis. "The Dark Lady: Demise of a Theory." *Shakespeare Newsletter,* 23(1973): 24.

Martin, Philip. *Shakespeare's Sonnets: Self, Love and Art.* Cambridge: Cambridge University Press, 1972.

Maxwell, J. C. "'Hero and Leander' and 'Love's Labour's Lost'." *Notes & Queries,* 197(1952): 334–335.

Melchiori, Giorgio. *L'uomo et il potere: Indagine sulle strutture profonde dei «Sonetti» di Shakespeare.* Torino: Guilio Einaudi, 1973, paper.

Meres, Francis. *Palladis Tamia: Wits Treasury.* London: 1598.

Miller, Perry. *The New England Mind: The Seventeenth Century.* Cambridge, Mass.: Harvard University Press, 1939.

Minto, William. *Characteristics of English Poets from Chaucer to Shirley.* 2nd ed. Edinburgh: 1885.

Mizener, Arthur. "The Structure of Figurative Language in Shakespeare's Sonnets." *Southern Review,* 5(1940): 730–747.

Muir, Kenneth, and Sean O'Loughlin. *The Voyage to Illyria.* 1937. Reprint. London: Methuen, 1970.

Ness, Frederic W. *The Use of Rhyme in Shakespeare's Plays.* Yale Studies in English. New Haven: Yale University Press, 1941.

Nowottny, Winifred. "Formal Elements in Shakespeare's Sonnets: Sonnets I–VI." *Essays in Criticism,* 2(1952): 76–84.

Nowottny, Winifred. *The Language Poets Use.* New York: Oxford University Press, 1962.

Noyes, Alfred. *New Essays and American Impressions.* New York: Henry Holt, 1927.

Oakeshott, Walter. *The Queen and the Poet.* London: Faber and Faber, 1960.

Oberman, H. A. *The Harvest of Medieval Theology.* Cambridge, Mass.: Harvard University Press, 1963.

O'Dea, Raymond. "The King of Men in Shakespeare's Early Work: Time." *Discourse,* 11(1968): 141–144.

Omond, Thomas S. *English Metrists.* 1921. Reprint. New York: Phaeton Press, 1968.

Ong, Walter J. *Ramus: Method and the Decay of Dialogue.* Cambridge, Mass.: Harvard University Press, 1958.

Ong, Walter J. *Ramus and Talon Inventory.* Cambridge, Mass.: Harvard University Press, 1958.

Palmer, George Herbert. *Intimations of Immortality in the Sonnets of Shakspere.* Boston: Houghton Mifflin, 1912.

Palsgrave, John. See Volder, in this section.

Panofsky, Erwin. *Studies in Iconology: Humanistic Themes in the Art of the Renaissance.* 1939. First Icon ed. New York: Harper & Row, 1972, paper, esp. pp. 95–128 and Plates XLI–LVII (Cupid).

Partridge, A. C. *Orthography in Shakespeare and Elizabethan Drama.* London: Edward Arnold, 1964.

Peacham, Henry. *The Garden of Eloquence.* London: 1577.

Pearson, Lu Emily. *Elizabethan Love Conventions.* 1933. Reprint. New York: Barnes & Noble, 1967.

Peterson, Douglas L. *The English Lyric from Wyatt to Donne.* Princeton: Princeton University Press, 1967.

Poetics, no. 12, 3(1974, no. 4). Eds. Joseph C. Beaver and J. F. Ihwe. Essays on metrics.

Poetics, no. 12, 4(1975, no. 4). Ed. Joseph C. Beaver and J. F. Ihwe. Essays on generative metrics.

[Puttenham, George?] *The Arte of English Poesie.* London: 1589.

Quintilian. *The Institutio Oratorio of Quintilian.* Trans. H. E. Butler. 4 vols. The Loeb Classical Library. Cambridge, Mass.: Harvard University Press, 1921.

Ramus, Petrus. *Dialecticae Libro Duo.* London: 1574.

Ramus, Petrus. *The Logike of . . . P. Ramus Martyr.* Trans. Roland McIlmaine. London: 1574.

Ramus, Petrus. *The Logike of . . . P. Ramus* (1574). Trans. Roland MacIlmaine. Ed. Catherine M. Dunn. Northridge, Calif.: San Fernando State College Press, 1969.

Ransom, John Crowe. *The World's Body.* 2nd ed. Baton Rouge: Louisiana State University, 1968, paper.

Richards, I. A. "The Places and the Figures." *Kenyon Review,* 11(1949): 17–30.

Richmond, H. M. *The School of Love.* Princeton: Princeton University Press, 1964.

Riding, Laura, and Robert Graves. *A Survey of Modernist Poetry.* London: William Heinemann, 1927.

Robb, Nesca A. *Neoplatonism of the Italian Renaissance.* 1935. Reprint. New York: Octagon Books, 1968.

Rowse, A. L. *Christopher Marlowe.* New York: Harper & Row, 1964.

Rowse, A. L. "Revealed at Last, Shakespeare's Dark Lady." *London Times,* 29 January 1973, p. 12. [See Chapter 2, n. 5, for dates of some responses.]

Rowse, A. L. *Sex and Society in Shakespeare's Age: Simon Forman the Astrologer.* New York: Charles Scribner's Sons, 1974.

Rowse, A. L. *Shakespeare the Man.* 2nd ed. London: Macmillan, 1973.

Russ, Jon R. "Time's Attributes in Shakespeare's Sonnet 126." *English Studies,* 52(1971): 318–323.

St. Clair, F. Y. "Drayton's First Revision of His Sonnets." *Studies in Philology,* 36(1939): 40–59.

Saintsbury, George. *Historical Manual of English Prosody.* London: Macmillan, 1910.

Saintsbury, George. *A History of English Prosody.* 2nd ed. 3 vols. London: Macmillan, 1923.

Schaar, Claes. *An Elizabethan Sonnet Problem: Shakespeare's Sonnets, Daniel's Delia, and Their Literary Background.* Lund Studies in English. Lund, Sweden: C. W. K. Gleerup, 1960.

Schaar, Claes. *Elizabethan Sonnet Themes and the Dating of Shakespeare's Sonnets.* Lund Studies in English. Lund, Sweden: C. W. K. Gleerup, 1962.

Schipper, Jakob. *A History of English Versification.* Oxford: Clarendon Press, 1910.

Schoenbaum, Samuel. *Shakespeare's Lives.* Oxford: Clarendon Press, 1970.

Scholl, Evelyn H. "New Light on Seventeenth Century Pronunciation from the English School of Lutenist Song Writers." *Publications of the Modern Language Association,* 59(1944): 398–445.

Sells, A. Lytton. *The Italian Influence in English Poetry: From Chaucer to Southwell.* 1955. Reprint. Westport, Conn.: Greenwood Press, 1971.

Siegel, Paul N. "Christianity and the Religion of Love in *Romeo and Juliet.*" *Shakespeare Quarterly,* 12(1961): 371–392.

Sipe, Dorothy L. *Shakespeare's Metrics.* New Haven: Yale University Press, 1968.

Smith, Barbara Herrnstein. *Poetic Closure.* Chicago: University of Chicago Press, 1968.

Smith, C. Gregory, ed. *Elizabethan Critical Essays.* 2 vols. Oxford: Clarendon Press, 1904.

Smith, G. C. Moore. "The Use of an Unstressed Extra-Metrical Syllable To Carry the Rime." *Modern Language Review,* 15(1920): 300–301.

Smith, Hallett. *Elizabethan Poetry.* Cambridge, Mass.: Harvard University Press, 1952.

Smith, Hallett. "The Nondramatic Poems." In *Shakespeare: Aspects of Influence.* Ed. G. B. Evans. Harvard English Studies. Cambridge, Mass., and London: Harvard University Press, 1976, pp. 43–53.

Sonnino, Lee Ann. *A Handbook of Sixteenth-Century Rhetoric.* London: Routledge & Kegan Paul, 1968.

Southem, B. C. "Shakespeare's Christian Sonnet? Number 146." *Shakespeare Quarterly,* 11(1960): 67–71.

Steadman, John M. "'Like Two Spirits': Shakespeare and Ficino." *Shakespeare Quarterly,* 10(1959): 244–246.

Steane, J. B. *Marlowe*. Cambridge: Cambridge University Press, 1965.

Stein, Arnold. "Donne and the Couplet." *Publications of the Modern Language Association*, 57(1942): 676–696.

Stirling, Brents. *The Shakespeare Sonnet Order*. Berkeley and Los Angeles: University of California Press, 1968.

Tannenbaum, Samuel A. *The Assassination of Christopher Marlowe*. 1928. Reprint. Hamden, Conn.: Shoe String Press, 1962.

Thompson, Charles. *The Sonnet*. 1874. Reprint. Folcroft, Pa.: Folcroft Press, 1970.

Thompson, John. *The Founding of English Meter*. London: Routledge & Kegan Paul, 1961.

Thomson, Patricia. "The Date Clue in Shakespeare's Sonnet 98." *Neophilologus*, 50(1966): 262–269.

Timberlake, Philip. *The Feminine Ending in English Blank Verse*. Menasha, Wisc.: George Banta, 1931.

Tottel's Miscellany. Ed. Hyder Edward Rollins. Introd. Douglas Bush. 2nd ed. 2 vols. Cambridge, Mass.: Harvard University Press, 1966.

Towne, Frank. "Logic, Lyric, and Drama." *Modern Philology*, 51(1954): 265–268.

Turner, Frederick. *Shakespeare and the Nature of Time*. Oxford: Clarendon Press, 1971.

Tuve, Rosemond. *Elizabethan and Metaphysical Imagery*. Chicago: University of Chicago Press, 1947.

University of Wisconsin Department of English. *Shakespeare Studies . . .* Madison: University of Wisconsin, 1916.

Van Dam, Bastiaan, and Cornelis Stoffel. *Chapters on English Printing, Prosody, and Pronunciation (1550-1700)*. Anglistische Forschungen. Heidelberg: Carl Winter, 1902.

Van Dam, Bastiaan, and Cornelis Stoffel. *William Shakespeare: Prosody and Text*. Leiden: E. J. Brill, 1900.

Viret, Pierre. *The Worlde Possessed with Deuils*. Part 2, translated by Thomas S[tocker]. London: 1583.

Viswanathan, S. "'Time's Fickle Glass' in Shakespeare's Sonnet 126." *English Studies*, 57(1976): 211–214.

[Volder, Willem de.] *The Comedye of Acolastus*. Trans. John Palsgrave. London: 1540.

Vyvyan, John. *Shakespeare and Platonic Beauty*. London: Chatto & Windus, 1961.

Vyvyan, John. *Shakespeare and the Rose of Love*. New York: Barnes & Noble, 1960.

Walker, William Sidney. *A Critical Examination of the Text of Shakespeare*. 3 vols. London: 1860.

Wardropper, Bruce W. "The Religious Conversion of Profane Poetry." In *Studies in the Continental Background of Renaissance English Literature: Essays Presented to John L. Lievsay*. Ed. Dale B. J. Randall and George Walton Williams. Durham, N. C.: Duke University Press, 1977, pp. 203–221.

Webbe, William. *A Discourse of English Poetrie.* London: 1586.

Whitaker, Virgil. *Shakespeare's Use of Learning.* San Marino, Calif.: Huntington Library, 1953.

Wiggins, Elizabeth Lewis. "Logic in the Poetry of John Donne." *Studies in Philology,* 42(1945): 41–60.

William of Ockham. *Philosophical Writings.* Ed. Philotheus Boehner. Indianapolis: Bobbs-Merrill, 1964, paper.

Williams, Franklin B., Jr. "An Initiation into Initials." *Studies in Bibliography,* 9(1957): 163–178.

Williamson, C. F. "Themes and Patterns in Shakespeare's Sonnets." *Essays in Criticism,* 26(1976): 191–208.

Wilson, F. P. *The English Drama 1485–1585.* Oxford: Oxford University Press, 1969.

Wilson, F. P. *Marlowe and the Early Shakespeare.* Oxford: Clarendon Press, 1953.

Wilson, Thomas. *The Art of Rhetorique.* London: 1585.

Wilson, Thomas. *The Rule of Reason.* London: 1580.

Wimsatt, W. K. *Hateful Contraries.* Lexington: University of Kentucky Press, 1965.

Wimsatt, W. K. "The Rule and the Norm: Halle and Keyser on Chaucer's Meter." *College English,* 31(1970): 774–788.

Winny, James. *The Master-Mistress.* London: Chatto & Windus, 1968.

Winters, Yvor. See in section "Poets."

Wolff, Max J. "Petrarkismus und Antipetrarkismus in Shakespeares Sonetten." *Englische Studien,* 49(1916): 161–189.

Index